Praise for *1984* ||||||||||||||||||| *y*

D0255202

"*The reception of Orwell's novel* _____ *_es.*
Until the end of the Cold War, the emphasis was on the politics
and the cruelty of living in a totalitarian state. More recently,
the focus has been on surveillance. This volume finally brings
together these and other approaches in a meaningful way, with
reference to the current political climate. An excellent and timely
collection of essays, which demonstrates why Orwell's great novel
still matters!"

> — MICHAEL NAGENBORG, co-editor of *Ethics and Robotics*
> (2009)

"*If 'Freedom Is Slavery', may philosophy be the liberator. In the*
fight against oppression, 1984 and Philosophy *is an exceptional*
tool. Read carefully, however, Big Brother is watching."

> — JIM BERTI, co-editor, *Rush and Philosophy: Heart and*
> *Mind United* (2011)

"*It's the best book* they *already know you will be reading!*"

> — GERALD BROWNING, author of *Demon in My Head* (2011)

"*Orwell's monumental* 1984 *may be even more important today*
than when it was first published, and the international array of
philosophers whose essays are collected in this book explains
why. Their essays broach important topics such as torture, mass
surveillance, revolution, resistance to authoritarianism, news
and media, freedom, history, and thought control. It's fascinating
reading for people with any interest in philosophy and a must-read
for anyone with even a single political bone in their body."

> — PETER S. FOSL, co-author of *The Philosopher's Toolkit*
> (2002)

"*Winston Smith learns in excruciatingly painful detail how a*
fascist regime operates. But, even as the rats eat his face, he never
learns why. This book reveals Big Brother's real thoughts."

> — KEVIN GUILFOY, Associate Professor of Philosophy,
> Carroll University

"This is an indispensable companion for anyone remotely interested in resisting Newspeak, the thought police, and the other despotic tools of the super state in Orwell's brilliant dystopian classic."

— CHARLES TALIAFERRO, Chair of the Department of Philosophy, St. Olaf College

"Why are we still having serious discussions about 1984? It's because concerns about control of bodies, state oppression, alternative facts, federal-level spying, identity politics, techno-augmentation and body modifications, and social media concerns are as real for us today as for the people in Oceania. The contributors to this book tackle these, and other, issues by examining how George Orwell, through Winston, brings discussions about these key social issues into sharp relief to help shed light on what it means to speak truth to power. The most important question raised by 1984 and Philosophy is whether resistance is futile. The answer is No."

— CLINT JONES, co-editor of The Individual and Utopia (2015)

"Irony abounds in high schoolers being forced to read 1984. The richness and, as recent history seems to indicate, the relevance of Orwell's work could be lost. 1984 and Philosophy has salvaged this essential read for another generation. It's an important companion to the original and whether you buy it for the radical flair it will give your classroom discussion or simply as a born-again reader, partake and enjoy . . . BIG BROTHER DEMANDS IT!"

— DAN MIORI, author, physician assistant, dissolute bastard

"Thought police, fake news, neoliberalism, mass incarceration, the pressure to continuously function like our technology, anyone? This team of philosophers present us with various philosophical and political views that help put Orwell's issues in their proper context. The volume reads like one long, entertaining discussion of the ideas Orwell so artfully presented to us, surely for the sake of provoking analyses like these. While fans of 1984 will love this volume, it is also going to create some new admirers of Orwell's genius."

— JENNIFER BAKER, Professor of Philosophy, College of Charleston

"The Party would like you to know that this book is subversive and dangerous; the Ministry of Truth has concluded that it fails to live up to the standards of our carefully crafted society. Anyone reading this book will be confused by its philosophical discussions of sexual enlightenment, government resistance, media manipulation, and doublethink. The Party has warned you!"

— COURTLAND LEWIS, author of *Way of the Doctor: Doctor Who's Pocketbook Guide to the Good Life* (2017)

"Is there a more pointed, potent allegory of contemporary civilization than Orwell's prescient post-World War II book, 1984? Supposing one lives through the rise of fascism, as the author did, its recrudescence seems highly plausible. Couple that return with advancing technologies that outpace human care and control, and tyranny's reassertion will be that much more vicious and capacious. The best way to counter the Thought Police is to think. This capable roster of scholars and critics does just that: discern ways to defend freedom, articulate the distinctions between truth and falsity in an age of simulacrum, and advance prospects for responding philosophically to the dictates of an encroaching tyranny that is anything but a fiction."

— DAVID LAROCCA, editor of *The Philosophy of War Films* (2014)

"Technological advances and recent concerns over censorship make many of the themes in 1984 extremely relevant. The authors in this book unpack many of the philosophical concerns over these issues. A great read!"

— MARC W. COLE, University of Leeds

"Philosophy is the love of wisdom, but the only universal truth is the love of BIG BROTHER."

— NATHANIEL GOLDBERG, author of *Kantian Conceptual Geography* (2014)

"Beware! If Ignorance is Strength, this book will turn you into a ninety-eight-pound weakling."

— ERIC J. SILVERMAN, author of *The Prudence of Love* (2010)

1984 and
Philosophy

Popular Culture and Philosophy® Series Editor: George A. Reisch

For full details of all Popular Culture and Philosophy® books, visit www.opencourtbooks.com.

Popular Culture and Philosophy®

1984 and Philosophy

Is Resistance Futile?

Edited by

EZIO DI NUCCI AND
STEFAN STORRIE

OPEN COURT
Chicago

Volume 116 in the series, Popular Culture and Philosophy®, edited by George A. Reisch

To find out more about Open Court books, visit our website at www.opencourtbooks.com.

Open Court Publishing Company is a division of Carus Publishing Company, dba Cricket Media.

Printed and bound in the United States of America.

1984 and Philosophy: Is Resistance Futile?

ISBN: 978-0-8126-9979-1.

Library of Congress Control Number: 2018933984
This book is also available as an e-book.

Contents

Thanks

We would like to thank the following people for helping us make this book: Diana Adela Martin, Ursula Di Nucci, Michael Nixon, Anna Vera Jørring Pallesen, George Reisch, Albert von Schrenck-Notzing, David Ramsay Steele, Aaro Tupasela, and also the many authors—too many to name—who submitted chapter proposals that we could not include. Finally, Ezio would also like to thank Stefan for coming to him with this brilliant idea.

Are We Living in *1984*?

EZIO DI NUCCI AND STEFAN STORRIE

W hen the future is already in the past, then there is no more
hope left. That's what's so depressing about discussing, in 2018,
a book about 1984 published in 1949; but a book that turns out
to be, today, more relevant than ever before.

Are we living in 1984? Surely not: it is, after all, 2018! But
while living in 2018 is incompatible with living in 1984, it is
not incompatible with living in *1984*—as in, George Orwell's
Nineteen-Eighty-Four. It really is unpleasant to think of perpetual war, global surveillance, and deliberate mass distortion
of objective facts. Should we consider such possibilities?

Orwell's *1984* has been written off as no longer relevant
numerous times. In retrospect such dismissals look laughably
naive. Isaac Asimov, in his 1980 review of the book, complained
that the specter of tyranny was no longer alive. Sure, at the time
of its publication in the late 1940s, with Stalin still in power, it
might have had some relevance; and sure, during the McCarthy
era in the 1950s it might have had some relevance. But not anymore, declares Asimov: long gone are the days of Hitler,
Mussolini, Franco, Mao, and Stalin. "If anything," Asimov muses
"governments of the 1980s seem dangerously weak."

A generation later Richard A. Posner, the most-cited legal
scholar of the twentieth century, painted a rosy picture of the
future where any possibility of the Orwellian nightmare will be
left far behind. The reason? "Freethinking among even deeply
religious people is the order of the day, not everywhere (in particular, not in all Muslim nations), but in most quarters of the

wealthy nations and many of the nonwealthy ones as well." Divested of its political relevance, Orwell's novel amazingly becomes almost pastoral for Posner: "As the political relevance of *Nineteen Eighty-Four* fades" Posner declares, "We can see it better today for what it is—a wonderfully vivid, suspenseful, atmospheric, and horrifying . . . romantic adventure story." Posner's paper was written in 2000.

Asimov's and Posner's dismissal of *1984* were exceedingly optimistic in their time of writing and such cosy assurances are now but a faded memory. The events of 9/11 in 2001 heralded a new era of world-wide constant terrorism and sectarian divide. The Iraq war that started in 2003 was premised on deliberately inaccurate claims about Iraq's weapon capabilities and Iraqi co-operation with al-Qaeda. A 2008 study by the Center for Public Integrity found that the US President and top administration officials had made 935 false statements in an orchestrated campaign to sway public opinion for the war between 2001 and 2003, and that the press was complicit in the push for war by its uncritical reporting on the alleged facts.

From Edward Snowden's 2013 global surveillance disclosures we know that the NSA's core purpose is to collect every retrievable communication event in the world. Advances in communication technology have for the first time allowed both state and non-state actors to create personalized propaganda content which should be properly understood as the weaponization of social media. The blatant disregard for truth and objectivity in the 2016 UK referendum on membership in the EU and the 2016 US presidential election led Oxford Dictionaries to declare "post-truth" the "international word of the year." On cue, in January 2017, US Counselor to the President Kellyanne Conway, faced with White House Press Secretary Sean Spicer's false statement regarding the number of attenders at Donald Trump's inauguration as President of the United States, chose to relativize the notion of truth rather than accepting the falsity of Spicer's claims by coining the iconic term "alternative facts." Orwell's *1984* was at this point the world's best-selling book.

You may understandably believe that this book should really have been about the powerful man who shall not be named—well, we already did name him actually; then call him the man whose name shall not be repeated all too often. And indeed there was between the end of 2016 and the beginning of 2017 a correlation between his election and renewed interest in Orwell's novel. But the Orwellian nature of the modern world transcends the events of November 2016—indeed, those regrettable events may be argued to represent an exception to the algorithmic predictability of modern life. Trump's not the problem: still, the exemplary nature of his political abuse of technology already brings us closer to home; and, inevitably, to *1984*.

On Super Bowl Sunday, January 22nd 1984, Apple ran a TV advertisement that declared: "On January 24th, Apple Computer will introduce Macintosh. And you'll see why 1984 won't be like *Nineteen Eighty-Four*." This is not surprising: the marketing department was apparently already back then the most innovative unit in Cupertino. But technology, such as Apple smartphones, is not the antidote to *1984*—indeed, it is much more likely to be part of the problem. The antidote is called *Philosophy*.

Before beginning to explain the role of philosophy—which is really the task of the whole book—it's worth looking further into the relationship between technology and what we may call 'Orwellian concerns' (which is just short-hand for our original question of whether we are living in *1984*). It's ironic that Apple would back in the 1980s advertise their Macintosh as a solution to Orwellian concerns, because it is not just today that we recognize the oppressive potential of technological innovation—that's already there in Orwell's book which, let us not forget, was published in 1949—before Steve Jobs was even born.

Here we have to be careful: it's undeniable that technology also has empowering potential for individuals and not just for institutions—such as for example oppressive governments like the Party in *1984*. This is—on a charitable reading—what the Apple marketing department was getting at—remember, it was a Super Bowl ad. Likely, then, that they were appealing to that typically American frontier spirit of anti-government individual empowerment. It was, after all, the dawn of the *personal* computer, bringing computers in every home, office or cubicle— just the way in which decades before cars had allowed for individual empowerment (which in American English should probably really just read: freedom).

So could we not just conclude that technology is, basically, neutral? Namely that the interesting normative questions are

all about the legitimate and illegitimate uses of technology by
both individuals and institutions but that there is nothing particularly concerning—in the Orwellian sense—about technology?
This question goes not only beyond the scope of this short introduction but also of the whole book: what's relevant here is the
perceptiveness and creativity with which Orwell—in the 1940s—
anticipated the way in which technology could be effectively used
for the manipulation of information—and here the complex
bureaucratic structures of totalitarian states should probably
themselves count as forms of—if you like—*political technology.*
So please don't just think of the telescreens—which may have an
astonishing resemblance to today's smartphones in their
omnipresence and inescapability but are probably not the most
terrifying instrument deployed by the Party—think for example
instead of the Party's complex apparatus for the re-writing of history or its dictionary 'streamlining', and how these elements,
when brought together and integrated, amplify oppression.

How, then, is philosophy the solution? Philosophy teaches us
to examine the foundations of those beliefs that guide our
thinking about politics, morality and our everyday life. It
allows us to become aware of our assumptions and what the
credible alternatives are, and allows us to weight and compare
different competing views. It makes us reflective and self-
aware and therefore less likely to be swayed by bad arguments
or by outright lies. At the same time, these skills can allow you
to influence and deceive the majority of people who are not
trained in these areas.

Everyone with an interest in political power knows this,
despite the bad press philosophy often gets. Leaders such as
Martin Luther King, Robert McNamara, Bill Clinton, John
Paul II, Aung San Suu Kyi, Emmanuel Macron, as well as virtually every British politician and prominent media person
have studied philosophy at university level.

Winston knows this too. "His heart sank as he thought of the
enormous power arrayed against him, the ease with which any Party
intellectual would overthrow him in debate, the subtle arguments
which he would not be able to understand, much less answer."

Philosophy enhances our ability to understand concepts, to
pose questions and answer them, to analyze problems and possible solutions. Philosophy supplies us the with tools to resist
oppression.

I

War Is Peace

1
Revolutionary from the Waist Down

STEFAN STORRIE AND DIANA ADELA MARTIN

At the heart of *1984* lies an erotic love story between Winston and Julia. Love and the enjoyment of sex are forbidden by the Party. According to the Party, sex should be an act of procreation not to be enjoyed (certainly not by the woman), but to be barely endured as a "duty to the Party." The Winston–Julia liaison is therefore a political act in opposition to the powers that be. But our two heroes have quite different views of *how* their relationship challenges the Party.

Winston sees their relationship as a rebellion, ultimately aimed to *overthrow* the oppressive society in which he lives. When Julia takes her clothes off, first in his dream, later in reality, it seemed to Winston "to annihilate a whole culture, a whole system of thought as Big Brother and the Party and the Thought Police could all be swept into nothingness by a single splendid movement of the arm" (pp. 31, 125). He thinks that sex is by its nature subversive and that it cannot fail to attack the regime, ultimately tearing it to pieces. According to Winston "the sexual act, successfully performed, was rebellion" (p. 65). And so, as Winston sees it, sex is a positive political force for societal change.

For Julia, on the other hand, the political function of sex is to put up resistance *within* the established political framework. "Life as she saw it was quite simple. You wanted a good time; "they" meaning the Party, wanted to stop you having it; you broke the rules as best you could." A bit later we find the thought that "any kind of organized revolt against the Party, which was bound to be a failure, struck her as stupid. The

clever thing was to break the rules and stay alive all the same"
(p. 131).

The political aspect of their relationship is for Julia a limited revolt where she seeks to carve out a space for personal
freedom and enjoyment within an oppressive system. This is
why, when Julia and Winston go to O'Brien to join the resistance, she point-blank refuses to never see Winston again for
the sake of the cause. For her, the relationship with Winston
trumps the political martyrdom of the Brotherhood.

Winston thinks Julia is naive in not acknowledging the
power that erotic relations can have in a society and admon-
ishes her half-hearted rebellion by saying, much to Julia's
amusement, that she is merely "a revolutionary from the waist
down." Julia, on the other hand, thinks organized revolution
against the party is an impossible dream, indeed, that it is "stupid." Who is right?

We "Other Oceanians"

In *The History of Sexuality* French philosopher and historian
Michel Foucault examined the relation between sexuality and
power. He presented and rejected the *repressive hypothesis*, the
widespread belief that sexuality was socially repressed from
the late seventeenth to the early twentieth century, which he
calls the Victorian Era, before the partial sexual liberation
began in the 1960s.

According to this hypothesis, the rise of the middle class and
the emergence of the capitalist industrial society resulted in
the social organization that centered on the family unit. The
couple became the model of sexuality, the privacy of the parents' bedroom became its "utilitarian and fertile" locus (*History
of Sexuality*, p. 3). By sexuality becoming a private matter it
also became something secret and not talked about. All of this
suited the emerging economical order because by repressing
sexuality it diminished the waste of labor energy.

However, the repression hypothesis, Foucault argues, is simplistic and inaccurate. It is simplistic because it sees the relation between power and sexuality merely as prohibition. In
doing so it sees the relation in strictly negative terms and fails
to acknowledge the many different active ways that sexuality
is used to gain control and power. As Foucault puts it in

Politics, Philosophy, Culture "the interdiction, the refusal, the prohibition, far from being essential forms of power, are only its limits, power in its frustrated or extreme forms. The relations of power are, above all, productive" (p. 118).

For example, Foucault argues, while religious confession became less sexually direct in the Victorian Era, at the same time it demanded that the confessors gave progressively more (albeit veiled) detailed accounts about sexual sins. Similarly, children's sexuality came to be seen as abnormal and as a consequence it became heavily regulated, but at the same time it became something that was copiously examined, studied, and taught.

The idea is that while greater efforts were made during the Victorian era to control sexuality and that sex then became something to be ashamed of, it is not accurate to see this merely in terms of repression and silencing. Rather, the process leads to a new way of speaking, thinking and acting in relation to sex, and doing so profusely. It has become more complex and scientific, more an object of knowledge than a source of pleasure. This means that those who control this knowledge, such as social scientists, educationalists, and those involved in certain forms of government policy, become more important and powerful.

As the repressive hypothesis is wrong, according to Foucault, an important question to consider is why modern western society was so ready to believe in the repressive hypothesis. His answer is that by portraying the Victorian era as sexually repressed, it allowed us "Other Victorians" to

> speak out against the powers that be, to utter truths and promise bliss, to link together enlightenment, liberation, and manifold pleasures; to pronounce a discourse that combines the fervor of knowledge, the determination to change the laws, and the longing for the garden of earthly delights. (*History of Sexuality*, p. 7)

Does this sound familiar? Winston believes in a version of the repressive hypothesis—his model of how sexuality is understood in Oceania is simply that the Party represses sexuality, and if it is let free it will destroy the current order. For this reasons he thinks that sex, because it can affect society, must do so in a revolutionary way.

Is Winston right? We say that the answer is *no*.

Winston's belief about repression does not map on to the facts of the situation, but is more likely based on the desire to see himself, this "Other Oceanian," as utterly different from his fellow citizens, and to allow himself to imagine a straightforward solution to the nightmare of existence in *1984*.

You might not be convinced that we can find the relevant similarities between Western culture in Victorian times and the Ingsoc regime. After all, bourgeois culture at, say, the turn of the twentieth century, was rather pastoral compared to the totalitarian nightmare of *1984*. It might therefore be instructive to consider the political use of sexuality in a society more like that of the Orwellian nightmare.

Orwell took his dystopian inspiration from a number of sources such as his experience of British colonialism in Asia and the British Labour party after World War II. But a central inspiration was always the Soviet Union. The political Left in Britain was in Orwell's view accepting and forgiving of the vast transgressions in Soviet Russia because the Communists were mistakenly seen as political allies. For this reason, shining a light on the atrocities perpetuated by Communism was urgent. It is the central theme of *Animal Farm* and also permeates *1984*.

Springtime of the Soviet Libido

In 1917, Lenin promulgated the Decree about the Dissolution of Marriage. Man and woman were now allowed to form or dissolve a family without registering themselves with the authorities as married. It was sufficient for one of the partners to request the end of the relationship, and no party had obligations towards the other after separation. Other measures led to the decriminalization of group sex and public exhibitionism.

This was an unprecedented thawing of restrictions related to sexuality. It was in Soviet Russia that the term "sexual revolution" was coined in a brochure promoting the policy of non-interference into sexual matters written by Dr. Grigorii Batkis. He was the director of the Moscow Institute for Sexual Hygiene and also led the Soviet delegation to the World League for Sexual Freedom conference in Berlin in 1923, where the initiatives presented were seen at the forefront of a liberalized sexuality.

But the socialist sexual revolution, praised in many quarters in the Western world as liberal and enlightened, was Janus-faced. Under the call for free sexual practices lay acts of subjugation. At the heart of the Stalinist sensual revolution's motto of sexual happiness for all, there is a political strategy of ensuring the continual power of the state.

US newspapers of the time, as well as a Senate Committee testimony of an American traveller in Soviet Russia, drew attention to sexual practices which resembled more a 'collectivization of women' than liberalization. In writing *1984*, Orwell took as a model the 1921 novel *We* by Russian writer Yevgeny Zamyatin, even writing a review of it in 1946, two years before the publication of *1984*.

In the dystopian society of *We* people are referred to as numbers and the ruler promulgated a sexual law that states that "each cipher has the right to any other cipher as sexual product." This, as Orwell notes in his review, is done by registering your preference at a special office where you receive a pink voucher showing your partner's number.

In his travel journal across Soviet Russia in 1916–18, Constantin Constante takes note of a conversation he had with a firm believer in the erotic liberation promised by the sensual revolution. Asking him how he sees the application of this ideal, the revolutionary proceeds by explaining that

> a commissariat of public love will be created, such that every citizen will be entitled to a love making voucher per day. Upon presentation of this voucher, the socialist woman will be obliged to put her body at his disposal, without opposition or expecting financial benefits. The children born from these second-long marriages will become property of the Soviet State, who will raise them and take care of them. These children, bearing no affection for their families, will be the most ardent and honest supporters of the Soviet family which is represented by the Soviet state. (p. 64)

While a wide range of sexual activity was permissible, new obligations were also being put in place, and sexual activity was controlled and sanctioned by the state. The Soviet Sexual Revolution, as Orwell knew, was not a liberation but a subjugation; sex was a means of state power. However, this exercise of power was rather creative and productive, certainly not reducible to probation and repression.

Big Brother Is Father to All the Children

Other Communist regimes were less creative and more draconian—perhaps the repressive hypothesis can find its confirmation here? During the rule of Nicolae Ceausescu in
1965–1989, Romania was under a dictatorship that showed
many similarities with Orwell's dystopia. Extreme surveillance, food rations, censorship, and propaganda transformed
communist Romania into an Orwellian state—one in which
Orwell's *1984* was banned!

As a measure to boost natality, the dictator Ceausescu
issued in 1966 the *770 Decree*, and with it an entire generation
came into being—a generation subsumed under the derisory
name of "The Decree Generation—Decreteii." The sexuality of
the Romanian woman of that period was depicted as being put
to the service of building socialism. Abortion was banned and
contraceptive methods were kept off the market, making
women relate differently to their bodies, by directing them to
the very specific function of making children. Ceausescu's political body clock was ticking. Every woman was expected to conceive four or five children, and all Romanian women together
were "the Mothers of the Nation."

Children born in the years of 1972 up to late 1980s were
used to hearing as early as kindergarten or in the overpopu-
lated orphanages spread across the country that Ceausescu
was their father. "In many cases, this is in a macabre sense
true" concludes Herta Muller in her powerful essay *Death or
Prison or Children* written in 1998 for the German journal *Taz*.
What better way for the state of Big Brother to strengthen its
hold than to take on the father figure? Muller goes on to ask
what could drive such an insane policy in regards to sexuality,
which can only lead to a rapid growth in population, already
subsisting on inadequate resources. She answers: "The knowledge that precarious standards of living are a precondition for
creating a large population of 'subjects'—as opposed to a small
population of citizens."

The state put in place a framework of policy and support
structures that encouraged procreation and child-raising by
creating crèches and child-care facilities. It also punished
those who were unmarried after the age of twenty-five, or
were married but did not have a child in their first two years

of marriage, with ten percent salary cuts. Gail Kligman, in her book *The Politics of Duplicity*, notes that the concept of "family planning" acquired an ironic connotation, given that the state did the planning with the aim of "achieving the right number of children suited to the family and to society" (p. 10). Ceausescu and the Communist Party "appealed to the entire population, to urban and village workers, to understand that to ensure normal demographic growth is a great honor and patriotic obligation for every family and for all of our people" (p.9). In the case of Socialist Romania, the family lost the capacity for self-determination in order to serve as an object of government.

This in turn diminished considerably the parents' private influence over their own children. The aim was to recreate the family structure ultimately making Ceausescu every child's father and therefore, surely, every mother's husband. While this exercise of power over human sexuality was draconian, its primary function was not the suppression of sexuality but a redirection for sexuality to be funnelled into service of a state gone insane. Again, as with the Soviet case, it was not simply a case of repression, but largely an active and productive change in state institutions, law, and propaganda. Foucault's position holds up again—power does not fear sex, it uses it for its own ends.

The Third Wheel

Before considering the repressive hypothesis in Oceania, it's worth asking what George Orwell meant to convey in *1984* regarding the subversive nature of sexuality. It might be thought that we are overthinking things. After all, isn't Winston Orwell's mouthpiece? Therefore, as Winston believes in the repressive hypothesis, so does Orwell, and therefore the 'meaning of the book' is to convey that hypothesis.

But identifying Orwell with Winston is a mistake. Orwell likes to cast his main character as a naive but principled male in his late thirties, where the hero's delusions are part of the unfolding tragedy. In Orwell's first novel, *Burmese Days*, the main character John Flory is a British teak merchant in colonial Myanmar. He attempts to escape his lonely and guilt-ridden existence by falling in love with Elizabeth Lackersteen, the only young European woman in town. He projects onto her an egalitarian understanding of the world, which in reality she does not hold in the slightest. The disillusion and betrayal he suffers as a consequence of this leads to his death.

Though Orwell's portrayal of Flory is largely sympathetic, he clearly sees him as flawed, and as lacking understanding of many things. Similarly, while we feel for Winston, he is not imbued with Orwell's intelligence and awareness. Winston gets closest to formulating a more sophisticated view on the relation between sexuality and power when he says: "The party was trying to kill the sex instinct, or, if it could not be killed, then to distort it and dirty it. He did not know why this was so, but it seemed natural that it should be so" (p. 66). Here Orwell expresses Winston's merely vague understanding of the complexity of the Party's wielding of sexuality.

What Julia, and of course the members of the Inner Party, and therefore, surely Orwell! understands, is that sex can also be used actively to uphold the status quo. Julia is well equipped to understand these complexities because of her job at the Pornosec subsection of the Ministry of Truth. At Pornosec they produce "the lowest kind of pornography" (p. 43), booklets with titles such as *Spanking Stories* and *One Night in a Girls' School*, which are used to entertain and pacify the proles.

True, the Outer Party members are more rigidly controlled in their sexuality by Big Brother. They are not supposed to have sex for enjoyment but only to have children. Chastity is highly valued. The Outer Party member's sexual energy is instead channelled towards hatred for the enemy—external and internal. At the same time prostitution is tacitly encouraged by the Party "as an outlet for instincts which could not be altogether supressed" (p. 65). This is quite a different strategy from the strict demands of chastity that the Party publicly endorses. Nevertheless, the acceptance of prostitution is also a method that Big Brother uses to control the population. While the Party controls sex, they do not control it absolutely, and the control they do wield is not reducible to simple repression.

While Winston's and Julia's relationship is seen as central for a large part of the book, it turns out that it is really a love triangle, also including O'Brien. It is through this third wheel, to put it mildly, that the reactionary channelling of sexuality that was so prevalent in Ceausescu's regime, crystallizes itself in Orwell's novel. O'Brien first charms Winston, and seduces him with the promise of the Brotherhood. At the beginning of the novel Winston confesses that he is "deeply drawn to him" (p. 11), in part because of the contrast between his "urbane manners" and "prizefighter's physique," as well as in the hope that O'Brien is not perfectly orthodox.

In the third part of the book this relationship takes a horrific turn as O'Brien tortures Winston. As Cass Sunstein has shown in "Sexual Freedom and Political Freedom," this is a "sustained scene of rape and castration" (p. 236). In an intensely jarring sequence at the beginning of the torture, O'Brien momentarily halts the pain causing Winston to look up gratefully at O'Brien. Winston is depicted as a grateful rape victim.

Orwell writes that Winston "had never loved him so deeply as at this moment." A bit later he continues: "In some sense that went deeper than friendship, they were intimates." As the next sequence of torture, which is an allegorical rape scene, is about to begin O'Brien explains: "We shall squeeze you empty, and then we shall fill you with ourselves." Winston is then connected to a torturing device that leaves him "not hurt, only prostrated."

Towards the end of the next torture scene, which represents castration, O'Brien orders Winston to take off his clothes and look at his broken emaciated body in a three-sided mirror. O'Brien grabs one of Winston's remaining front teeth: "A twinge of pain shot through Winston's jaw. O'Brien had wrenched the loose tooth out by the roots. He tossed it across the cell." He then tells Winston "Now put your clothes on again" (p. 272). Only when he is sexually broken is he ready for the rat torture during which he ultimately betrays Julia. Winston is now finally broken and O'Brien can easily redirect Winston's erotic attention to Big Brother. O'Brien has not merely repressed Winston's sexuality but directed eroticism and desire away from the human experience to a love for the empty abstraction of Ingsoc. Here sex *is* used to destroy, but then also to create something new.

Winston's simplistic understanding of what to revolt against and how to do it shows that Orwell's point is really this: only if the productive purpose of the vast, complex and often horrible machinery of domination and exertion of power is properly understood will effective resistance be possible. Winston's mistaken understanding of the relation between power and sexuality simply in terms of repression is a common one but also a dangerous one. By believing that power is exerted merely by repression you will believe that liberation only requires that certain prohibitions are lifted. However, this underestimates the complex productive relation between power and sexuality and will most likely lead to a breakdown in genuine resistance. Ironically, it is Winston who proves to be revolutionary only from the waist down.

2
Physical Jerks Ungood

Ezio Di Nucci

It's early morning on a weekday, and the sprawling ranks of Western middle classes are getting up to go to work. You will increasingly find that many of them will—between when they wake up and when they leave for work—make time for some form of exercise, be that a bit of stretching, yoga, going for a run or—the saddest of them all—a quickie at the local gym.

Indeed, many of these busy bees will have woken earlier than necessary for the pleasure of *working out before work*. And—truth be told—if I didn't have small children I would love to be one of those losers myself: getting up before 6:00 A.M. in the winter when it's dark, cold, windy, and probably raining too (and we'll have to add sweat and lycra to that happy list before the end of the work-out).

Do those poor sods remind you of anyone? In *1984*, Winston (along with all other 'office workers') is woken up every morning at 07:15 for the Physical Jerks:

> It was nought seven fifteen, getting-up time for office workers. Winston wrenched his body out of bed—naked, for a member of the Outer Party received only 3,000 clothing coupons annually, and a suit of pyjamas was 600—and seized a dingy singlet and a pair of shorts that were lying across a chair. The Physical Jerks would begin in three minutes. . . .
>
> "Thirty to forty group!" yapped a piercing female voice. "Thirty to forty group! Take your places, please. Thirties to forties!" Winston sprang to attention in front of the telescreen, upon which the image of a youngish woman, scrawny but muscular, dressed in tunic and

gym-shoes, had already appeared. "Arms bending and stretching!" she rapped out. "Take your time by me. ONE, two, three, four! ONE, two, three, four! Come on, comrades, put a bit of life into it! ONE, two, three, four! ONE, two, three, four! . . ." The pain of the coughing fit had not quite driven out of Winston's mind the impression made by his dream, and the rhythmic movements of the exercise restored it somewhat. As he mechanically shot his arms back and forth, wearing on his face the look of grim enjoyment which was considered proper during the Physical Jerks, he was struggling to think his way backward into the dim period of his early childhood. It was extraordinarily difficult . . .

It may not be funny but it's at least a bit ironic and maybe even mildly interesting, that the liberated middle-classes of the twenty-first century would impose upon themselves the very regime of exercise that the Party 'offered' its members in *1984*. Who needs an oppressor when we are so eager to oppress ourselves?

But what's the problem? Exercise is, after all, a good thing. Not just good for you per se, good for society as well, with its promise to reduce healthcare spending. And it's not just good for the body and the Ministry of Health—it makes you feel better as well (yes it does). So, you may wonder, why would the party ever be so generous to its members, given everything else the Party 'offers' Winston and company in *1984*?

Strength Is Weakness

Exercise may well be healthy, but that does not necessarily mean that it's good for you or, at least, that there isn't a price to pay whatever the benefits of exercise and sport; this was Orwell's intuition when he included the Physical Jerks in *1984*; and we ought to be mindful of that as we spin (or whatever it is we do on the treadmill while going nowhere). From *Ignorance Is Strength* to *Strength Is Weakness*.

Let's start from the obvious: exercise may be good for your health but—honestly—does anybody actually believe that's why folk do it? Allow a philosopher his thought-experiment: imagine a possible world where exercise—being as good for your health as it is in this world—made you fat or ugly. Wouldn't that be a dream? Assuming, anyway, that in this possible world lack of exercise made you thin, fit, or whatever it is that it's in vogue these days—strong?

Anyway, you may object to my little thought-experiment on the grounds that you cannot, *conceptually*, separate, say, unhealthy from fat or ugly. But that's clearly false: fashion magazines really did manage to convince a generation of girls (and their mothers too) that skinny models looked good—and whatever those models are, they certainly are not healthy. So it is not through concepts that we will get out of this mess.

More optimistically we could hope that part of the reason why we think that fat is ugly is not just that fat is, indeed, ugly but also that fat is not healthy. Otherwise, you may just as well think that what distinguishes our world from the possible world of our little thought-experiment is sheer luck: what makes you healthy also makes you look better—what a happy coincidence!

Now, reality is surely much more complex than that, but, for our present purposes, it will be enough to hypothesize that, in the possible world of our thought-experiment where exercise makes you healthier but also uglier, lycra and treadmill companies would be a tad less successful than they are in our world. This, I submit, is a modest and plausible hypothesis (that's philosophers' speak for: self-evident).

Even admitting the superficial nature of exercise, though, why would Orwell include it in the Party's oppressive structures? It surely can't be that bad. The answer—my answer—is that to understand the oppressive potential of exercise and sport we should focus on the activities that exercise takes time from: sleep, for example; or reflection—think of the final bit of Orwell's quote above:

> As he mechanically shot his arms back and forth, wearing on his face the look of grim enjoyment which was considered proper during the Physical Jerks, he was struggling to think his way backward into the dim period of his early childhood. It was extraordinarily difficult . . .

Orwell here is literally suggesting that exercise makes it more difficult for Winston to think and, crucially given the context of *1984*, to remember—which is exactly what the Party does not want Winston to do. Now, we may be twisting Orwell's words— or anyway at least his meaning here—a bit too far: still, the point is a simple one and it is independent of Orwell; namely that the time and energy that we invest in exercise (not to mention the bloody money it all ends up costing) could be employed elsewhere.

The Party, after all, wants a workforce which is fit enough to go to work and be productive—so they must not be too tired or sick; but crucially the Party also wants a workforce that lacks the energy and focus to free itself from oppression—a distracted and exhausted workforce is easier to deal with. Please notice the way in which here Orwell's *1984* Party may be used to represent two different players in modern societies: yes, government, obviously; but also employers, which—suspiciously enough—seem to have the same interests as governments: a productive workforce which lacks the time, energy, and resources to cause trouble.

I hope that at least some of this will sound familiar to you: after all, the oppressive character of passive sport as entertainment is at least as old as the Roman Empire. Juvenal's classic *panem et circenses* (bread and circuses) has always been used to refer to the political benefit of making sure not just that people had enough to eat but also that they'd be too distracted or entertained to challenge their leaders. And it's too easy to take this out of the *Colosseum* and apply it to modern sports, increasingly enjoyed not even live anymore but through our changing telescreens. From *panem et circenses* to *panem et iphones*. It's reassuring that some things never change—and I'm not talking about bread.

(Allow me to pause my argument here to make a point too tempting to go unsaid in the context of *1984*: from an Orwellian point of view, it's quite funny that it wasn't enough for us to have telescreens (such as TVs and computer screens) all over our houses and offices—we had to go and make them, first, portable and, finally, mobile; thanks very much, Apple, for having out-Orwelled Orwell. Back to sport and exercise.)

So the oppressive nature of passive sport is well-documented and almost as old as philosophy. But surely that has nothing to do with exercise, you will object: we should be delighted if people—instead of laying on their sofas, beer, chips and all—actually get up early to go for a run: think of all the fresh air!

War Minus the Shooting

The similarities between the passive consumption of sport and an active and healthy life (as in, exercise) are, I'm afraid, as obvious as the differences. Yes, from a health and fitness point of view we should welcome the bursting energy of those early-raising, go-getting, lycra-wearing members of society. But what about the political side of things? As the Romans and Orwell remind us, the sofa, beer, and chips crowd may be just as distracted as the pedometer, treadmill, and lycra gang.

Indeed, the latter gang may be even worse off when it comes to their ability to, say, engage politically: they are, after all, literally knackered—and they haven't even been to work yet. Talking of passive sport, we should mention here that George Orwell wasn't very fond of that either: "Serious sport has nothing to do with fair play, it is bound up with hatred and jealousy, boastfulness, disregard of all the rules and sadistic pleasure in unnecessary violence. In other words it is war minus the shooting" ("The Sporting Spirit").

More interestingly for our purposes, Orwell in *1984* has this to say about the role of sport in controlling the proles: "Heavy physical work, the care of home and children, petty quarrels with neighbors, films, football, beer, and above all, gambling filled up the horizon of their minds. To keep them in control was not difficult . . ." So exercise for Party members and football for the proles: things really have not changed since *1984* (Yes, I do know it's a work of fiction) with the modern obsession for training and fitness very much a middle-class phenomenon. Gyms are, after all, an expensive rip-off.

Aristotle had this crazy idea that participating in the political life of the polis was necessary for the good life. You don't have to agree with Aristotle to concede that political engagement or at least political awareness are crucial to the democratic process (even though some contemporary philosophers—see Jason Brennan's book *Against Democracy*—will try to convince you that the less people engage in politics, the better). So it's worth posing the question of what kind of effect obsessive exercise has on how political today's citizen is and, crucially, will become.

Here's another thought-experiment (let me know when you've had enough): imagine you had to choose between voting and exercising; which one would you drop, if you had to drop one? And, crucially, which one do you think the government cares more about? After all, the beneficial effects of exercise are well-documented; while you never know with voting, you may end up opting for the wrong party.

Health institutions usually recommend that you spend at least half an hour a day exercising. Think of the amount of politics that could get done instead—it's 3.5 hours a week, more than a hundred hours a month, over 1,200 hours per year! And when I say politics, you don't need to think of it in terms of re-tweeting *Politico* articles about 2020 hopefuls—that's the sofa, beer, and chips version of politics; I'm thinking, for example, of volunteering, charity, and so forth. Or it may even be spending a bit more time with your kids to make sure they understand what's going on. Or it may be something as banal as reading a book.

Okay, before you say it: I know that many of the busy bees listen to audio-books or podcasts while they exercise. But that's the point: we're so desperate to exercise that we have other people read on our behalf. You don't have to worry about forgetting how to read to find this strange. But, now that I'm at it, it is actually worrying: how can we expect our children to learn how to read properly if we ourselves delegate that to actors so that we can go on the treadmill?

I'm not exactly saying that exercise makes us stupid: but it does get in the way of other activities and it does so twice, because of the time spent exercising (and do include preparation and showering with that—which easily end up doubling the time of the actual work-out) plus the fact that you have less energy afterwards. There's also another relevant consideration: we're so desperate to exercise that we very often end up going for the more solitary (probably because more practical and less time-consuming) forms, such as running or treadmill plus headphones in a gym full of treadmills with everyone wearing headphones.

Mark Greif tells us how he came to his epiphany:

> I was standing in the usual stance of mutual disregard, pretending not to notice my neighbors sweating through skintight pyjamas and making their angry—or, I suppose, fierce—faces. I tried not to look up when someone grunted or shouted, and kept my eyes politely on the

calories ticking by on my readout, just as in a lift I'd keep my eyes on the floor numbers. But then I breached convention and looked around, and was struck down by the sort of vision that must have come to William Blake, a glance into heaven and hell, suddenly manifest in his garden in Felpham. There was a young man crucified on a lat pull-down. There was a young woman whose legs were madly turned by a spinning bike. No one looked happy: they either looked like executioners, grim as death, or victims. Certainly no one looked sociable—though this might be the space with the most people, together, supposedly at ease and enjoying leisure time, that they would enter all day. I turned from one unseeing face to the next, each chasing some number, and I said: "You are condemned. You are condemned. You are condemned." I, too, was condemned. I got down from the treadmill." ("Get Off the Treadmill")

So exercise may also have the potential to *alienate* us. Again, the time spent exercising on our own could be spent socializing instead, making society more cohesive—which long-term and collectively may be a more important good than individual or public health. Social tensions and wars are never the result of people being unfit while often being the result of not understanding each other. This is another obvious example of what I have been referring to as the price of exercise—and again in this respect we see that, actually, passive sport may be less worrying—as it tends to be more social than exercise.

Before moving on we should probably make a distinction that you would have thought obvious, but you never know: when I say "exercise" I mean physical activity which does not serve any other purpose than fitness; so obviously what I am saying does not apply to professional sports nor does it apply to, say, cycling to work or carrying your kids to school on a cargo bike (yes, your honor, I confess: I live in Copenhagen) or even taking the stairs instead of the elevator. Those are functional physical activities and—while I'm sure you can also take them too far—are excluded from my argument here.

Enough, I think I have made my and Orwell's point clearly enough: the Physical Jerks have—whatever their health benefits—a price and so it's no surprise that the Party makes 'office workers' do them every morning: it's just another way for the regime to control its subjects.

Social Injustice Is Lazy

The modern obsession with exercise and fitness may be healthy for those who do it but it also furthers inequality and class division. It's no coincidence that the lycra crowd is primarily middle class, nor does it have much to do with the price of trainers (even though gyms are expensive—have I said that already?). Can you imagine someone whose shift at the construction site starts at 7:00 A.M. sharp waking up at five to go for a run? Or, even worse, coming home after eight to ten hours' work at the site to then leave again for the gym? It makes no sense—and the same goes for waiters or kitchen staff on their feet all night, or even nurses and factory workers; truck drivers may be an exception here, given the nature of their work—even though, in collective imagination, truck drivers are always fat, go figure. So the answer is, again, to be found in George Orwell's Physical Jerks, since in *1984* this activity is reserved for "office workers."

Through exercise, the middle classes—who are already healthier (because richer) than working-class people; data on life expectancy shows its class and income dependence, for example—further class inequality. And, given the nature of the kinds of jobs available to those who do not go to university, we can't very well object that working class people should start exercising more as well. Exercise is just not an option in many cases—so the middle classes aren't just furthering their privilege, period; they're unfairly enhancing their privilege through means that are inaccessible to working-class folk.

You may think this argument is crazy (and maybe it is): you may say that people have the right to exercise simply because they have the right to do with their free time whatever the hell they like—including exercising, whatever its health benefits or intellectual price. A society in which middle-class folk were not allowed to exercise on the grounds that exercise increases their privilege would, after all, be no better than Orwell's dystopia. And still, the principle is pretty simple. Take any means by which someone can further their privilege—add the fact that others do not have access to the same means—and you get an inequality problem. Private school is the obvious analogy here: it furthers the privilege of the rich over the poor and it does so unfairly because the poor have no access to it, since they lack the funds.

Exercise works in exactly the same way as private school, with the only difference being that what working people lack in the case of exercise is not necessarily the funds but more like time or—isn't it ironic?—the energy. But given that making more time is just as impossible for many working-class people as making more money, this difference is not relevant from the point of view of equality.

It should be no surprise that exercise is problematic from the point of view of inequality, as it is—along with its increasing solitary character—one of the most self-centered and egotistical things you can do with your time. You may only work for the money but, in almost every case—whatever it is you do in order to get your paycheck—your work will have some benefit or function to others as well, otherwise you'd probably be out of work soon—it's the market, stupid (I know, I know: that's why I said "in almost every case"). But that doesn't apply to exercise: if it's beneficial at all, it benefits you and you alone.

So next time you get up in the dark hours of an early morning to go for a run and think to yourself how hard it is, don't be fooled into feeling good about it being hard; rather, think back to *1984*'s Physical Jerks: there's a reason why it's hard. Nature wants to warn you off the bourgeois pointlessness of it all. And if you're really that desperate for bourgeois pointlessness, read some philosophy.[1]

---

[1] Disclaimer (you've probably guessed it already): I am one of these early morning lycra runners myself and this chapter has been written *under that influence*. I would like to thank Michael Nixon, Aaro Tupasela, and Stefan Storrie for their helpful comments on this chapter.

3
Why Don't the Proles Just Take Over?

GREG LITTMANN

"If there is hope, it lies in the proles" Winston repeatedly tells himself. He thinks, "If there was hope, it MUST lie in the proles, because only there in those swarming disregarded masses, eighty-five percent of the population of Oceania, could the force to destroy the Party ever be generated."

Revolution would be easy for them:

> the proles, if only they could somehow become conscious of their own Strength . . . needed only to rise up and shake themselves like a horse shaking off flies. If they chose they could blow the Party to pieces tomorrow morning. Surely sooner or later it must occur to them to do it? And yet——!

And yet they never do! "They are helpless, like the animals," O'Brien assures Winston. The Party forces the proles to live in gruesome poverty, barely above the starvation level. Given that they are so oppressed, but have the power to overthrow the Party in order to replace it with something better, why don't they?

It's a problem Orwell wrestled with in the case of real-world societies in which he thought the masses were exploited, like England, Russia, and the entire capitalist and communist world. The exploited majority had the numbers to replace the system with something better for them, so why didn't they? In democracies like England and the US, the exploited majority wouldn't even need to fight, since they could elect anyone they chose. Instead, wealth and power were being concentrated in

23

fewer and fewer hands. Orwell writes in "James Burnham and the Managerial Revolution" (1946) that "For quite fifty years past the general drift has almost certainly been towards oligarchy. The ever-increasing concentration of industrial and financial power . . ."

These exploited workers weren't necessarily as identifiably "proletarian" as the bottom eighty-five of Oceania's workforce. Orwell notes in *The Road to Wigan Pier* (1937) that many English white-collar workers who would never think of themselves as "proletarian" or "working class," have small and insecure incomes, and so are effectively in the same position as manual laborers. They "have the same interests and the same enemies as the working class."

In the modern US, there has been a historically unprecedented concentration of wealth at the top, even as many Americans struggle to get by. The bottom ninety percent of Americans own only 22.8 percent of the nation's wealth, while the top one percent own 38.6 percent (*Federal Reserve Bulletin*). Meanwhile, wages stagnate, especially at the lower end, and healthcare, education, and social services are inferior to that in most first-world nations. As in Orwell's day, the question remains: Why do the masses tolerate being exploited?

It isn't necessary, for our purposes, to identify exactly who is to count as one of the "masses," though as a rough benchmark, the poorest sixty percent of the population will suffice, since such a group is large enough to vote in any system of government it wants. That's everyone earning about $70,000 a year or less, high enough to include many middle-class workers, but far from rich, and together possessing only a small proportion of the nation's wealth.

The lower sixty percent are certainly pissed off. When Donald Trump won the presidency, he did it promising to fight the "elites" and the "establishment," and to do something for ordinary workers suffering from the fallout of the global economic crisis. Yet there'll be no fundamental improvement in the condition of ordinary Trump supporters. See if I'm wrong!

In *1984*, Winston diagnoses why there has been no proletarian revolution: The proles are unaware of the nature of their own exploitation. He observes that

> even when they became discontented, as they sometimes did, their discontent led nowhere, because being without general ideas, they

could only focus it on petty specific grievances. The larger evils invariably escaped their notice.

Their ignorance creates a vicious cycle, because there would need to be a rebellion before they could be educated. Winston concludes, "Until they become conscious they will never rebel, and until after they have rebelled they cannot become conscious."

Orwell saw the masses in the real world as being similarly unconscious. He writes in "Looking Back on the Spanish War" (1942), "The struggle of the working class is like the growth of a plant. The plant is blind and stupid, but it knows enough to keep pushing upwards towards the light . . ." He agreed with Arthur's Koestler's claim, modified by Winston above, that, "Without education of the masses, no social progress; without social progress, no education of the masses" ("Arthur Koestler," 1944).

Presumably, Orwell would judge today's masses to be similarly unaware of their condition, and so explain their failure to govern in their own best interest. But how can the masses be unaware of their situation in an age of mass communication? *1984* and the political philosophy of George Orwell can help us tackle that question.

Ignorance Is Strength

In Oceania, the citizens are exposed to only one opinion: that of the Party. The Party lies constantly, but since it has complete monopoly over the media, the Party's lies become the people's reality. Orwell wrote in "The Prevention of Literature" (1946) that the "immediate, practical enemies" of intellectual liberty in his day are "monopoly and bureaucracy." Given "the concentration of the press in the hands of a few rich men, the grip of monopoly on radio and films, the unwillingness of the public to buy books," people rarely got to hear different points of view.

Today, the masses have an unparalleled ability to communicate. Anyone with an internet account can set up their own website or YouTube channel and share their ideas with the world. Yet monopoly over the mainstream media has grown much more extensive since Orwell's day and is increasing. Already, about ninety percent of the American media is controlled by only six corporations: CBS, Disney, GE, News Corp, Time Warner, and Viacom.

Even with media monopolies in place, different media sources report radically different views of the world. If you check CNN.com, FoxNews.com, and the popular right-wing Breitbart.com over a few days, you'll find very different accounts of what is going on, and very different views of which events are newsworthy. For example, CNN leads with one Trump blunder after another, while Fox and Brietbart focus on Democratic scandals. As I write this, every top story on CNN is about the fallout from a press conference in which Trump said there were "very fine people" among the white national-ists who marched with neo-Nazis and KKK members at a Charlottesville protest at which a white nationalist terrorist drove a car into the crowd of counter-protestors and killed Heather Heyer. The story isn't presently on the Fox front page at all, though there is a top story about the threat of anti-Trump "fake news."

When we decide what media to trust, we almost always decide to listen to only one point of view. In Oceania, the most important censors are the Party. In the modern West, the most important censor determining what an individual will hear is the individual themselves. Whereas Oceanians live in a reality-bubble of Party propaganda, we tend to live in a reality bubble we tailor to ourselves, listening only to those who think the same way we do.

Orwell noted that people are often so locked into their view of what is going on in the world that they refuse to believe that anyone genuinely holds any other view. Instead, they assume that anyone claiming to have a different take on the facts is being dishonest for political purposes. He writes in "The Prevention of Literature," "The Catholic and the Communist are alike in assuming that an opponent cannot be both honest and intelligent. Each of them tacitly claims that 'the truth' has already been revealed, and that the heretic, if he is not simply a fool, is secretly aware of 'the truth' and merely resists it out of selfish motives."

We see the same phenomenon in the US today. It seems to be an article of orthodoxy on both the left and right that what distinguishes the two sides is a difference in values. Yet if you listen to mainstream politicians and journalists on all sides, you'll find the values appealed to are largely the same: freedom, justice, equality, compassion, patriotism, the public good, and so on. In fact, the fundamental political divides between Americans seem not to rest on differences in values, but on difference in opinion over facts. For instance, most people who support gun rights believe gun rights make us safer, whereas most people who believe in gun control believe gun control makes us safer. Most people on either side would support the other side instead if they had the same beliefs about what makes us safer. Likewise, most supporters of President Trump believe illegal immigration from Mexico is seriously harming American workers and refugees from Muslim nations pose a serious terrorist danger, while the average liberal believes neither of these things. Presumably, if the Trump supporter and the liberal had each other's opinion of the facts, they would be a lot likelier to support each other's immigration policies.

Of course, someone's decisions about what facts to believe may be influenced by the values they hold. For instance, it seems likely that someone who hates black people will be more liable to believe that Black Lives Matter is anti-white. Still, our political disagreements almost always require disagreement over facts.

Among the facts we disagree on are the motivations and plans of political movements. As in Orwell's day, it's routine for commentators to assume bad faith when offering accounts of the motivations and plans of those they disagree with. So, for instance, when conservatives offer justifications for reduced welfare spending in terms of the economy or welfare fraud, liberals often dismiss these justifications as rationalization to cover the fact that conservatives only care about money and not people. Likewise, when liberals offer justifications for increased welfare spending in terms of hardship and need, conservatives often dismiss these justifications as rationalization to cover the fact that liberal politicians want to buy the votes of the lazy by handing over the money of hard working Americans. Such assumptions of bad faith make people not want to bother listening to arguments offered by the other side. Why listen to an argument from someone who doesn't believe what they are saying themselves, and are only trying to trick you?

Crimestop, Doublethink, and Reality Control

Citizens of Oceania are trained in mental techniques to remain orthodox. Crimestop is the skill of "stopping short, as though by instinct, at the threshold of any dangerous thought. It includes the power of not grasping analogies, of failing to perceive logical errors, of misunderstanding the simplest arguments if they are inimical to Ingsoc, and of being bored or repelled by any train of thought which is capable of leading in a heretical direction."

So, for instance, while Goldstein offers reasons in his book for rejecting the Party, the correct response, in accordance with Crimestop, is not to analyze his arguments, but to refuse to consider what he is saying. Winston's colleague Syme explains, "Orthodoxy means not thinking—not needing to think. Orthodoxy is unconsciousness."

Crimestop is just a version of our regular human tendency to ignore reasoning when it leads us to conclusions we dislike. Orwell observed that some political agendas aren't permitted to be contradicted by reality. For instance, in "Writers and Leviathan" (1948), he notes that among socialists, the question of lowering wages or raising hours to deal with economic events can't be discussed. The economy can never require this, as a matter of principle. The pressure to be orthodox was so intense that Orwell suggests it may be a bad sign if a political writer on the left isn't suspected of conservative tendencies.

Even if we are committed to being reasonable, we'll be fighting our instinct to use Crimestop. Can you imagine giving a fair hearing to an argument in favor of slavery, or anything else you find morally repugnant? Not making a habit of Crimestop could even harm your social position. How would it go down with the people you hang out with if you changed your mind on some of your core political positions? Even trying to fairly consider the best arguments of "the other side" is looked down on. Social groups are much more likely to approve of finding the *worst* arguments and most outrageous positions presented by someone on "the other side", just to demonstrate how awful people on the other side are.

In Oceania, citizens are expected to practice Doublethink— "To hold simultaneously two opinions which cancelled out, knowing them to be contradictory and believing in both of them." So for instance, as part of his job falsifying history in the

Records Department, Winston must believe he is falsifying history, and also that history has never been falsified.

It isn't clear exactly what the difference is between Doublethink and simply being self-contradictory and hypocritical, which is something all human beings do. Orwell writes that Doublethink must be both conscious and unconscious, which isn't obviously true of all real-world hypocrisy. Still, the technique clearly represents the self-contradiction and double standards Orwell found among the politically orthodox. For instance, while he thought the left was no more prone to inconsistency than anyone else, he accused leftists of his day of having "accumulated in our minds a whole series of unadmitted contradictions, as a result of successive bumps against reality" ("Writers and Leviathan"). For example, the left recognized that the British Empire had grown wealthy by exploiting Asia and Africa, but also believed that being just to Asia and Africa wouldn't damage the British economy and cause hardships for British workers.

Today, as always, Doublethink is practiced on all sides of politics, wherever there is a political orthodoxy to protect. There are conservatives who trust scientists when they need medical care, but not on climate change, and conservatives who champion Christianity, but see no duty to the poor, especially those living overseas. There are liberals who take it as obvious that a man can become a woman by identifying as a woman, and equally as obvious that a white person can't become a black person by identifying as black, and liberals who, as in Orwell's England, are outraged by inequalities within their nation, but forget that in international terms, first-world citizens are privileged exploiters more than exploited victims.

Did I just piss you off? No doubt, you don't think all of those are self-contradictory, but nothing hangs on whether you buy these specific examples. I'm sure you can come up with your own examples of Doublethink in political orthodoxy, if only the fact that leaks and filibusters are considered outrageous or not, depending on who benefits from them. Probably the most damaging case of Doublethink in the US is the combination of two beliefs:

1. Media outlets are often biased or dishonest.

2. I don't have to question the media I consume.

With this pair of inconsistent beliefs, an individual can't become aware that they are being misled by their media.

In Oceania, Party members must practice "reality control" by bringing their memories into line with Party accounts. When Winston replaces a story praising the now-disgraced Comrade Withers by inventing a story about the heroic Comrade Ogilvy, he is to immediately forget that Ogilvy isn't real.

"Reality control" is just a formal version of the memory rewriting we all naturally engage in. We often think our memories are accurate records, but in fact, we subconsciously edit them all the time, forgetting inconvenient facts and remembering things that never happened. Particularly distorting is "confirmation bias," the tendency to notice and recall information that supports our pre-existing beliefs, but not information that contradicts them. People often wonder how those on the other side of the political aisle can keep voting for their chosen party, given that party's track record. Yet people on different sides of the political aisle will genuinely remember different track records.

War Is Peace

Oceania is constantly at war with either Eurasia or Eastasia. Though the war poses no real danger, the Party ensures that "war hysteria is continuous and universal." The news, accompanied by "strident military music," presents gory descriptions of the annihilation of enemy armies, and shows footage of massacres, like that of the woman and boy Winston watches being "blown to pieces" by a helicopter. Popular music celebrates hatred, as in the case of the aptly named "Hate Song": "Roared out by hundreds of voices to the tramp of marching feet, it was terrifying. The proles had taken a fancy to it . . ." The hanging of prisoners of war is a popular spectacle that children in particular "always clamored to be taken to see."

Goldstein explains, "the object of the war is not to make or prevent conquests of territory, but to keep the structure of society intact." It does this in two ways: "It eats up the surplus of consumable goods, and it helps to preserve the special mental atmosphere that a hierarchical society needs." Surplus production must be destroyed so the proles remain poor, for otherwise, they "would become literate and would learn to think for themselves," and thus recognize their own oppression. The special mental atmosphere is one in which every Party member is a "credulous and ignorant fanatic whose prevailing moods are fear, hatred, adulation, and orgiastic triumph." Their fear and hatred of their enemies distracts them from the wrongs done to them by the Party, and makes them rely on the Party for protection. War hysteria isn't as constant among the proles, though they are "prodded into frenzies of fear and hatred" as necessary.

It's unlikely that any real-world government has deliberately destroyed production through war. On the other hand, war has often functioned to distract the masses from their condition. Orwell was aware of how the two world wars had subdued the labor movements, as workers pulled together to fight for their nation instead of their class. After these wars, the Cold War focused attention on the threat of communist nations. Today, Americans are called on to unite against foreign threats like North Korea and Russia, and above all, against ISIS and other Islamist organizations. Hostile governments and terrorist groups are frequently represented in conservative media as being primarily motived by hatred of American freedoms and the American way of life.

In Oceania, citizens are kept alert for traitors in their midst who seek to betray the state to its foreign enemies. Goldstein is said to be the commander of the Brotherhood, "a vast shadowy army, an underground network of conspirators . . ." Any citizen who opposes the Party is branded as such a traitor. Goldstein and his minions pretend to be fighting for the public good, but it's a trick. At the Two Minutes Hate, Goldstein cries from the screen that the revolution has been betrayed, and calls for free speech, while "behind his head on the telescreen there marched the endless columns of the Eurasian army."

Likewise, during the Cold War, it was widely believed that American's foreign enemies were being helped by a network of traitors. These "reds under the bed" were thought to be particularly active in the labor movement, and supporting workers' rights was often portrayed as siding with the "commies."

Modern America also fears internal traitors, including those who, like Goldstein, are pretending to be fighting for the good of the people. Some say President Trump sold the US out to the

Russians, others that liberal politicians are plotting to establish a communist state, or to abolish religion, or are secretly Muslim and wish to impose Sharia law. Americans of all political persuasions fear being murdered by terrorists inspired by ISIS. Such fears provide a powerful distraction from economic inequality.

Oceania, 'Tis for Thee

One of the Party's key tools for social control is the manipulation of identity. War hysteria can only be maintained by preventing Oceanians from realizing what they have in common with ordinary people everywhere. Goldstein muses: "all over the world, hundreds of thousands of millions of people just like this, people ignorant of one another's existence, held apart by walls of hatred and lies . . ."

If the proles were to identify as part of an international proletariat, they might understand the proletariat's position, and overthrow the ruling caste. So the Party has them identify themselves in ways that alienate them from foreign proletariats and bind them to the Party. Specifically, they ask them to be nationalists and identify as Oceanians. As the anthem says, "'Oceania, 'tis for thee," and all must stand to attention when they hear it. Foreigners become people to defend Oceania against, rather than natural allies.

Orwell saw the exploited workers of England as lacking a common identity. He urges in *Wigan Pier*, "all people with small, insecure incomes are in the same boat and ought to be fighting on the same side." Nor did English workers share a sense of identity with those overseas. In "Looking Back on the Spanish War," Orwell wrote, "To the British working class the massacre of their comrades in Vienna, Berlin, Madrid, or wherever it might be seemed less interesting and less important than yesterday's football match."

In the modern US, citizens are encouraged to identify as American. Patriotism is celebrated and flags abound. American schoolchildren even perform a morning ritual of pledging allegiance to the flag. One product of American nationalism is a common insistence, as a point of principle, that the US is the best place to live, and a corresponding lack of interest in how things are done elsewhere. Among other effects, this keeps many Americans ignorant of the numerous nations with higher standards of living. Goldstein explains, "so long as [the masses] are not permitted to have standards of comparison, they never even become aware that they are oppressed."

History classes in American schools tend to focus heavily on the history of the nation. Particular attention is paid to America's wars, especially the Revolutionary War, Civil War, and World War II, in all of which the US was fighting for good causes. Yet the story of a nation is only one narrative we could follow when considering history. For instance, we might instead follow the story of democracy, educating students about the English Civil War, the French Revolution, and the spread of democracy in Africa, as part of *their* history. Alternatively, the narrative followed could be that of the oppressed masses, enduring thousands of years of toil for the benefit of kings and wealthy nobility before slowly growing conscious enough to rise up and demand change. Instead of celebrating the triumphs of nations, we might celebrate the triumphs of an international proletariat.

Orwell rails against "nationalism," though he uses the word in a special sense that goes beyond partisanship towards nations. In "Notes on Nationalism" (1945), he defines "nationalism" as "first of all the habit of assuming that human beings can be classified like insects and that whole blocks of millions or tens of millions of people can be confidently labelled 'good' or 'bad' . . . But secondly—and this is much more important—I mean the habit of identifying oneself with a single nation or other unit, placing it beyond good and evil and recognizing no other duty than that of advancing its interests." His examples of nationalisms include "Communism, political Catholicism, Zionism, Antisemitism, Trotskyism and Pacifism . . . Jewry, Islam, Christendom, the Proletariat and the White Race . . ." Given the way feminists are represented in *Burmese Days* (1934) and *Keep the Aspidistra Flying* (1936), it seems Orwell saw some feminists as "nationalists" too.

Orwell thought such nationalism blinds people. He wrote: "All nationalists have the power of not seeing resemblances between similar sets of facts . . . Actions are held to be good or bad, not on their own merits, but according to who does them, and there is almost no kind of outrage . . . which does not change its moral colour when it is committed by 'our' side . . . The nationalist not only does not disapprove of atrocities committed by his own side, but he has a remarkable capacity for not even hearing about them."

Americans are divided by many non-national "nationalisms." Perhaps the most obvious is that of some white workers who direct their resentment at black and Latino Americans. On the other hand, too many middle-class liberals pontificate about white male heterosexual privilege without showing any awareness that the average poor white straight male is less privileged than almost any middle-class person. Wherever we find groups of people in conflict, we find partisan "nationalists." Where there is such partisanship, there is an impossibility of understanding one another and co-operating, let alone finding a common identity.

A particularly problematic form of "nationalism" is "nationalism" towards political movements. People identify as "conservative," "liberal," "green," or what have you, and treat the victories or humiliations of the movement as personal victories or humiliations. They cannot admit that a person with their political views has done something wrong, or that a person with contrary political views has done something right. Admitting that "your side" has made a mistake would be tantamount to letting the "other side" win. So, for instance, many poor white Americans whose interests would best be championed by a party on the left identify as "conservatives," and so support the GOP. It's no accident that economic conservatives, who want low taxes, have made common cause with social conservatives, who want to retain cultural norms. Orwell writes in *Wiggan Pier*, "Economically, I am in the same boat with the miner, the navvy, and the farm-hand; remind me of that and I will fight at their side. But culturally I am different from the miner, the navvy, and the farm-hand: lay the emphasis on that and you may arm me against them."

Until They Become Conscious They Will Never Rebel

In *1984*, the proles remain oppressed because they are unconscious of their situation. They are kept ignorant by the reality bubble of Party propaganda, aided by the psychological skills of Crimestop, Doublethink, and reality control. They are prevented by war and nationalism from focusing on their own subjugation or from understanding the common condition they share with the proletariat internationally.

In the modern US, there are many reasons why the masses are exploited, but the most important, as in *1984*, is that they don't understand the nature of their exploitation. Citizens are often isolated in reality bubbles. Our basic human irrationality, hypocrisy, and willingness to rewrite the past, are harnessed and used against us. International conflicts stoke nationalism and prevent the masses from finding a common identity with the masses worldwide. Within the US, conflicts between different social groups pit the masses against one another, and prevent them from recognizing their common condition.

Acknowledging this doesn't give us a blueprint for political improvement. But it gives us reason to resist demonizing those who disagree with us politically, to look for opportunities to make common cause with them, and to engage them in genuine dialog, rather than just denouncing them. The better the masses understand their situation, the better political decisions they are likely to make.

4
Non-State Enemies of Freedom

ERIN J. NASH

One of George Orwell's most important philosophical and political achievements in *Nineteen Eighty-Four* was to bring into sharp relief the profound way that our freedom and unfreedom, as individuals, and as societies, is bound up with the ability of words to *do things*, something scholars like J.L. Austin, Catharine MacKinnon, and Rae Langton would later emphasize.

But the full force of this insight, and what we can learn from it, has been obscured by the almost universal interpretation of *Nineteen Eighty-Four* as a critique of state power. Has this monoculture fallen out of a blind spot that Orwell himself suffered from? Or have we largely been misreading *Nineteen Eighty-Four*?

My impression is that Orwell wanted to impart a very different point than what has typically been assumed about who threatens our freedoms via the manipulation and control of our public information systems. Moreover, this deeper message will enable us to more fully grasp the problematic features of our contemporary political landscapes, and to develop better responses to these issues.

How to Oppress People with Words

The Party in *Nineteen Eighty-Four* deploys several mutually reinforcing communications-based strategies to distort reality and deceive and indoctrinate Oceania's inhabitants: it alters historical records, disseminates propaganda and misinforma-

tion, destroys evidence, and provides 'education' that leaves
children ". . . unwilling and unable to think too deeply on any
subject whatever" (p. 241). The *pièce de résistance* is 'Newspeak',
an official language the Party invents, and that it gradually
culls the vocabulary of. Syme boasts that this has the effect of
narrowing the scope of people's consciousness, and thus the
range of thoughts a person can possibly think (pp. 60–61).

If a person's consciousness and thought is circumscribed,
then so too is what they can subsequently *say* and *do* in turn.
If a person is literally unable to *think* 2 + 2 = 4, for example,
then they cannot *say* "2 + 2 = 4." If they cannot say "2 + 2 = 4",
then their freedom to assert this proposition has been cur-
tailed, and they have been subjected to a type of *silencing*.
Similarly, if we are unable to think that 2 + 2 = 4, we won't be
able to carry out practical activities that turn on such knowledge. One of Orwell's favorite examples was that two and two
must make four if you want to successfully design an airplane
(a point Orwell makes in "The Prevention of Literature" and
has Winston make in *Nineteen Eighty-Four*, p. 227). Hence,
because Oceanians have been deprived of the necessary capacities to recognize their oppression, voice their dissatisfaction,
and retaliate, the Party considers a revolt of the masses to be a
risk 'in theory' only.

Orwell therefore illuminates the way our very autonomy—
that is, having *sufficient control* over determining our own values and ends, and over whether our acts succeed in realising
those values and ends—can be affected by others' speech.
Whilst nineteenth-century philosopher John Stuart Mill
emphasized the importance of freedom of speech for fostering
the conditions under which thought, consciousness, and autonomy can flourish, *Nineteen Eighty-Four* predominantly focuses
on the other side of this equation: the way that certain agents'
freedom of speech—primarily, their freedom to spread
untruths—can be used to construct barriers to, or actively
erode, others' freedoms.

The State as an Agent of Oppression

Ever since seventeenth-century poet and scholar John Milton
protested the government's control of the printing press, the
actor whose freedoms have been viewed as a threat to our own,

and consequently, whose power needs to be constrained, has invariably been the state.

Interpretations of *Nineteen Eighty-Four* have only served to fuel this perception, as readers from across the political spectrum have generally taken *Nineteen Eighty-Four* to be a straightforward critique of collectivism and 'big government'; at times, it was even explicitly marketed as an anti-Soviet and anti-Communist tract. Accordingly, many readers have assumed *Nineteen Eighty-Four*'s key warning to be about the potential, and even propensity, for governments to inevitably slide down a slippery slope into totalitarianism, with the manipulation and control of language and speech playing an instrumental role in achieving and sustaining this tyranny.

In many ways, this is a very reasonable interpretation. The domination and oppression of citizens by the state under the twin specters of Nazism and Stalinism was of course a key feature of the political era within which Orwell penned *Nineteen Eighty-Four*. And we naturally associate the Party in Oceania with an organized political party that had gained power; just like governments, it had Ministries, and carried out activities that resembled the development and implementation of public policy. It also appeared to have a military, and was supposedly at war with other states.

We also know that Orwell anguished over the post-war state of socialism, particularly in England. He was especially disturbed by the widespread allegiance to Stalinism he observed among the intellectual left, despite the presence of overwhelming evidence of the evils of Stalin's regime. Orwell thought there were "strong tendencies towards totalitarianism in the English literary intelligentsia" ("Writers and Leviathan"). These frustrations seem to have motivated him to call the Party's ideology in *Nineteen Eighty-Four* 'Ingsoc' ('English socialism'). His observations of the habits of thought and speech of these intellectuals and elites also provided the inspiration for 'newspeak', 'blackwhite', and 'doublethink'. Orwell protested that "nearly the whole of the English Left has been driven to accept the Russian regime as 'Socialist', while silently recognizing that its spirit and practice is quite alien to anything that is meant by 'Socialism' in this country. Hence there has arisen a sort of schizophrenic manner of thinking, in which words like 'democracy' can bear two irreconcilable meanings."

So, unlike many of his fellow left-wing bourgeois colleagues, Orwell maintained a strong connection to reality, and unlike Winston, was able to preserve his sanity.

There was a reversal of this trend, however, in the second half of the twentieth century, which saw an abundance of intellectuals who, like Orwell, weren't under any illusions about the dictatorships that had blighted, and were still devastating, much of Europe. They feared the power of states over citizens, and their writings honed our understanding of this threat and lent power to interpretations of *Nineteen Eighty-Four* as a warning about governments.

Three philosophers, all of whom had first-hand experience of life under totalitarian regimes, are particularly noteworthy here for the connections that can be drawn between their scholarship and *Nineteen Eighty-Four*: Karl Popper, Hannah Arendt, and Isaiah Berlin.

Popper, a philosopher of science, wrote both *The Poverty of Historicism* (1944) and *The Open Society and Its Enemies* (1945) as responses to his experiences of Nazi Germany. An important aspect of these works was a critique of theories of history that take the past to be inevitably unfolding according to universal laws. Like Orwell, Popper viewed such deterministic understandings of history and society to be a key aspect and driver of totalitarian ideologies.

Hannah Arendt's first major book was *The Origins of Totalitarianism* (1951). In it she traces the roots of Nazism and Stalinism, and argues that these administrations represented a novel type of government in that they used terror to subjugate the masses, rather than taking aim only at their political adversaries. Later, in *Eichmann in Jerusalem* (1963), she coined the phrase "the banality of evil" to describe the way that ordinary people commonly conform to mass opinion and obey orders without conscious thought, and therefore without regard to the consequences of their actions or inaction. This passive state is exhibited by many of the characters we meet in *Nineteen Eighty-Four*, like Winston's colleagues at the Ministry of Truth, and especially his 'goodthinkful' wife.

Finally, Isaiah Berlin, in his most famous work "Two Concepts of Liberty" (1958), distinguished between two key ways liberty could be understood: negative liberty, based on non-interference, and positive liberty, based on the development of the individual. Under the negative conception of liberty, a person is free to the extent that they do not face obstacles, barriers, or constraints to their actions, whereas under the positive conception, a person is free to the extent that their actions are self-determined—they control and master their own life, in alignment with their own interests. Berlin's preference for negative liberty is implicit in the essay, with much of it dedicated to an exposition of the dangers of positive liberty, and a historical account of the uses and abuses of it by totalitarian governments.

Popper's and Berlin's scholarship in particular, is representative, and perhaps even a significant driver, of the general intellectual drift towards liberalism in political philosophy since the middle of the twentieth century. As Lorna Finlayson has argued, academic political philosophy today is almost synonymous with liberalism. The focus has increasingly been on the individual, and on the state as *the chief* threat to individuals' freedoms. The key questions asked are predominantly about the extent to which governments can rightfully interfere in the lives of individuals, and hence, how its influence over our lives needs to be constrained through, for example, strong protections for freedoms of speech and of the press.

But has this focus on the state as the subjugating agent, in interpretations of *Nineteen Eighty-Four,* and within academia and popular culture more broadly, functioned as a distraction, and blindsided us to the variety of wellsprings of domination and oppression within our societies? And if so, was a neglect of these threats partly responsible for the recent political upheavals across large parts of Europe and the English-speaking world?

The Under-Appreciated Threat of Non-State Actors to Our Freedoms

The "denial of reality" is not only a "special feature" of Ingsoc and its rival systems of thought (p. 226); it has also been a prominent part of our own political terrain. Whilst the commentariat declared 2016 the beginning of the 'post-truth' political era, this assertion exaggerates the novelty of the influence of false, inaccurate, and misleading speech on politics.

'Fake news' is at least as old as the printing press itself, and older still if you count false rumors as fake news; it's probably as old as human civilization, and hence politics, itself. Even the claim that it's the extent of the phenomenon that is new, not its presence, is debatable; commercial actors and ideologues from political think tanks have, increasingly since the 1950s, utilized and hidden behind their 'free speech rights', and the virtue our culture attributes to 'dissenters', to propagate misinformation.

These 'alternative facts' induce ignorance and doubt, which works to disempower the public politically and delay societal responses to issues that have significant negative consequences for many people's lives. Historians of science Naomi Oreskes and Eric Conway have dubbed these tactics the 'Tobacco Strategy', due to their use in the tobacco industry's fifty-year campaign denying the relationship between smoking and cancer. It has since become the strategy of choice of free market fundamentalists in particular, who have replicated and deployed it to a long list of issues, from acid rain and anthropogenic climate change, to the impact of chemical waste disposal on human health.

However, more moderate organizations and experts that nominally represent the 'public interest' have, deliberately or unwittingly, frequently engaged in reality distortion in attempting to secure political ends too. In his book *The Divide* (2017), anthropologist Jason Hickel exposes the deceitful creative accounting practices and misleading declarations of bodies such as the United Nations and the World Bank. Whilst these organizations tell us that global poverty rates are declining and that extreme poverty will soon be eradicated, Hickel says these assertions are simply not true. His analysis demonstrates that poverty is not disappearing as quickly as these organizations claim it to be, and that, by some measures, it has in fact been getting significantly worse. It's almost as if these organizations have been heeding Goldstein's advice, that "it is necessary for a person to believe that he is better off than his ancestors and that the average level of material comfort is constantly rising" (p. 242).

Similarly, economics journalist Aditya Chakrabortty has stressed that the proponents of free trade, many of whom are representatives of organizations Hickel refers to, such as the International Monetary Fund and the World Trade Organization, "peddle their own untruths. They have insisted that black is white, even as the voters beg to differ." Notice here Chakrabortty's reference to the Orwellian practice of 'black-white'. Scientists and analysts, or those who report on their work, can spread falsities and misleading statements when they erroneously characterize their assertions as facts, and overlook the way that these statements are value-laden. (K.C. Elliott's book *A Tapestry of Values* is an introduction to the ways much of science can be value-laden.)

But unlike Chakrabortty, much of the corporate mass media does not call this propaganda out; rather, it plays a symbiotic role in aiding and abetting its mass distribution. This flies in the face of the popular image of the 'free press' as society's guardian of truth and upholder of democracy, and moreover, as a reliable place citizens can turn to for accurate and unbiased information to use in their own decision making. In *Nineteen Eighty-Four* we are told that, "The invention of print . . . made it easier to manipulate public opinion, and the film and the radio carried the process further" (p. 235). Can you imagine then, what the world of *Nineteen Eighty-Four* would have been like with the internet and social media in Big Brother's hands?

What the commentariat's long overdue epiphany about post-truth politics does reveal though, and is indicative of, is the long-standing general neglect of the existence of horizontal threats to our freedoms, such as the speech acts and manipulation and control of language, data, information and knowledge by various *non-state* actors, and the downplaying of the seriousness of these dynamics whenever red flags were waved. As many of the state's powers have been reined in after the political shocks of the twentieth century, non-state actors' influence within and over society has correspondingly expanded. At first blush, it seems like such threats were Orwell's blind spot in *Nineteen Eighty-Four.*

Oligarchy within *Nineteen Eighty-Four*

However, it's also possible that Orwell's vision did not suffer, and that we have largely been misreading *Nineteen Eighty-Four* and what it was that Orwell was trying to warn us about. This becomes apparent if we read *Nineteen Eighty-Four* not as a critique of Stalinism, Communism, Socialism, or the threat of a large, centralized government, but as a cautionary tale about the oppressive potential of *any* concentration of power; that is, about the presence of oligarchies in society.

This interpretation fits with Orwell's interest in the theories of philosopher and political theorist James Burnham. In *The Managerial Revolution* (1941), Burnham suggests that capitalism is disappearing, but that—in contradiction to Marxist theory—it is not being replaced by socialism. Burnham speculates that what is in ascendance is a new kind of planned, centralized society, but not one that is capitalist nor, in any genuine sense, democratic. Burnham thinks that the rulers of this society will be those who control, rather than own, the means of production: business executives, technicians, bureaucrats, and soldiers. These 'managers' will organize society so that all power and economic privilege remain in their hands. A hierarchy within society will persist, but at the top will be an aristocracy of *talent* rather than inherited wealth, with a mass of semi-slaves still residing underneath.

If this sounds familiar, you probably recall that in *The Theory and Practice of Oligarchical Collectivism*, Emmanuel Goldstein notes that, "What kind of people would control this world had been equally obvious. The new aristocracy was made up for the most part of bureaucrats, scientists, technicians, trade-union organizers, publicity experts, sociologists, teachers, journalists, and professional politicians" (p. 235). That Orwell chose to draw on Burnham's philosophy to write Goldstein's manual and set the scene of *Nineteen Eighty-Four* is unsurprising considering he thought that Burnham's theories, at least those about the present and the immediate past, were probably more right than wrong ("Second Thoughts on James Burnham").

However, Orwell also had significant disagreements with Burnham's philosophy. He took the real question to be, "not whether the people who wipe their feet on us during the next fifty years are to be called managers, bureaucrats or politicians: the question is whether capitalism, now obviously doomed, is to give way to *oligarchy* or true democracy?" There are at least three options for what Orwell might have meant by this statement. The first is that there is no meaningful difference as to who the power-holders are within an oligarchy; whether they are state or non-state actors, the outcome, and its consequences, are essentially the same. Remember

Goldstein asserts that, "*Who* wields power is not important, provide that the hierarchical structure remains always the same" (p. 240).

Alternatively, Orwell could be intimating that state and non-state actors within capitalist societies ultimately work in concert to oppress the population at large, or even that they may eventually become indistinguishable if government machinery is captured by non-state actors. Such possibilities are hinted at in *Nineteen Eighty-Four* when we learn that citizens in Oceania have been "shaped and brought together by the barren world of monopoly industry and centralised government" (p. 235). This feature has been borrowed from Zamyatin's *We*, which Orwell took to be aimed not at any particular country (such as Soviet Russia), but at what capitalist industrial civilization suggests about the direction social and economic development will be under increasing pressure to move towards. That Zamyatin and other writers had already posited this is why Orwell says of Burnham's scholarship that: "The notion that industrialism must end in monopoly, and that monopoly must imply tyranny is not a startling one."

Political philosopher Sheldon Wolin claimed that such societies suffer from a form of 'inverted totalitarianism'. He coined this term to describe what he believed to be the emerging governance structure of the United States. Wolin argued that one of the main ways governments could be understood to be enacting an inverted form of classical totalitarianism was that, whereas the state-dominated economic actors under totalitarianism's classic form, within an inverted totalitarian society, non-state actors, such as corporations, come to dominate and control the state, through financial contributions, lobbying power, and other means, such as those we explored earlier, for instance through the Tobacco Strategy. In working to manipulate voters' understanding of reality and shape their political preferences and behaviors, these methods are able to maintain a much more covert grip over the state and its citizens.

The third possibility is that Orwell wanted us to understand that it's plausible that totalizing forces can endure without the deliberate actions of any physical person or thing. Orwell warns, again through Goldstein's manual, that

the 'older kind of Socialist' "did not see that the continuity of
an oligarchy *need not be physical* . . . The essence of oligarchical rule is not father-to-son inheritance, but the per-
sistence of a certain world-view and a certain way of life,
imposed by the dead upon the living" (p. 239). By capitalizing
the P of 'Party', perhaps Orwell was suggesting—by indicating we should understand this as a doublespeak or blackwhite term—that the 'Party' does not simply correspond to a
standard political party, and that it should be understood to
be something entirely different.

Likewise, we never find out who, or what, the 'infallible' and
'all powerful' Big Brother is. Could Big Brother and the Party
be something more abstract then, perhaps akin to the market
or the internet? Such a possibility seems less far-flung when
we find out that Oceania is *not* centralized in *any* way, except
for its language (p. 238), which remember, has an in-built ideology. This fact simultaneously renders an interpretation of
Nineteen Eighty-Four as a warning about the 'big state' and the
centralization of government much less credible. What Orwell
shows us is that there need not be a centralized government,
traditionally understood, for totalitarianism to be brought
about and sustained.

Finally, it's also clear from letters Orwell wrote after the
release of *Nineteen Eighty-Four* that he intended it as a warning
about totalitarian methods *in general*, regardless of their source.
In a letter to a union leader in June 1949 he emphasized that

> My recent novel is NOT intended as an attack on Socialism or on
> the British Labour Party (of which I am a supporter) but as a show-
> up of the perversions to which a *centralized economy* is liable and
> which have already been partly realized in Communism and
> Fascism.

In another letter the following week he laments that right-
wing newspapers in the US have been using *Nineteen Eighty-
Four* propagandistically against their left-wing rivals. But
contrary to any partisan interpretation or use of *Nineteen
Eighty-Four*, Orwell wanted us to understand that, given certain concentrations of power, totalitarianism could arise in any
society or period, from any part of the political spectrum, and
be dressed in many different disguises.

Resisting Big Brother and the Emergence of an Oceanic Society

Nineteen Eighty-Four was also Orwell's passionate plea to fight against totalitarianism, and its pages contain a great deal of advice for how we can go about resisting Big Brother types and the emergence of Oceanic-like societies. These crucial facets of the book have often been overlooked because many have taken its ending, with Winston's eventual submission to Big Brother, to suggest that Orwell was pessimistic and believed totalitarianism to be irresistible and unavoidable. This, however, could not be further from Orwell's deepest convictions.

One of his most significant disagreements with Burnham was that Burnham took the future socioeconomic trajectory he had prophesized to be inevitable, whereas Orwell rejected this kind of determinism and, like Popper, wanted to resist any suggestion of inexorable laws. This is most obvious when we look carefully at the *Principles of Newspeak,* which is an appendix to *Nineteen Eighty-Four.* This document refers to a *past* time, signalling that Ingsoc was eventually defeated. Winston's and Julia's actions throughout the book therefore leave us clues as to how the regime may have been overcome, and hence how we can contribute to ridding our own societies of domination and oppression. I see the following as two of the most pertinent of Orwell's lessons in *Nineteen Eighty-Four* for our current era.

Firstly, there is the importance of *evidence.* We never find out what happens to Winston's diary, but it's possible that it was found and used by others as a "standard of comparison," a concept which Orwell thought was indispensable and that is emphasized at several places within *Nineteen Eighty-Four.* Through his diary, perhaps Winston did succeed in passing on the 'secret doctrine' that 2 + 2 = 4. But because collecting, processing, storing, and interpreting evidence is generally carried out by experts (Burnham's 'managers') often necessarily without the participation of lay-citizens, the integrity and public accountability of the systems that generate and disseminate and report on data, information, and knowledge, are critical to our freedoms and the health of society.

The second is the value of democracy. Orwell held strong beliefs about the capacity for public opinion, in the ideal, to help society avoid errors and injustices. He put Nazi Germany's destruction partly down to its undemocratic, 'managerial' structure: "Mistakes of this magnitude can only be made, or at any rate they are most likely to be made, in countries where public opinion has no power. So long as the common man can get a hearing, such elementary rules as not fighting all your enemies simultaneously are less likely to be violated" ("Second Thoughts on James Burnham"). This is also reflected in Winston's unwavering confidence that the only hope for humanity lies in the Proles.

Notice that these two values are entangled: public opinion and democratic processes are only valuable to the extent that these opinions are not based on significant factual inaccuracies, and are sufficiently peoples' own; evidence, on the other hand, is only valuable to the extent that it actually does further our understanding of the world, and contributes to enhancing our freedoms. We can therefore only achieve comprehensive freedom and social progress if the entities and processes that generate, distribute, and use all forms of knowledge are democratically orientated and trustworthy.

Whether or not Orwell intended *Nineteen Eighty-Four* to be interpreted as I have suggested in this essay, I suggest that we can learn more from it if we do interpret it that way.

Nineteen Eighty-Four is itself an exemplar of freedom-enhancing speech.[1]

---

[1] Thank you to Sarah Buchanan, Ruth Crook, Sally Davies, and Stefan Storrie for very helpful feedback on earlier drafts of this chapter.

5
Ministry of Truth Handbook: Excerpt on the Strategic Use of Fallacious Reasoning for Thoughtcrime Prevention

PREPARED BY PARTY MEMBER ELIZABETH RARD

Welcome to your new role as an upper planning agent at the Ministry of Truth. If you are reading this handbook then you have been granted top clearance and are now a key asset in the ongoing war against an informed population, which, as you know, is the most dangerous threat to the safety and stability that comes with total government control.

Note: If you do not have the appropriate clearance, and rather have come across this publication through unapproved avenues, please remain calm. Agents from the Ministry of Love will be with you shortly to alleviate the burden of your awareness of the existence of this document. Rest assured that the fine citizens at the Ministry of Truth will make all necessary corrections to the historical records so that they are consistent with the facts of your nonexistence.

It was long ago determined that as long as populations were allowed access to the truth they would inevitably come to realize that those in power did not need to stay in power. Hierarchical societies are by their nature unstable as those at the top become complacent while those in the working class become dissatisfied with their status. Whenever it is discovered that those at the highest levels of a society are fallible (and perhaps do not have the best interests of the people as a main motivating goal) power tends to shift and a new regime takes the place of the old leadership.

Big Brother understands that the root of these upheavals lies in a population that is too clever for its own good. If we are to maintain the order of the established hierarchy we must focus on two things: poverty and ignorance. The enemy of the state is independent thought. Those who think independently will question the status quo, they will ask whether things might not be better if different individuals were in charge, they will discover that the party is not the salvation that is reflected in the daily news bulletins, and they will come to realize how the structure of society, and especially the leadership tier, might be changed.

This handbook will provide a working knowledge of the connection between rational thought and true belief, and will illustrate the ways in which rationality and belief can be separated. True belief is largely the enemy of our goals. We need the general population to believe without question that everything that is good in their lives, all of their food and security and happiness (such as it is), comes directly from Big Brother. In addition it must never even cross their minds that things should, or even could, ever be better than they currently are.

We must have control of every thought in Oceania. It will often be in the best interests of party control, and therefor society at large, for the general population to hold beliefs that are not actually true. To ensure that the proper beliefs are in place we must be able to create false beliefs in our citizens just as easily as true beliefs. To guarantee that evidence and facts do not interfere with this goal we must utilize methods of persuasion that will support the creation of false beliefs just as easily as the creation of true beliefs.

Rational thinking is notoriously biased in favor of true belief and as such we must wherever possible remove the ability to think rationally from our citizens. Fallacious reasoning as it is outlined in this handbook has one important virtue; it can be used to produce belief in false propositions just as easily as true propositions.

Ignorance Is Strength

The goal of rational thought is often considered to be the attainment of true beliefs. One argument for such an assumption might run something like this. The world actually is a certain way. We, as rational humans, have certain goals such as surviving and prospering, being happy and finding food, and not being horribly mangled in a biking accident. It is much easier to achieve these goals if we actually have beliefs that reflect the way the world is. Hence true beliefs (ones that reflect the way the world is) are generally quite useful, and as such are a worthy goal of rational thought.

But we in the party have come to realize that truth is the enemy of stability. People generally cannot be trusted to make decisions about their own well-being. They may not realize that the best place for them is in the loving care of Big Brother. In order to allow our citizens to trust in Big Brother completely we will remove from them the burden of dealing with confusing truths, and rather feed them a reality that will allow them to trust completely in the system.

Most of the teachings of the old philosophers have been erased by the Ministry of Truth, and as such never existed in the first place. We can however reveal a fragment of philosophy that has been reconstructed, as it is crucial to the internal justification of Party policy. Plato (whom you won't remember was removed from the approved list of intellectuals deemed safe for public consumption) argued that sometimes it is in the best interests of the citizens of a nation to not know the truth about certain things. Sometimes to get people to act in the best interest of themselves and society a few people are justified in lying to everyone.

For example if there was a small chance that a disease might cause an epidemic, but there was nothing anyone could do to change the likelihood that the disease would continue to spread, a government might keep the information from its citizens in order to avoid widespread panic, which would lead to death and destruction. Plato called such a justified and well-intentioned deception a *noble lie*. You can think of your mission here at the Ministry of Truth as a continuation of Plato's dream.

Plato had the right idea when he realized that people need to be lied to for their own good. But the problem with having just one noble lie in a society, especially one that is generally well-educated and allowed access to mostly truths, is that the lie becomes apparent quite quickly. Anyone with the slightest bit of critical reasoning ability will begin to notice the inconsistencies that pop up in a generally true belief system with only a few lies mixed. The only way to avoid such an inconvenient eventuality is to have complete control over all the beliefs of the citizens, and to remove their ability to reason about their beliefs in such a way that internal inconsistencies might become apparent.

The majority of the population can be kept almost completely ignorant of the way the world actually is. The Proles will be kept tired and poor. They will work until they are too exhausted to ask questions, and they will not be educated beyond what's needed to complete the menial tasks we give them. They will have a vague love for Big Brother, a patriotism sufficient to ensure their continued compliance with labor demands placed on them. When they have a complaint it will be that some specific need has not been met. But they will not have the resources to formulate a criticism of the system. Rather they will accept any explanation that blames their misfortune on the enemies of the state, and they will be content to accept their lot in the world order because they will be too tired to think further on the matter.

The difficulty arises in controlling those who are needed to perform the more cognitively demanding tasks, those moderately intelligent individuals who work in the ministries themselves, who must have the minimum education and cognitive resources to perform the complex tasks that are required to keep our technology running and our surveillance effective.

These are the most dangerous because they have the potential brainpower to understand the distribution of power within our society (it is, of course, not actually distributed since all power lies solely with Big Brother). They could figure out that the war makes no sense. They could figure out that the government has not actually done a fantastic job of providing food to the citizens.

In order to control these individuals and to keep them free of thoughtcrime we must use every tactic at our disposal to confuse their ability to reason generally, blocking all inferences save those that are required for the completion of their assigned tasks. It is to this end that the Ministry of Truth, in co-operation with the other Ministries, has implemented a plan of strategic irrationality. This irrationality is achieved through the constant use of fallacious reasoning to control the thoughts of our citizens so that the content of the minds of our workers is safe from the inconveniences of truth.

Strategic Fallacy Deployment

In this section you will be introduced to some of the particular fallacies that the Ministry of Truth has found to be useful for controlling the beliefs and reasoning abilities of the general population. Study these fallacies, for they are the key to creating whatever reality suits the current purposes of Big Brother. Fallacies are common errors in reasoning, ones that are common because they tend to be very persuasive. As such they can be readily exploited to manipulate the beliefs of individuals regardless of what conclusions the evidence might support.

Ad Hominem

This fallacy is an excellent bit of manipulation because it allows you to counter anyone's argument without even needing to engage the argument. Take for example the positions of Goldstein. As we know Goldstein is a main threat to the Party as his actual arguments expose the methods and motivations of the Party. But we cannot simply ignore him, as knowledge of his existence is widespread throughout Oceania. Were we to simply pretend he never existed people would become suspicious and would seek to find more details of his position. Rather we start by making the citizens dislike the man, through careful character assassination, so that they lose interest in his arguments.

During the Two Minutes Hate (one of our most ingenious methods of belief correction) we show a version of Goldstein to the people. His features are to always be portrayed as similar to those of a goat. Indeed, his very voice must sound like the shrill bleating of a goat. Through this characterization of Goldstein people will come to identify him not as an intellectual to be listened to, but rather as an animal, dumb and disgusting. Once they think of Goldstein as this repulsive goat-like creature, they will not for a moment think his positions would be worth considering. The great beauty of this approach is that it does not matter if Goldstein is right, or that we cannot give any good argument to show why he is wrong, it only matters that we make people hate him. Once this task is accomplished no one will even consider his position to be worth a second thought.

Straw Man

The *ad hominem* will go a long way to dissuade people from pursuing Goldstein's teachings, but there is still a chance that some might be curious enough to overlook the repulsiveness of the man. Curiosity is a dangerous threat to party control. An individual citizen consumed by curiosity will go to great lengths, even risking personal harms, in order to satisfy such curiosity. Threats will not necessarily quell the longing for understanding. The best way to dissuade citizens from seeking the teachings of Goldstein, or worse yet trying to use their own intelligence to recreate the arguments, is to give them (in a sense) exactly what they want. We satisfy the curiosity of misguided citizens by presenting them with a version, albeit a bastardized version, of the position that they wish to comprehend.

During the Two Minutes Hate, when the caricature of Goldstein is bleating at the audience, we have him actually explain a position, an argument against the party, but we ensure that the content of the argument is so suspect, the logical thread of the reasoning so flimsy, that anyone anywhere could see immediately that the reasoning is poor. This approach, of creating a straw man version of Goldstein's actual position, helps control the beliefs of the population in several ways. First, they have their curiosity concerning Goldstein's arguments satisfied, and so no longer feel compelled to pursue his teachings on their own. In addition they are given an argument that is truly and obviously unpersuasive, and so they conclude on their own that Goldstein must be wrong. In fact, his reasoning is so poor that they decide he is an incompetent fool, and conclude that only such a fool as he would go against the Party.

But the really brilliant bit is this. We include just enough actual argumentation that, while people see the flaws for themselves, there is some small worry that others may be fooled. This creates an army of citizens who will continue to explain to anyone and everyone why Goldstein's positions must be rejected.

Suppressed Evidence

The suppressed evidence fallacy is the bread and butter of the Ministry of Truth. This fallacy is committed when someone omits some piece of information that would, were it to be known, weaken their argument. Traditionally this fallacy merely involved leaving the weakening evidence out of the argument, which still left open the possibility that an industrious person might take it upon themselves to look for, and possibly find, the missing information. We here at the Ministry of Truth have taken this fallacy to the next level. As you know the Ministry devotes considerable effort to identifying and destroying all evidence that would support any claim that is contrary to the narrative that the Party has approved. By destroying evidence that could weaken the arguments that the Ministry puts forward we make our position appear stronger since there is no apparent evidence against the Party's position.

Special Use of Emotional Distraction:

In this section you will find additional fallacious techniques employed by our office. Central to these tactics is an exploitation of the irrationality that comes with heightened emotions. Aristotle, who also never existed (of course) famously never said that man is a rational animal. Humans are particularly well equipped to use their reason to understand and make predictions about the world around them. This is no good. Big Brother decides what people need to believe. We can't have them running about using their faculty of rationality to form their own beliefs.

Fortunately Aristotle also gave us the key to thwarting rationality. He thought that in order to facilitate rational thought we must each learn to control our emotions so that we would not be at the mercy of extreme emotional reactions that would directly interfere with our ability to think and act rationally. Aristotle held up such disgusting virtues as courage and wit among the character traits that could be achieved through a careful balancing of one's emotions. The clear answer then is to trigger extreme emotions in the citizens in order to both hamper their ability to think rationally, and to persuade them to adopt the set of Party-approved beliefs.

Appeal to Fear

In an appeal to fear we begin by creating a fear in the individual we are targeting, or bringing out an already existing fear. For example we release records and stories of the way the world was before the Party came to power. It does not matter if these representations are accurate, for we have wiped the world clean of any evidence of the way things actually were before the great state of Oceania arose.

We carefully paint a picture of a people terrorized by the monster capitalists. In our narrative the capitalists owned everything, all the land and houses and factories, and especially all of the money. Everyone else was their slave, and people who disobeyed lost everything. They were fired, had their homes taken away, and were even starved to death.

Once we have made the citizens sufficiently fearful of the way things were we then present Big Brother as their salvation. Big Brother is the only thing that stands between citizens and a return to the despair of the capitalist era. The strategy here is beautiful in its simplicity. We make people so afraid of a world that is worse, we prey on their fears of loss, starvation, and death, and then we offer them the solution. Embrace the new world order, love Big Brother, and you will be safe from the terrors of a capitalist world. People are so afraid of the way things could be, and so grateful that they have been offered salvation and continued security, that they never stop to ask for any proof that things are better now, or that Big Brother is the best way to keep their situation from getting worse.

Appeal to Force

This is our last resort, and it is necessary when we are dealing with a particularly clever and willful individual. You might well wonder why we do not simply erase such individuals, but we have found that these sorts of people can sometimes prove very useful, when they can be controlled.

The method here is simple. If all other means have failed to produce the appropriate beliefs in an individual we simply confront them with a fate so horrifying that their own sense of self-preservation overrides their rational brain and produces the desired beliefs in their mind.

One instance of a successful deployment of this tactic occurred when a thoughtcriminal named Winston was treated for his unapproved beliefs. Winston had begun to use his own reason to question the authority and supremacy of the Party. Worse yet he had ceased to love Big Brother. He began to seek out the teachings of Goldstein, and was committed to taking any action that would aid in overthrowing the Party. He proved immune to our normal techniques of thought control and so he had to be taken into custody.

In order to finally correct his thinking we tortured him for months, beating him and depriving him of food. Gradually his beliefs began to fall in line with those that were approved. After much work Winston reached a point where he accepted that anything could be true, anything the Party said was true was thereby true, regardless of any fault that logic may imply in the positions of the Party. Winston was able to will himself to believe that the very laws of gravity themselves were subject to revision. In the end we were able to purge him of his belief that he loved another traitor by attaching a cage filled with starving rats to his face. In that moment he abandoned completely his naive attachment to rationality and instead gave himself over completely to the will of the Party.

We are pleased to report that, through threat of great bodily harm, we were able to rehabilitate Winston fully. He no longer attempts to use rational thought and argument to arrive at his beliefs. Rather he unreservedly accepts whatever the Party tells him as the truth.

We Must Be Ever Vigilant

These fallacies, these instruments of thought control, are the most powerful tools at the Party's disposal. It is clearly in the best interest of this Party to have the ability to create false beliefs in our citizens. There is a danger, though. Were people to become aware of the fallacies that are being used to persuade them they might develop an immunity to them. Once someone sees why a *straw man* argument, for example, is not the sort of argument that is likely to lead to true beliefs, that person may be able to both identify such a faulty argument, and even resist its powers of persuasion.

6
Big Brother Ltd.

DARREN BOTELLO-SAMSON AND KAYCE MOBLEY

> He has no freedom of choice in any direction whatever. On the other
> hand, his actions are not regulated by law or by any clearly formu-
> lated code of behavior. In Oceania there is no law. . . . Many of the
> beliefs and attitudes demanded of him are never plainly stated, and
> could not be stated without laying bare the contradictions inherent in
> Ingsoc.
>
> —GEORGE ORWELL, *1984*

In 1961, Erich Fromm wrote in an afterword to *1984*, "The
reader will find many other features of our present Western
society in Orwell's description in *1984*, provided he can overcome enough of his own 'doublethink'" (p. 266).

What Fromm noticed about Orwell's cautionary tale is the
applicability of its critique to the general exercise of power over
and upon humanity. While Orwell wrote *1984* directed towards
the abuses of Stalinism, which is why the novel is frequently
read as a critique of socialist and communist governments,
Fromm is arguing that it can also be read as a representation
of authoritarianism more generally, including the kind exercised by politically conservative governments. And Fromm
identifies an important tool used in the exercise of that power,
what Orwell called Doublethink, or "the power of holding two
contradictory beliefs in one's mind simultaneously, and accepting both of them."

In the quote that opens this chapter, Orwell is referring to
the members of the Outer Party and the manner of control
exercised over them by the Inner Party. If the Inner Party were

to articulate specific rules of conduct for members of the Outer Party, their power would be limited to those rules and the power of the Inner Party would not be absolute. But the appeal to the power of the Inner Party must be made on the basis of truth and law, otherwise their claim to power would be as arbitrary as anyone else's.

So to be a good member of the Party, either Inner or Outer, requires holding these two contradictory positions, law and lawlessness, at the same time. In "The Theory and Practice of Oligarchical Collectivism," Goldstein's handbook for the Brotherhood, it is revealed that the pursuit of power is sought by the Party for its own sake. Therefore, the dystopic visions of *1984*, including the phenomenon of Doublethink, should remain applicable, as warnings if not descriptors, in our current political environment.

That current political environment is neoliberalism, a political force that rose to prominence in the 1980s and, in the United States, has gained acceptance by both the Republican and Democratic parties, both of which pursue policies and reforms aimed at tailoring government to operate more like a business. The values of such a system may seem at odds with *1984*.

A party with "Freedom Is Slavery" as a slogan would seem to not offer many insights into a political ideology that emphasizes individual property rights, personal consumer freedom, and limited government. However, a closer look at neoliberalism reveals a paradoxical relationship with democracy. While arguably not matching the degree of authoritarianism in *1984*, the manner in which the neoliberal governments within the United States exercise power, both domestically and internationally, parallels that of Ingsoc.

The Theory and Practice of Neoliberalism, by Emmanuel Goldstein

The ideology of neoliberalism is rooted, which should be no surprise, in the ideology of liberalism. Political liberalism has a historical meaning that may cause confusion to those more familiar with the word's contemporary usage. When John Locke wrote his famous *Two Treatises of Government* in 1689, his main target was Sir Robert Filmer, who defended the divine right of kings. Locke's critique of this traditional monarchical defense of authority rested upon what would become the influential foundational principles of liberalism: political equality, individual liberty, and natural rights.

These ideas would lay the basis for US constitutionalism and an advocacy for a government limited to the preservation of individual liberties. In the words of John Locke, "The end of Law is not to abolish or restrain, but to preserve and enlarge Freedom" (p. 306).

Neoliberalism grows as a specific branch out of this tradition of liberalism, coming to prominence in the US political environment in the late 1970s, growing more accepted among political elites of both parties throughout the 1980s and 1990s.

In his book *A Brief History of Neoliberalism*, David Harvey, an anthropologist and social theorist, has identified the central tenet of neoliberalism as the idea "that human well-being can best be advanced by liberating individual entrepreneurial freedoms and skills within an institutional framework characterized by strong private property rights, free markets, and free trade" (p. 2). These basic values are not unique to neoliberalism; the principle of *laissez faire* is accepted within traditional liberalism as well as contemporary US conservatism (itself a branch of traditional liberalism).

For neoliberalism to be something other than liberalism, something "neo" (or new) must be added to it. In an article titled "American Nightmare," the political theorist Wendy Brown argues that the new element "is that it depicts free markets, free trade, and entrepreneurial rationality as *achieved and normative,* . . . not simply as occurring by dint of nature" (p. 694).

Within the tradition of liberalism, John Locke would claim that private property was naturally occurring. Adam Smith argued the same about free trade. In other words, these things did not rely on government intervention to occur. Liberals and neoliberals alike prefer minimal interference from the government. However, neoliberalism is marked by a perceived necessity of governmental institutions, such as courts, the police, and the military, to create environments in which markets can flourish.

According to Harvey, the ideology of neoliberalism has substantially influenced several elements of US foreign and domestic policy. In foreign policy, military and diplomatic efforts are generally guided by "the assumption that individual freedoms are guaranteed by freedom of the market and of trade" (p. 7). In terms of domestic economic and social welfare policy, "the freedom of businesses and corporations (legally regarded as individuals) to operate within this institutional framework of free markets and free trade is regarded as a fundamental good" (p. 64). This means that policy is not necessarily evaluated by its effects on society, but by an underlying assumption that certain policy directions, such as deregulation and privatization, are inherently preferable. According to Brown, one of the hallmarks of neoliberalism is that all political problems are understood from the point of view of the market and are, therefore, seen not as public problems, but as "individual problems with market solutions" (p. 704).

It is on this point that the world of *1984* resembles the world of neoliberalism, despite the former representing a planned economy and the latter a free-market society. Brown has observed that, under neoliberalism, where the government is remade on the model of the firm, the language of government becomes more like the language of the market, and traditional political values are replaced by business norms, such as "productivity and profitability" (p. 694).

Although it would be hard to imagine today's business leaders seeing a friendly business environment in the London of Airstrip One, the Party effectively reduced all things down to their economic elements to the point that even the writing of books is no different from the production of jam or bootlaces. In both the fictional world of *1984* and the contemporary world of neoliberal politics, power is exercised with an eye toward corporate efficiency and underlying contradictions are worked out through Doublethink.

The Doublethink of Administrative Law, or Accountableindependence

One area of government that is the focus of both Orwell and neoliberalism is bureaucracy. Orwell paid special attention to the minutia of bureaucratic inner-workings and the interiors of the various labyrinthine ministries. So much of the terror of the novel comes from the portrayal of a bureaucracy that to the contemporary reader is all too relatable.

Anyone who has spent time at the Department of Motor Vehicles could imagine an Ingsoc version, likely called something like Minidrive, and might opt for the less torturous rat-cage-face-mask. Neoliberalism also focuses on bureaucracy, suggesting a set of reforms to administrative law, the body of law that governs governmental procedure. These reforms utilize Doublethink to forge a particularly neoliberal relationship between the two principles around which administrative law is constructed: independence and accountability.

When administrative law pursues independence, it is trying to ensure that bureaucrats are free to make decisions within their area of power. Although Winston clearly has superiors who may override his decisions, the Ministry of Truth, as a whole, is free to publish propaganda as it sees fit. In US administrative law, this principle is protected by a concept know as *Chevron* deference, which was developed in the 1984 Supreme Court decision, *Chevron v. NRDC*. This principle means that, whenever an action of a bureaucracy is challenged in a court as inconsistent with the law the bureaucracy is enforcing, the court will generally defer to the agency's interpretation of the law, provided it is not entirely unreasonable (at 365).

This deference gives burcaucrats significant power, which is not to say that such power is never justified. Bureaucracies house the experts of government and, when a government is charged with performing a task that requires some expertise, those experts should be listened to. Even in Orwell's London, Winston must have had some degree of comfort in knowing that the bureaucrat in charge of the production of Victory Gin knew enough about distilling to at least produce non-poisonous gin.

In any sort of democratic government, accountability plays an important role in both limiting and justifying the exercise of power by non-elected bureaucrats. While governmental experts need a degree of independence with which to exercise their power, that power is confined by rules meant to keep bureaucrats accountable, such as the US Administrative Procedures Act, which lays out the basic rules that all agencies must follow when they create policies and enforce them. Likewise, a court may rule that an agency is either exercising a power not given to it by Congress or has exceeded what authority has been given.

It would be easy to dismiss accountability as having any influence over the administration of law in *1984*. One of the most basic standards used to overturn bureaucratic decisions is that the decision was arbitrary, and much of the exercise of power in *1984* is just that, arbitrary. Winston lives his life knowing that it is only a question of when, not if, he will be killed by the Party. This arbitrariness is due to an abandonment of standards of truth.

O'Brien declares that the Party exercises power purely for its own sake, making every action arbitrary, and Winston's job of correcting media reports is made challenging by having no standard of truth to which he can direct his corrections. However, this does not mean that the ministries in *1984* operate free from the mechanisms of accountability. Julia reveals that Pornosec, the section of the Ministry of Truth that produces pornography, only employs unmarried girls on the theory that male "sex instincts were less controllable than those of women." This demonstrates one form of governmental accountability, the avoidance of conflicts of interest.

As a policy goal, neoliberalism prefers deregulation, privatization, and a generally limited level of government control over economic activities. Therefore, neoliberal reforms generally prescribe strong accountability measures that limit the reach of government. However, neoliberalism is also based on an awareness of the necessity of government to create the conditions of free exchange and entrepreneurialism. According to Harvey, threats to unrestricted use of labor, property, or capital frequently come in the form of public majorities and, for this reason, neoliberalism is "profoundly suspicious of democracy. Governance by majority rule is seen as a potential threat to individual rights and constitutional liberties. . . . Neoliberals therefore tend to favour governance by experts and elites" (p. 66).

In a form of Doublethink, however, this governance needs a veneer of democratic accountability. This is provided with a set of neoliberal Newspeak buzzwords, such as "stakeholder" and "customer-driven government," buzzwords that reflect the ideology's reliance on the business world as its model for government. Winston's associate, Syme, the dictionary writer, keenly (yet joyfully) observed that "the whole aim of Newspeak was to narrow the range of thought."

When used as a part of rulemaking, these words redefine who the public is. Whereas the Inner Party and Big Brother were able to define the continuation of their power as what was really in the best interest of the people, neoliberalism can valorize business interests and free trade as general political values, assuming that they are truly in the public's best interest. Brown has identified the result as something of a paradox, where the essential values of participation and democracy are used to remake "the state on the model of the firm," which then empowers the state in a manner "unacceptable to a democratic culture or within a democratic table of values" (p. 705).

Political scientists Christine Harrington and Z. Urum Türem have written that, under such conditions, democratic participation in government is "'maximized' for nongovernmental actors but 'minimized' for the public at large" (p. 208), all in the name of democracy.

Whistleblowing in Front of a Telescreen

Just as Doublethink is used by neoliberalism to redefine the private as public, it is also used to negotiate between conflicting identities of persons within and under government, namely, the bureaucrats themselves. To be employed by any of Big Brother's ministries is to dedicate your entire life to that cause, to identify the interests of the party as your personal interests.

The degree to which Winston had interests that were not the same as the interests of the Party made him a problem for the Party. Therefore, the Party exercised a policy of encouraging loyal members to report thought-criminals. The ability to get children to report their parents demonstrates clearly how personal and public interests are understood in *1984*. Normally, we would expect a child to see the interest of her parents as consistent with her own, even if only for the selfish reason of needing to eat. By reporting their parent as a thought-criminal, the children were demonstrating an early awareness of their own interests as being perfectly represented by the interest of the Party.

The life of a contemporary bureaucrat is a bit more complicated, as the split identity of the same person as a bureaucrat and a citizen is more readily recognized. As a bureaucrat, you are a representative of the government. You have power to exercise in the furtherance of policy. But as a citizen, you have interests in how bureaucrats do their jobs. As your tax dollars pay the salaries of bureaucrats and fund their activities, you have an interest in that money not being wasted.

Furthermore, you have an interest in the outcome of policy, an interest which may conflict with your interest as an employee of the government. As an employee, your interest is to keep your job by doing it correctly, which means, according to the law. If that law dictates that you only monitor water pollution at a less-than-preferable level, your interest as a water-drinking citizen may be different than your interest as a bureaucrat.

The Ingsoc bureaucrat has a singular identity: bureaucrat *as* citizen. A contemporary bureaucrat has a split identity: bureaucrat *and* citizen. This difference affects the way in which bureaucrats can evaluate their own actions and the actions of others. When Winston discovers irrefutable evidence that the Party is pushing a lie through its propaganda, his only obligation is to the Party. A contemporary bureaucrat observing malfeasance on the part of the government has an obligation as citizen to the citizenry to inform the public that its trust in its government is being abused, in other words, to blow the whistle.

In the United States, government employees are protected from retaliation in response to blowing the whistle on government misdeeds by the Whistleblower Protection Act (WPA). However, neoliberal reforms aimed at modeling government on private sector corporations risk diminishing the bureaucrat's identity from citizen to mere employee.

In *Pickering v. Board of Education*, the US Supreme Court decided that, while the speech of a government employee could be restricted as it relates to job performance, the employee still enjoyed free speech as a citizen; therefore, any effort by the government to punish an employee for what they say must be balanced against the public interest in free speech. More recently, however, in *Garcetti v. Ceballos*, the Supreme Court has ruled that any speech made "pursuant to their official duties" (at 421) is categorically exempt, and the Constitution affords that speech no protection. Furthermore, efforts aimed at bureaucratic cost saving and efficiency have created a heavier reliance on collaborative, non-judicial forms of dispute resolution.

A government whistleblower who believes that she's being punished by her employer settles such grievances before the Merit Systems Protection Board. The administrative judges on this board, however, are essentially employees of the same government being challenged in a whistleblower case and are less likely to properly oversee governmental misbehavior. The end result of this reform is a change in the relationship of a government employee with the government from a bureaucrat that retains a separate identity as a citizen to a mere employee and less of a citizen.

Making the World Safe for Big Brother

Within *1984*, the writings of Goldstein argue that a perpetual state of war provides both the material and psychological bases for the maintenance of the power of the Party. Such war consumes the products of labor, maintaining an artificial scarcity, which further justifies a concentration of power into the hands of a small elite. The stated purpose of war, and even simply maintaining an outsized naval presence abroad, in a neoliberal society is to create environments conducive to free-market enterprise, thus expanding wealth.

Within US foreign policy, President Trump's promise to hammer out better "deals" abroad embodies a neoliberal approach to foreign relations. However, the "Washington Consensus," a set of neoliberal economic policies broadly advocated by Western states and Western-led development agencies since the 1970s, exemplify Orwellian Doublethink in foreign policy.

After a major food crisis in the early 1970s, the International Monetary Fund and other actors that provided international loans began requiring most developing countries to dismantle their protectionist agricultural policies, such as subsidizing fertilizer and seeds, in favor of free-market systems that determine production through the ability of a nation to produce a good more cheaply than a competitor. In an act of Doublethink, however, many developed countries, including the United States, refused to liberalize most of their own agricultural policies, arguing that they had a comparative advantage in agricultural production and that importing food was more efficient for developing countries than domestic production.

US Agriculture Secretary John Block summarized the idea in 1986 by stating that "the idea that developing countries should feed themselves is an anachronism from a bygone era. They could better ensure their food security by relying on US agricultural products, which are available in most cases at lower cost" ("How to Manufacture a Global Food Crisis," pp. 450–51). The developing countries accepted this logic largely because these ideas were tied to desired and needed structural adjustment loans. Western industrialized countries manipulated the rules in a way that favored their preferred ideology, neoliberalism, without following it themselves and in a way that kept developing countries subservient.

Over the last forty years, developing countries have become dependent on agricultural imports from the West, which are priced artificially low because of the West's proclivity for agricultural subsidies, and have therefore become more subject to the volatility of the world market. According to the food anthropologist Tom Marchione in his article, "A Time to Rethink the Global Food Regime," neoliberalism treats "food as if it were a commodity no different than gold or oil—with no inherent human value, subject to the whims of global traders and commodity fund speculators with only peripheral interest in human needs" (pp. 5–6).

The policies of the Washington Consensus pushed the majority of the least-developed countries from being net food exporters in the 1960s to being net food importers just a few decades later. These policies contributed to, among other fiascoes, the food price crisis of 2007–08, in which world grain prices doubled, leading to riots in more than sixty developing countries. Policies that were implemented with the stated purpose of free and efficient production produced scarcity.

Political interpretations of *1984* often view the work as either a critique of real authoritarian governments from long ago or as a critique of all existing and potential authoritarian governments more broadly. However, modern audiences can benefit from considering what it has to say about democracy as well. Because both authoritarian states and democracies depend on bureaucracies to carry out orders and enforce rules—everything from waging wars to issuing drivers' licenses—using this lens to view *1984* can help us to apply its insights about Oceania to our own technocratic societies.

All bureaucracies must balance the competing ideas of authority and autonomy, of accountability and independence; all government employees must weigh competing incentives from their roles as both bureaucrats and citizens; and all governments are at least tempted to pursue their own economic interests at the expense of others. Because all of these tendencies have real consequences for citizens both at home and abroad, we would do well to consider the lessons of neoliberal critiques along with those of Orwell, lest we be sweet-talked by bureaucratic lingo or sideswiped by Doublespeak.

II

Freedom Is
Slavery

7
Big Brother, We're Watching You!

TORBJÖRN TÄNNSJÖ

> At the end of the hall, a poster covered one wall. It showed an enormous face, more than a metre wide: the face of a handsome man of about forty-five, with a large, black moustache. The man's eyes seemed to follow Winston as he moved. Below the face were the words: BIG BROTHER IS WATCHING YOU. Winston gazed at the poster and thought silently to himself: If only I could see him the way he sees me, I wouldn't mind!

How could Winston have reached this conclusion, had this quotation been a true account? Let's dig into Winston's fictional mind and explain!

Mass Surveillance

We live today in a state of mass surveillance even more efficient than the one that faced Winston Smith in *1984*. Is that a problem? It is, but it would not be such a problem if we could handle matters in the right manner—at present, we don't.

Correctly handled—handled in a reciprocal manner, where the citizen is allowed to see Big Brother in the manner Big Brother sees the citizen—the state of mass surveillance is to be preferred to any of its feasible alternatives.

To be sure, we're not there, but the open society is a viable ideal and it also sets a more realistic goal than a return to a putative golden age where everyone could keep their secrets. What Orwell saw as the main problem with *1984*, the fact that you are or could at least always be observed, is something we will have to live with. Mass Surveillance is here to stay.

That's a claim that will be met with suspicion and resistance. I will therefore defend it against the best arguments I have come across.

Why Do People Fear Surveillance?

Why do some people think that mass surveillance is terrible? Here's a typical way of stating what is wrong with mass surveillance. First of all, it is said that surveillance violates our privacy. And why is our privacy so important? "Privacy is an inherent human right, and a requirement for maintaining the human condition with dignity and respect. It is about choice, and having the power to control how you present yourself to the world." These are the words of Bruce Schneier, both expert on, and a fierce critic of, the system of mass surveillance and author of *Data and Goliath*.

Here we meet, not one argument, but several. We need to look carefully at each of them. I'll start with the last one.

An Ethics of Honor

The idea that we have a right to control the public image of ourselves dates back to an ethics of honor, typical of the duelling classes way back in the history of Europe. At least this is the thesis in James Q. Whitman's article "The Two Western Cultures of Privacy." This ethics of honor has now taken a hold on everyone (at least in continental Europe), not just the nobility. And in order to guard our honor, we need not resort to duelling any more. Instead we can call the police (in Europe) or file a lawsuit (in the US). This is how Whitman characterizes this culture:

> Continental privacy protections are, at their core, a form of protection of a right to *respect* and *personal dignity.* The core continental privacy rights are *rights to one's image, name, and reputation* . . . They are all rights to control your public image—rights to guarantee that people see you the way you want to be seen. They are, as it were, rights to be shielded against unwanted public exposure, to be spared embarrassment or humiliation.

In a state of mass surveillance we *cannot* protect the putative right to control our public image. In particular, the press threatens this right for those who are rich and famous, but also, social media threaten it for each and every one of us. But why is this right of such importance to us? Could we not take on a more relaxed view of our public image?

An ethics of honor is, with good reason, looked upon with suspicion in other contexts. When a father kills his daughter because she has through her sexual behavior put his honor in jeopardy, we do not applaud him. Why not apply the same line of argument in this context as well? Why not give up the ethics of honor? Well, if I'm right in my argument, this kind of ethics of honor is something that just *has* to go. There is, and there will be, no place for us to hide, regardless of how we try to deal with the surveillance society.

Of course, in Oceania, only Big Brother owns a right to control his image. It is part of my proposal in this chapter that we should rob him of this exclusive right.

A Right to Privacy?

But is there not a *right* to privacy? This is the claim made by Bruce Schneier. However, there is no such right, at least not if we listen to moral philosopher Judith Jarvis Thomson, who does defend the idea of moral rights in general, but not this one. I think she's correct. Even if a moral theory of rights should turn out to be true (a claim I am prepared to question), there is no specific right to *privacy*.

What we call a right to privacy, according to a theory of moral rights, is just a consequence of our right to *ourselves* and to our private *property*. I own myself, according to the moral theory of rights. Hence, I have a right to do whatever I see fit with myself, as long as I do not violate any rights of others. This means that I have a right not to be touched by anyone without my consent. I have a right not to be looked at, if I prefer to be hidden from the eyes of others. However, if I appear naked in the street I have implicitly consented to be looked at.

The same goes for my home. No one has a right to enter my home, or to eavesdrop on me in my home, if I do not consent to this. However, when I quarrel with my spouse with the window open I have implicitly consented to being listened to. This means that if someone gets access to embarrassing information about me, in my home, in a manner that did not violate my rights, the one who now has this information is free to circulate it. I have a right to my personal integrity but not to any control of my public image. If I invite you into my home, and you happen to find child pornography there, you can do as you see fit with this information.

Even if, abstractly speaking, there may be something to the theory of a right to privacy, there is no way that we can see to it that it is protected. So, once again, we had better take this right less seriously than we often do. If we do not want to give up on the moral theory of rights as such, then we could at least take these rights less seriously by just implicitly consenting to the kinds of violations we are bound to live with.

Dignity?

The idea that privacy relies on a notion of dignity alluded to by Schneier is popular but difficult to understand. However, a way of understanding it could be this. Dignity is a matter of autonomy. In order to respect the dignity of a person we need to allow this person the possibility of making autonomous choices. However, if we spy on her, she will not be able to make autonomous decisions. Hence, by spying on her we show disrespect for her dignity.

How could this be? You would think that our autonomy is jeopardized when we are manipulated or nudged into making certain decisions we would not otherwise make. But how can the mere fact that others *observe* us stop us from acting autonomously? The idea is, I believe, that if we are not allowed to deliberate privately, and to discuss matters only with a selected number of people, we will yield to the opinion of those who watch us. We are bound to become anxious and conventional in our way of life, if we are not allowed to consider and reflect on it alone.

There may be some truth to this argument as well. I suppose people are more or less vulnerable in this manner. And what is required by this argument is only that each individual has *some* absolutely protected place to retreat to. According to this argument we all need what Montaigne called a "backshop," wholly our own and entirely free. However, in practice there is no way to sustain this kind of respect for our privacy. There is no place where we're entitled to feel completely secure. We can never know that we're not observed. This is the lesson Winston and Julia learned the hard way. They assumed they were safe in the litter room above Mr. Charrington's shop. They weren't. Neither are we. Hence, we must find ways of dealing with the lack of this kind of (absolute) privacy.

Privacy Is Not One Thing but Many

These privacy arguments are typically put forward against a system of mass surveillance. They are a mixed bag. They imply very different ideals of privacy. To allow you to control your own image is different from having a safe place to retreat to which, in turn, is different from self-ownership. Which one of them should we rely on, if we want to come up with a way of handling the issue of surveillance?

One could of course think that, since they are all controversial, why not try to satisfy all of them? In that way, we could have an overlapping consensus in the defense of our system of surveillance. But this is not a live possibility. Moreover, if we want to assess these arguments, we need to be clearer about the alternatives we are facing. In which ways can we possibly handle the surveillance society? The relevance of the arguments should be assessed in relation to the real alternatives facing us.

What Can We Do about Our Situation?

It may seem as if, roughly, there are four different possibilities facing us.

- First of all, we could think of a society where there is an *absolute* protection of our privacy.

- Secondly, we could think of a society where there is surveillance, but only of a *targeted* nature (against criminals and those who are for some reasons suspect).

- Thirdly, we could think of a society of *mass* surveillance of the kind with which we are only too well acquainted. A primitive version of this kind of society is Orwell's *1984*. Ours is just more sophisticated.

- Finally, we could think of a society of *total* surveillance, a society where there is absolutely *no* privacy (where even our inner thoughts lie in the open to be read by everyone else).

However, in reality our choices are much more limited than this.

Mindreading?

First of all, there is no technical possibility of realizing a situation where we can read the inner lives of others. Mass surveillance is one thing, total surveillance something quite different.

Total surveillance may even be conceptually impossible. To the extent that our inner life can be captured by definite sentences, the idea of mindreading does perhaps make sense. However, there is much in our inner life that doesn't take a definite verbal form. So it's hard to say what it would mean to "read" that part of ourselves. Not even Orwell in his *1984* contemplates this possibility.

Yet it's interesting to *speculate* about this possibility (to the extent that it is a possibility). Many religious people believe that at least their favored god can read their inner thoughts. They seem to be comfortable with this state of affairs. The American philosophers Thomas Nagel and James Rachels, however, have defended the common-sense view that this would be terrible. Nagel has stressed the importance of a secret *inner* life if we want to be able to go on with our *social* life; if people could read my thoughts about them, especially when these thoughts are nasty or sexist, our co-operation would be blocked.

Rachels has stressed the need for us to distribute our more intimate thoughts in a varying degree among our fellow human beings. We would not be able to have friends if we could not privilege some people when we share our thoughts with others. To our friends go our most intimate thoughts, to the others the more mundane ones. Without this kind of separation there would be no such thing as friendship.

But is this correct? The English philosopher Jonathan Glover claims that it would only mean that friendship would be something different, and less exclusive. Our friends would simply be those people we like to be close to. He seems to think that this kind of friendship would be more valuable than a friendship that presupposes exclusion of those who are not your friends. He may be right about this.

This is a fascinating matter, but it is not a live possibility in our dealings with surveillance.

Why There Is No Escape

Secondly, and more importantly in the present context, even the first suggested alternative seems hopeless. There can be no such thing as *absolute* privacy. There is no way in which we can satisfy all the arguments above and guarantee everyone even *one* secret place, where she can feel confident that no one listens to her. The very presence and spread of mighty surveillance techniques means that there is always a possibility that someone is, if not reading your thoughts, at least secretly listening to what you say and watching what you are doing.

The primitive telescreens in *1984* could in principle be turned off. However, the way we interact with one another, with the government and with firms electronically, there is no way of ensuring that we are not watched. This is an important difference between our surveillance culture and the surveillance culture of *1984*. In *1984* people are passive victims of it. We contribute willingly to it. But this means that there are really only two options facing us. Either we accept mass surveillance in roughly the form we know it, or we go for something I have referred to as targeted surveillance.

Targeted Surveillance

The difference between a society with mass and with targeted surveillance is not crystal clear. Those who advocate this line of thought list all sorts of measures that could be taken if we want to opt for targeted rather than mass surveillance.

At the core of this proposal is the idea that only hostile nations, terrorist groups, and criminal elements, should be the intended subject of surveillance. And a court order should always be required before governmental agencies are allowed to spy on its citizens. Let us suppose that this kind of reform is possible. Would it also be desirable?

We should note that even targeted surveillance is at odds with the arguments given above. You can always turn out to be a suspect. You need not do anything wrong in order to become a suspect. It is sufficient if you happen to socialize with people who do something wrong—or with people who socialize with people who do something wrong. Winston was well aware of this. Moreover, the risk that you will, because of fear of the eyes of others, be incapable of thinking freely about your life and politics, will still be a real one. If you can't think freely when you are observed, then the mere *possibility* that you are observed is probably enough to stop you from thinking autonomously. This is what people in Oceania had to fear. They didn't know if anyone was watching them, but it was always possible that they were being watched.

Furthermore, with targeted surveillance people who belong to dissenting groups will now feel *extremely* insecure. They know not only that they are targeted, just like anyone else, but also that an *extra* effort has been put into the attempt to get hold of *their* secret thoughts. They will belong to the same category that Winston and Julia did, once they had started secretly to question Big Brother. But if we value autonomy because we see it as a source of social reform, these people, the dissidents, are the ones who most need protection. And given targeted surveillance they will have the least of it.

I think it's preferable to have a situation where we *all* know that we can be observed to one where only "suspect" people need to feel insecure. It's true that social change takes time. First people have to hold all sorts of secret beliefs among themselves, before it's time to go public. Just think of the gay movement. A way of making a gay lifestyle, not only legal but also generally accepted as a part of normality, has been, at first, secretly to meet and to discuss how to pursue the political project of gay liberation. Then came a time of civil disobedience. Finally, there was legal reform and a change of thought in general. In a society of mass surveillance these people, who initiate the political movement, know that they are observed. But this would be so even more in a society with targeted surveillance, where these people would understand, not only that they were kept under surveillance, *as everyone else*, but also that they were subjected to *extra* efforts intended to stifle their ambitions. Or, take the example of forensic DNA-registers. Should we not prefer a situation where all, rather than only suspect people, are included in them? If we are all in the register no special stigma goes with being there.

None among the arguments discussed above seems to indicate that we should prefer a system of targeted surveillance to a system of mass surveillance. If these arguments are sound they point to the impossible: a society with an *absolute* protection of privacy. Hence, with regard to these arguments, it seems that we could just as well live with mass surveillance. However, this does not mean that there are no problems with the system we now live under. These problems are obvious and well known.

When Big Business and the government have a lot of information on us there's always a possibility that they will use it against us. This may happen even if we have nothing to hide, at least not from the point of view of criminal justice. There may still be things we are ashamed of. When exclusive knowledge about these matters is granted to Big Business and government there is a risk that we will be in so many ways blackmailed or threatened by the prospect of bad exposure.

These problems are exaggerated in Orwell's *1984*, where those who rule have absolutely no good intentions and where the system of surveillance is used to keep a terrible political and social order in place, but even in a modern democracy they are real; we need no abstract principles to do with honor, moral rights, or dignity to realize this. They are of a simple pragmatic nature, to do with the possibility that we're taken advantage of when we're being watched. But there may be ways to reduce these problems. There may be ways of handling these risks in a state of mass surveillance. There may be measures of harm reduction that we can undertake. And indeed, there are.

The Open Society

We should opt for as much transparency as possible. We should always recognize that others might know what we communicate and do. And in order to render this common knowledge innocuous, we should see to it that it is *truly* common; the information gathered should not be allowed to stay in the dark. I suppose this is the insight that Winston got in the opening "quotation" in this chapter. He can accept that Big Brother watches him if he can watch Big Brother. Let's see how we can achieve such a goal.

First of all, we should strive for legislative reform. The authorities now possess enormous and unprecedented techniques for surveillance. We voluntarily provide input into their system when we communicate electronically. In return, we should demand openness from them. They are so mighty that they can afford all sorts of losses in efficiency, in exchange for transparency.

Even if a transparent system is slightly less effective than a closed one, with regard to the aim of going for the bad guys, selling products with designed ads, and so forth, those who run the system can afford some loss in terms of efficiency. So, transparency is what we should aim at. We should argue that there should be no such thing as secret diplomacy (a demand the British philosopher Jeremy Bentham made already during the eighteenth century). We should demand that the secret services such as CIA and NSA render all their records public, at least after five years. The same goes for ordinary criminal investigations. At least all the information should be shared *with the person who was once a suspect*. And we could go on almost indefinitely with suggested reforms to the same effect. The customer should have a right to know what the company knows about her, and know how the information is put to use.

Secondly, to the extent that the fight for political reform turns out to be, at least at first, in vain, there are things we can do. Even if we could have these laws in place (which is a big IF), we must suspect that those covered by them would not really abide by them. But again, there are measures available for us. We should then resort to public gossip. We shall encourage people to become whistle-blowers, go public when the law is not followed, and we shall not hesitate to take advantage of the information provided by whistle-blowers, to disseminate it further, discuss it and adopt a reflected stance towards their findings.

Finally, we should treat those who dare to go public as the true heroes of our time. This means not only that we should honor them in our thoughts and writing, but also that we should work energetically to have them free of legal sanctions. Asylum for Edward Snowden in a country like my own (Sweden), for example, would be fine, but yet, for all that, it would be only a poor substitute for what we *really* owe him: a safe haven in the country of his own choice. The successful campaign to free Chelsea Manning is something to be proud of.

We need more of the kind.

Given such a policy of transparency we should be prepared to welcome a society of mass surveillance, roughly as we know it. We should do so since targeted surveillance is even worse, while a world of total privacy is an impossibility. And remember that there are also nice aspects of openness. We should not hesitate to reap the fruits of an open society in terms of security against unjust arrest and punishment as well as against crime. We should enjoy the relaxed style of life where we can shamelessly appear in public the way we truly are.

We should be prepared to appear naked in front of Big Brother, in the way I have speculated that Winston did, but only if we're allowed to undress Big Brother as well. Until the point where he accepts, or is forced, to appear naked in front of us, we should not hesitate to peep in on him.

8

Human Enhancement for Freedom

POLARIS KOI

Part of the disconcerting allure of Orwell's *Nineteen Eighty-Four* lies in our worry that a totalitarian future might be a genuine possibility.

Many of the technologies of total domination used by Oceania's rulers are more freely available than ever. For example, far from being limited to the constant information flow and ongoing supervision of living-room telescreens, we now carry smartphones which both provide us with a steady stream of information and are capable of tracking our every movement with GPS, microphones, and cameras.

But technology isn't a one-way street to dehumanization and oppression: it can also be used to prevent totalitarian regimes from gaining foothold.

In *1984*, the Party subjugates citizens largely by undermining their human capacities: the proles are intellectually stinted, constrained to a reality of false rumors and entertainment, such that "Until they become conscious they will never rebel, and until after they have rebelled they cannot become conscious" (p. 74). Meanwhile, the intellects of Party members are directed to conform to its ideology, their physical and emotional faculties suppressed under stone-faced self-discipline.

Since the time of Aristotle, we've known that well-being and the exercise of our capacities are important for positive social functioning and a productive political life. Sarah Buss has argued that our very autonomy—our capacity to act in accordance with our own wishes—depends on our flourishing, that is, on having our basic human needs met. The value of flourishing

for our capacity to function has also been empirically demonstrated: for example, nutrition has a powerful effect on IQ.

The power of the state to regulate our access to food, shelter,
healthcare, and—as *1984* demonstrates—even love and com-
panionship, means it has power to cause us to languish, thereby
undermining our capacities and making us easier to bring
under the yoke. Orwell thus directs our attention towards an
important aspect of the human condition: that even the ingenious, adaptable, and capable species we are, our ingenuity is
easily undermined by external conditions.

But what if we were different? What if humans had abilities
that made us less vulnerable to such manipulation? Could we
become more resilient towards dystopian futures by improving
on our human nature?

Oxford philosophers Ingmar Persson and Julian Savulescu
think we could. While their major concern isn't the onslaught
of a totalitarian regime, they are concerned that our human
capacities simply aren't well suited for the social and political
challenges we now face, and that in order to avoid a global catastrophe, we need to become different. While education may
have helped the situation somewhat, Persson and Savulescu
are skeptical that it would suffice in preventing what they call
"ultimate harm." In their book *Unfit for the Future*, they recommend that we research and implement biomedical methods
for improving on human capacities, in order to create a humanity capable of avoiding a disastrous future.

The idea that we could become better human beings than
we currently are, that by biomedically modulating something
in us we could become resilient to the kinds of oppression
Orwell describes, may sound like science fiction. Then again,
many of the technologies described in Orwell's *1984*, which
then seemed like science fiction, have now been surpassed.
Besides, if the threat of a dystopian future is as real as the bur-
geoning surveillance industry and the boom of internet disinformation are, it may well be worth looking into any possible
means to avoid it.

Human Nature Is Faulty

All states have ideas about what their citizens should, ideally, be
like. For Ingsoc, the ideal is "a nation of warriors and fanatics,

marching forward in perfect unity, all thinking the same thoughts and shouting the same slogans" (p. 77). For present-day capitalist democracies, the ideal is a healthy, law-abiding, productive citizen, educated enough to make informed choices in elections.

For both ideals, human nature presents dire challenges. While most people are quite naturally law-abiding and, as Orwell illustrates, easily fall for various group mentalities, we are also sometimes reckless, violent, eccentric, or rebellious, we get sick or injured, and we tend to come up with various pursuits, goals, and values which sometimes are at odds with those preferred by the state.

Methods for coaxing the people towards these ideals are diverse, from education and propaganda to surveillance and the distribution of wealth. In the modern world, these methods include medical ones, such as immunisation programs and pre-natal screenings. O'Brien describes how Ingsoc is working on medical means for improving the citizens' loyalty: "We shall abolish the orgasm. Our neurologists are at work upon it now. There will be no loyalty, except loyalty towards the Party" (p. 280).

While Orwell already speculated on neurologically making us into better citizens (by Ingsoc's standards) in 1948, the philosophical discussion of biomedically enhancing human capacities started decades later, when Jonathan Glover wrote *What Sort of People Should There Be?* The year was 1984. Glover's slim volume was the first philosophical discussion on human genetic choices and on what has since become called 'neuroethics'—the ethics of how we should responsibly use bio-medical neurotechnologies, from psychiatric drugs and gene editing to brain-computer interfaces and brain stimulation.

In the subsequent decades, the debate of what human capacities we could, or should, try to enhance, burgeoned. As neuroscience leaped forward, the prospect of improving our capacities using biomedical methods became more and more credible. Medical ethicists agreed that they should discuss the ethical implications of such technologies before they became reality, but this proved to be a difficult task.

Too Smart to Be Subjugated?

Abilities that have, to date, been suggested as possible targets of enhancement range from mood and empathy to life span and physical strength, but perhaps the most discussed has been intelligence. Considered by the prominent political philosopher John Rawls to be a "primary good," that is, something that every rational person would want because it is helpful in leading any kind of life, intelligence does appear to be something most of us want more of.

As Oxford philosophers Nick Bostrom and Rebecca Roache point out, many laws and regulations are already in place in Western democracies to protect and improve our cognitive capacities, including mandatory education, bans on alcohol for minors, and the regulation of lead in paints and in tap water.

The ethical debate surrounding the enhancement of intelligence, however, has raised a number of questions: what happens to our authenticity and sense of self if we get considerably smarter than we used to be? To what extent is intelligence even something that's in the brain and thus biomedically alterable? What about justice: if only some can afford to get smarter, doesn't that increase the gap between rich and poor? And if everyone would get enhanced, what about freedom to say no to it? To this bundle of concerns, Persson and Savulescu add another: what if we used our improved intelligence to do something incredibly bad?

It's not that all of us would. But it only takes one villain, hell bent on destroying the world and capable of devising a foolproof plan to do so, to end the game for all of us. This, Persson and Savulescu argue, is reason enough to be wary of a bump in intelligence.

In *1984*, intelligence is a two-edged sword. On one hand, the Party runs on intellectuals who use all their wits and cunning to coldly calculate the most efficient path to its omnipotence. On the other, the Party is doing its best to keep the citizens of Oceania, whether proles or members of the Outer Party, less capable of thinking straight. Whether by keeping them in poverty so that they need to focus on survival alone, or by lulling them with an imaginary lottery, the cognitive capacities of the proles are diminished, ensuring that they remain unable to devise a plan for revolt.

Meanwhile, members of the Outer Party are dumbed down with Newspeak, which strips them of vocabulary they would need to articulate their ideas, even to themselves. The eradication of history, even recent history, causes a profound distrust of our own thoughts, memories, and experiences that also serves to undermine independent thought; and the constant flow of propaganda is used to direct any remaining cognitive functioning into Party-approved functions. Obviously, the Inner Party thinks that an intelligent population would pose a threat to its reign—otherwise they wouldn't put so much effort into undermining the people's cognitive capacities.

So could intelligence enhancement prevent us from ever being subjugated by a totalitarian regime? Some statistics on national average IQs make it look promising. Richard Lynn and Tatu Vanhanen, who have extensively researched national IQs, say that countries with higher national IQs have lower rates of corruption. So would that mean that if our IQs were higher, we'd be less vulnerable to poor government? Unfortunately, this would be too hasty a conclusion to draw.

Correlation does not equal causation: just because two things occur together doesn't mean that one of them causes the other. While it's true that some countries have a higher average IQ than others, that is mostly because education, nutrition and general well-being improve IQ. This means that generally, the wealthier nations have a better shot at a high national average IQ—depending, of course, on how that wealth is distributed. It happens that corruption is more common in developing countries. A similar problem occurs when looking into other correlates of intelligence on a statistical level: intelligence tends to walk hand in hand with relative wealth and well-being, and for many phenomena, differences in health and wealth are more plausible explanations than differences in intelligence are.

These practical difficulties needn't deter us from looking into intelligence as a possible safety mechanism against poor government. Perhaps high intelligence would make us more likely to revolt against a totalitarian regime: famous revolutionaries have tended to be brainy. From Karl Marx to Emma Goldman, whether or not you like their ideas you have to hand it to them that they were among the sharpest minds of their times. But it's harder to say whether people who resist oppression are more intelligent in general, or whether we only ever hear of the bright ones.

Nevertheless, there's some indication that liberalism tends to walk hand-in-hand with high intelligence. There's been a number of studies comparing the IQs of Democrats and

Republicans, and while most studies show democrats to have higher IQs on average, the results haven't been conclusive. Some researchers have explained this by saying that *all kinds of liberals* tend to have higher IQs: while Republicans who are socially conservative have lower IQs in average, Republicans who support economic freedom tend to have higher IQs. Similarly, socially liberal Democrats tend to have higher IQs. To sum it up, there is some indication that bright people are more likely to appreciate fiscal and civil liberties, but also likely to disagree about which party best promotes them.

So would we all love liberty if we were smarter? And if we did, would this make sure that we wouldn't fall for totalitarian movements like the Party? Not necessarily. A study on American college students found that among high-school students, the most gifted were the most likely to embrace extremist right-or left-wing political views. While people with high general intelligence might be likely to rebel against a totalitarian regime, the same kinds of people might also be the most likely to get the totalitarian Party started.

There are good reasons to think that intelligence enhancement might make us more resilient to Orwellian futures. But the relationship between intelligence and politics is too complicated to draw any quick conclusions, and trying to avoid a totalitarian regime by means of intelligence enhancement would, at best, be an educated gamble.

Amping Up Our Empathy?

Even without super-villains or the Party, things aren't going that well for the human race. Persson and Savulescu write, "The twenty-first century is the century in which humans will pose the greatest threats to themselves, in virtue of their nature" (2011, p. 497). This is because humans have created living conditions for themselves that are drastically different from the groups of around 150 hunter-gatherers we have genetically adapted to.

Those adaptations include our common-sense "gut" morality, which, for a large part, evolved to facilitate living in such small units. As a result, we care more about not causing harm than we do about doing good (for example, it is more important not to kill than it is to save a life); we care more about the near future than we do about the distant future; and we care more about people close to, or similar to us, than we care about people on the other side of the globe.

These adaptations are ill suited for acting ethically in a global community, and may partly explain why so many developed nations shirk from shouldering their responsibilities towards the developing world. They also help explain why the global community has failed to co-operate in avoiding environmental harms, such as a climate catastrophe. Adequately responding to worrying phenomena such as global climate change, loss of biodiversity, and deforestation has been on the global community's agenda for decades, yet the contemporary world appears not to be capable of taking sufficient action.

Skeptical about the prospects of our current methods for alleviating these matters, Persson and Savulescu propose that we try to devise a biomedical way of making our moral psychology better suited for contemporary challenges. Our present-day technology could be used to create an immense amount of welfare instead of, say, nuclear weapons. While such technology is not yet available, if we were to find a means of morally modifying ourselves into more altruistic, caring people, a doomsday scenario could be avoided.

To sum things up, Persson and Savulescu have the threat of a global harm—nuclear warfare, terrorists spreading smallpox, or climate catastrophe—in mind. But they wrote their article and book in 2008 and 2012, when many would still have been surprised by the momentum that clickbait disinformation, citizen surveillance, and personality-cult leadership have since gained, and many genuinely worry that this development may end in a *1984*-like future. They suggest that a global catastrophe may be averted by making us more altruistic and empathetic. Could the same means be used to prevent a totalitarian regime from gaining foothold?

In Orwell's *1984*, Party members are expected not to form close relationships with each other. Expressions of empathy are discouraged. Intimacy is shunned, and people are expected to keep a stiff upper lip at all times. The Party appears to work hard to dissociate people from their feelings of empathy. Could it be, then, that empathy—understood not just as being able to feel what the other person feels, but also more broadly as sympathising with their situation—is the key to revolt, the feature of our human nature that makes us difficult to suppress? And if we were more empathetic, could it be that a government such as Oceania's simply couldn't sever us from the empathy we feel? Could a more empathetic humankind be insuppressible?

A number of writers and philosophers, from Steven Pinker to Peter Singer, have called for our capacity for empathy to be consciously improved on in order to meet the challenges faced in the present-day world. And indeed, empathy is something we might well be able to enhance in the future. In fact, we already modulate empathy in some people. The neurotransmitter and hormone oxytocin mediates empathy, promoting behaviors such as pair-bonding, generosity, and trust. It's naturally elevated through cuddling and sex. However, it is also available as nasal spray. With research into improving our empathy already underway in the form of researching oxytocin, we might well come up with a way to efficiently promote empathy in the future.

Given that the Party holds love relationships, such as that of Winston and Julia, to be so subversive, might a humankind that was more attached to each other, more caring of each other's welfare and more appreciative of intimacy be inherently more subversive, unswayable by any political instance that would sever those ties of attachment? It's a widespread belief that empathy plays a key role in a just society. However, even Martha Nussbaum, who holds empathy to be one of the cornerstones for social justice, admits that people are often too weak, confused, and isolated to carry out any political action— much like Winston, who wishes that someone would do something, yet can't even hold that two plus two equals four.

Perhaps if our capacity for empathy was so much stronger after enhancement, we could overcome that weakness and act on our empathy despite the risk. Even in that case, how, and towards whom, we display empathy would remain a largely political and cultural issue. Historian Steven E. Ascheim calls this "the political economy of empathy." What he means is that ideology, religion, race, politics and culture have a profound impact on *whom* we empathize with. For example, there's no reason to believe that Nazis were in possession of less empathy than, say, their Jewish contemporaries; but they had been taught to direct their empathy selectively only to a specific in-group, and to consider people of other ethnicities unworthy of such empathy.

Ascheim describes how empathy takes root within ethnic or national boundaries—boundaries which, in the Third Reich, excluded Jews. After the Holocaust, the German political climate changed drastically, which allowed for Jewish people to be included in the sphere of empathy. To give another example, Peter Singer has drawn attention towards the way we humans tend to have empathy towards animals with big, round eyes, such as baby seals—but not towards smarter animals that happen not to be as cute, such as pigs. In *1984*, the Party restricts the sphere of empathy to an extreme: you are expected to love the Big Brother only.

Empathy gets even darker than that: it can also motivate atrocities. In Orwell's *1984*, the citizens believe that the revolution that brought on the reign of the Party improved life on Airstrip One. It isn't just out of self-interest that they do not wish to return to life without Big Brother: it is clearly also out of empathy. This is evidenced by how the Party's propaganda draws on the citizens' disposition for empathy by telling horrid stories of child labor before the revolution. For someone who is no longer a child, there is no self-interested reason to be horrified by child labor: we adults are averse to it out of empathy.

Atrocities have also been motivated (or claimed to be motivated) by empathy in the real world. In 1939, a German family petitioned for a "mercy killing" of their blind, physically and developmentally disabled newborn: their petition was granted, and Hitler instructed his doctors to furthermore show the same kind of "mercy" to all similar cases. This developed into the first mass murder committed by the Nazis, preceding the Holocaust. Called the "euthanasia" program, it involved the mass murder of physically and mentally disabled children of up to seventeen years. Later, the same measures were also taken against disabled adults.

Clearly, empathy itself is no guarantee for doing the right thing. While empathy is necessary for fruitful relationships and peaceful coexistence, if we wish to safeguard ourselves from an Orwellian dystopia, we'd better not count on empathy alone.

Everyone's Cured Sooner or Later

So far, the prospects of amping up our intelligence or our empathy to avoid a dystopian future look pretty bleak. So should we abandon the idea altogether? Well, not quite yet. Perhaps we would do well to look into other abilities. Perhaps increasing our pain tolerance to make us less susceptible to giving in to torture in Room 101. But it looks like the same kinds of problems come up, wherever we look: whatever ability we think of as improving our odds at avoiding a totalitarian regime, we can imagine the oligarchy making the most of that ability, too.

Let's face it: even the most intelligent of us can be fooled, and even the most empathetic of us can end up participating in atrocities. Should we embark on a quest to improve our intelligence, our empathy, or some other ability under the notion that this will make us immune to totalitarianism, we'd only set ourselves up to be hoodwinked. But that doesn't mean we wouldn't benefit from improved intelligence or empathy.

In a quest for a world where no one needs to submit to masters as cruel as The Party, we need to keep improving our capacity for empathy. But we also need to develop our intelligence, to make sure that we know who is worthy of that empathy—the proles or Big Brother. If medical means can safely help us develop these abilities, we certainly should look into that. But if we truly want a future without totalitarianism, we should also not drop our guard. Instead, we need to take heed of what I think is the core message Orwell is trying to convey in *1984*: that none of us, however smart, compassionate, or rebellious we become, will ever be immune to the love of Big Brother.

9
24/7 Newsleep

JASON MATTHEW BUCHANAN

After the end of a long day, nothing seems better than a good night's sleep. Your eyes are tired and your brain is a bit fuzzy.

Beep! It's a text from a friend. Chirp! Someone has liked your Facebook post. Ding! CNN has a breaking story. You turn your phone to Sleep mode.

Yet you still know your phone is collecting information and keeping you plugged into a world that continues to spin even while you're asleep. You're never truly disconnected.

Sleep is one of the most restorative activities performed by our bodies. Sleep is essential to our well-being—it's as important as food and water. Yet, increasingly, the interlocking elements of globalization and technology create an environment where a good night's sleep becomes harder and harder to find.

This disruption of sleep is caused by large issues, like a 24/7 global economy that never stops, and small issues like a text from a friend. Sleep is a state in which our body doesn't just rest, but instead strengthens and develops the parts of our brain that help us keep our mental stability. There may be no exact real-world analogy to Big Brother, but our phones, computers, and watches are all keeping tabs on us with their "telescreens" and alerts.

Plugged In, Worn Out

George Orwell's *1984* is famous for its dystopian presentation of a world overloaded by information, which is a method for "the Party" to police, terrorize, and confuse its members.

Winston Smith is not only monitored by telescreens, microphones, and Thought Police but also is bombarded by a constant flow of information, disinsformation, and propaganda. His life is structured by constant stimuli that leaves him "gelatinous with fatigue" due to "an enormous debauch of work" (*1984*, Plume edition, p. 159).

It's not just the duties of his job that impact Winston's ability to rest and recuperate. The intense and invasive presence of technology always intercedes on Winston's thoughts, most often in the form of announcements for the "Two Minutes Hate" or the "trumpet calls" from the telescreens signaling "news" stories (p. 259). The Party keeps its people physically exhausted by constant work and constant stimulation.

Technology, especially technology that intrudes on the individual, is everywhere in Orwell's book and is a key part of his fear about how society could change for the worse. In discussing *1984*, Orwell claimed that the book isn't "intended as an attack on Socialism" or any other left-wing "kind of society," but instead is a warning about how a society like the one depicted by *1984* "could arrive" in the world ("Orwell's Statement on *Nineteen Eighty-Four*").

Orwell wasn't worried about his novel being true, but was worried about its possibly becoming real. An important part of the dystopia presented in Orwell's novel is the intrusive nature of Oceania's technology. This portrayal represents a fear about a shift in the role of technology that escapes the pages of the book and arrives as a part of our world. *1984*, as a work of speculative fiction, depicts a world where technology works hand-in-glove with a "post-Truth" authority. Winston's sense of reality is beset by doublethink, thoughtcrime, and Newspeak, all of which are heavily influenced by a diminished role of sleep. Big Brother is always watching and waiting, especially while Winston sleeps.

The environment of *1984* is a clear depiction of how the mundane actions of our lives can be fraught with political manipulation. Sleep is one such activity that Oceania uses to maintain control over its people. When thinking about a time before the rise of the Ingsoc government, Winston recalls a dream about his mother and sister that was a "continuation of one's intellectual life" where he could become "aware of facts and ideas which still seem new and valuable after one is awake." This dream about his family reminds him that this type of dreaming and thinking "could not happen today" because "no dignity of emotion or deep or complex sorrows" are felt by the citizens of Oceania. The Party robs its people of a good night's sleep and, by doing so, disrupts the parts of their brain engaged with deep emotions.

Don't Sleep on Philosophy

Sleep is often thought to be a moment when people can switch off their brains and recharge their bodies. Plenty of commercials for sleep aids, comfortable beds, and new pillows portray slumber as a time when all the worries and stresses of the day are put aside, at least for the moment. Sleep is usually considered to be the moment when thinking, thankfully, stops.

Yet, despite the more commonly-held ideas about sleep, there have always been those who have analyzed sleep as an active state of thought where, even if a person is not fully conscious, our brains are doing significant work.

Ancient cultures, including the Egyptians and Greeks, thought of sleep as a time during which divine messages or sacred truths could be revealed in the form of dreams. Aristotle rejected the sacred aspect of sleep but believed it to be an important time when, according to Joseph Barbera, our "perceptual mechanism," or imagination, was active and engaged in causing "agitated blood" or dream-like responses. Much later, Sigmund Freud categorized sleep and dreams as loaded with symbolic content that our mind is using to work through our desires and wishes ("The Interpretation of Dreams," p. 140).

Currently, neurologists find sleep to be an activity where "vivid conscious experience is possible, despite the sensory and motor disconnection from the environment" (Claudio Bassetti, p. 114). Sleep, therefore, is not like turning off a telescreen. There's no complete shutdown. Rather, sleep is a time when our brain re-focuses on other tasks. If we take a closer look, it's possible to see that sleep has a "history" which has been "shaped and reshaped by its social concepts overtime" (Michael Greaney, p. 59). Nobody just passes out when they sleep. Instead, our bodies are always looking for the right kind of sleep.

With everything that goes on behind our eyelids when we shut them, it would be unwise to sleep on, well, the role sleep plays in our thought process. Even when we're in a dreamless sleep, our brains are still in a state of consciousness. Our unconscious slumber is necessary for our brains to continue vital work. In other words, sleep is not the opposite of thinking. Sleep, however, is an act of thinking that occurs in a different way as we perceive our thoughts, desires, and memories through deep slumber (REM sleep) and dreams. In reality, any theories of human consciousness and any theories of sleep should be cut from the same (bed) cloth ("The Philosophy of Sleep," p. 7).

Sleep-Hacking by the Party

The importance of sleep to thinking is something Big Brother fears since the guiding philosophy of Ingsoc is opposed to the "empirical method of thought" and seeks to use technology only as a means for the "diminution of human liberty" (*1984*, p. 171).

The Party knows that their "hierarchical society," with the Inner Party at the top, could only exist by creating a world of "poverty and ignorance" (p. 169). They keep people just poor enough to live in order that they keep working to meet day-to-day needs. The Party also keeps people ignorant through the constant influence of propaganda and a scientific focus on discovering, "against his will, what another human being is thinking" (p. 172). The mad-scientist qualities of the Party show that piercing a person's consciousness is a way to maintain power. The guiding ethos of the Party realizes that a government must control thoughts to control bodies. A way to control thought is to control when, where, and how a person sleeps.

For the Party, sleep is a moment of potential resistance where an individual's mind could continue to grow and develop outside the messages of the Inner Party. Orwell's book underscores that sleep isn't a natural function that just happens. The Party works to "sleep-hack" Winston to make him a more pliable, ignorant, and pacified Party member. Unlike the current trend to find "hacks" to make life better or more efficient, the Party controls the rhythms and patterns of sleep to produce the proper mindset for "doublethink."

Winston describes doublethink as a way to "consciously induce unconsciousness and then, once again, to become unconscious of the act of hypnosis you had just performed" (p. 131).

Doublethink can be hard for a reader to wrap their head around, but in many ways, it's like making your life into a dream, then actively trying to forget that you're in a dream. It's the perfect reality as designed by Freddy Krueger.

The Party hacks sleep by making it the new way for Party members to be awake; namely, the Party mixes up the type of thinking you do while asleep with the thinking you do when awake. By jumbling together sleep and wakefulness, the Party has jumbled up the thoughts of its citizens and by jumbling the thoughts of its citizens it has made the confusing nature of doublethink *the only way to think*.

A Restless Environment

Even before *1984*, Orwell understood the role of sleep in the process of our thinking. His memoir, *Down and Out in Paris and London*, describes the tough lives of those existing on the edges of society. In one scene, he describes a flophouse where poor people could attempt to find a night's sleep on the "Twopenny Hangover."

The Twopenny Hangover was not a phrase related to the morning after a long night of boozing. In reality, it explained a unique set-up: men—and the flophouse was only for men— were placed shoulder-to-shoulder on a bench with a rope in front of them which they would "lean on . . . as though leaning over a fence" (p. 211). In the morning, "a man, humorously called the valet, cuts the rope."

Orwell recognized that the Twopenny Hangover highlighted that a lack of money often results in a lack of good sleep. His experiences with those "down and out" helped him understand that environmental factors impact sleep. Good sleep, it seems, was a privilege and not a right. In *1984*, he would take this recognition about good sleep and apply it to a new technological landscape that is actively harmful to sleep.

1984 takes this image of the rough sleepers on the Twopenny Hangover and expands it to an entire society. Airstrip One, formerly the British Isles, is a name that sounds like a military service station, and the London of *1984* is a beaten, gray, and rough environment that is practically designed to make sleep impossible. Also, due to the role of doublethink, Winston is clear that personal space doesn't exist in

Airstrip One, even during sleep. He states that a Party member "lives from birth to death under the eye of the Thought Police. Even when he is alone he can never be sure that he is alone. Wherever he may be, asleep or awake, working or resting, in his bath or in bed, he can be inspected without warning and without knowing that he is being inspected" (p. 187).

Winston highlights that this inspection occurs while sleeping or in bed. As an omnipresent force, the Thought Police are an insidious influence in a person's head while that person is trying to sleep. Winston is cognizant that while he's sleeping, he's also being monitored to make sure the doublethink is working in his brain. This is an inversion of how sleep should work; crucially, Winston's mind cannot switch to the type of thinking that happens during sleep. His mind is always tormented by outside stimuli in the guise of the Thought Police. Like the men on the Twopenny Hangover, Winston is always aware of the rope of the Thought Police and waits for it to be pulled out from under him. He's never fully asleep and never fully awake.

The world of *1984* is one where all but the most privileged people exist in a constant state of agitation. Only Inner Party members, like O'Brien, can turn off their telescreens. O'Brien's privilege of turning off his monitor is such a unique moment for Julia and Winston that it amazes them. For everyone else, there exists a "restless monologue" that constantly runs inside their head, reminding them that the Thought Police are always there (p. 7).

The Party would like to make humans into iPhones that, even in Sleep mode, are always collecting information and, at a moment's notice, are ready to pop awake and complete a task. Even in places where Winston believes himself to be safe from the view of the government, like Mr. Charrington's room, there exists only false hope. For people who have trouble sleeping, one of the most common issues is restless leg syndrome, which is when a person has an irritable and irresistible urge to move their limbs. Big Brother, the Thought Police, and the Inner Party bend the will of the entire populace to create an agitated society inflicted with restless mind syndrome.

Orwell's book imagines this half-waking, half-sleeping environment as a restless world trapped by "a disturbing extension" of "technocratic power," as Michael Greaney puts it, that reaches into "the bodily lives of its citizens" (Greaney, p. 58). Technocratic power, or technocracy, is the belief that society can be more efficiently run by a small group of scientific experts who exercise total control over everything. *1984* represents a dark realization of a technocratic society where the Inner Party, as exemplified by O'Brien, uses technology to maintain total power.

Winston's life represents the dark underbelly of technocratic societies when he notes that the energies of technology have undercut the advancement of an "earthly paradise" at the exact "moment after it had become realizable" (p. 181). The manipulation of sleep in order to influence the role of thinking is one strong example of technology being used to oppress the citizens of Airstrip One.

Newsleep

In *1984* Orwell creates a restless and agitated world that he hoped would never arrive. Big Brother's country, however, mirrors our always-on world of technology that connects each of us to the entire world. Airstrip One's pervasive technology facilitates a "banal exercise" of fear, isolation, and political powerlessness.

Jonathan Crary describes the way we live now as an "illuminated 24/7 world" that views sleep and rest as blockages to the goal of making "human life" into a state of "continuous functioning" (*Late Capitalism and the Ends of Sleep*, pp. 8–9). A direct line between our 24/7 world and the dystopia Orwell was worried about can be easily drawn: Nobody gets breaks. Nobody stops working. Nobody stops watching. Nobody has time to think.

The rough sleep, constant agitation, and ceaseless monitoring all come to a head when Winston experiences what I call Newsleep. The clearest example of Newsleep comes when Winston talks about a dream where he "meets" O'Brien. He describes a dream when a stranger cryptically says: "We shall meet in the place where there is no darkness" (p. 22).

Initially, Winston doesn't know who spoke the words but quickly becomes certain the voice came from O'Brien. He thinks it's O'Brien's voice despite not being certain that he had ever heard O'Brien's voice before the dream. That's right,

Winston is certain about the voice even if he can't be certain of the timeline of his experiences. As the novel progresses, this fact that Winston can't fashion a coherent timeline is made sinister. O'Brien's role in the novel makes it seem like this idea could've been planted in Winston's head while he was sleeping.

During the torture scene, which is the event that actually occurs in the place with no darkness, Winston describes how O'Brien knew everything about him, even the deepest areas of his mind. O'Brien is able to control Winston's mind by disrupting his sleep. Winston's torture distills every part of his life into a prolonged moment of extreme manipulation.

O'Brien changes Winston's sleep schedule to disrupt Winston's thinking to "control the present," which allows O'Brien to control the relationship between the past and the future in Winston's head (p. 221). O'Brien is very clear that the power of the Party resides in its ability to screw up the reality of it citizens. To make dreams into reality or make reality into dreams. To control how reality becomes a dream—and vice versa—is the goal of the Party.

For Winston, like the many others under the boot of the Party, sleep has become a derealized state. In a derealized state, Winston's reality is increasingly made to feel unreal and fabricated. His sleep-thoughts are dragged into his waking consciousness to break down his capacity to orientate himself in the world. He will never be sure what he consciously understood and what he dreamed. O'Brien's world of Newsleep pacifies Winston by making it hard for him to question his thoughts or find a moment to collect himself. Sleep is just another moment in the day where he can receive messages from the Party. O'Brien's long re-education of Winston encapsulates the entire function of Newsleep in that the border between past and present, reality and memory, has been smashed by a constant stream of information. Newsleep makes your brain fuzzy. It makes your brain confused. As a result, sleep will never just be sleep again.

Fake News and Newsleep

Orwell's development of Newsleep represents an intensely present part of the current global world where people are overrun by a 24/7 news cycle fueled by an "always on" social media that blurs the line between fact and fiction. Orwell's novel shows that restful, deep sleep is an impediment to the politics, commerce, and culture of a world in hyper-drive. Newsleep is, perhaps, most evident in President Donald Trump's use of Twitter to, like Big Brother, broadcast his major policy changes, declarations of "fake news," and threats to former political allies. Trump's confusing and contradictory declarations come at all hours of the night, forcing individuals into a state of Newsleep in order to receive information from the most powerful person in the country.

Orwell's Newsleep is found whenever our phones beep in the night to alert us to all types of news occurring at locations across the globe, from personal messages to important events. This environment of Newsleep is a key reason why many feel the world is becoming derealized by a fuzzy border between the observable reality of truths and the fantastical world of conspiracy theories and fake news.

1984 is, in part, Orwell's warning that we must guard our sleep.

10
Love, Truluv

Timothy Sandefur

Winston Smith is finally broken at the Ministry of Love. After a brutal regimen of torture and indoctrination, he comes at last to the realization that makes him a loyal subject. At the end of *1984*, "He loved Big Brother."

This famous sentence is key to one of Orwell's most important insights into the nature of totalitarianism. He saw as few others did that what made totalitarianism distinct was its demand that the subject *love* his oppressor. Kings and emperors of the past were content with obedience or loyalty, but the Hitlers, Stalins, Maos, and Big Brothers demanded more: they demanded love, and sought to create it by compulsion, to establish on Earth the changeless collective state of undifferentiated harmony that reflects the mystical image of supernatural love.

That effort, Orwell subtly argues, is doomed to fail, because faking love is ultimately impossible—it would require the faking of ultimate reality. Still, in the process of trying, totalitarianism causes unimaginable suffering—including the misery Smith experiences at the aptly named Ministry of Love.

Love Is Unequal

Defining love may forever preoccupy philosophers and poets, but it's clear at least that love consists of a willing union—a desire for co-operation with a special other person, in which the person who feels love seeks what is best for the loved one as well as—perhaps even more than—for himself.

Ideally, this feeling is mutual, as in a happy marriage. But the same is true of asymmetrical forms of love, as with a parent and a baby: the parent who loves *that* particular child, and wants that child to succeed and prosper and be happy, even if the child grows up to choose a path the parent herself would not. Or perhaps a woman loves a man who does not love her back—she nevertheless sincerely wishes him well when he marries another, because despite her own pain, she wants him to be happy. Whether mutual or not, love means an appreciation for the other person in his or her uniqueness—and that appreciation must be willing.

In other words, love is specific and selective. "To an ordinary human being," wrote Orwell in one essay, "love means nothing if it does not mean loving some people more than others." That marks the difference between human love and the religious notion of loving humanity as a whole, in which one "cannot give one's preference to any individual person."

Orwell contrasted this supernatural version of love with what he called the "essence of being human," namely, "that one does not seek perfection . . . and that one is prepared in the end to be defeated and broken up by life, which is the inevitable price of fastening one's love upon other human individuals." To love everyone equally and indiscriminately would actually mean not loving at all, because human love means appreciating the loved one *differently* from everyone else.

That means *inequality* is embedded in the act of loving: at a minimum, loving someone means recognizing those qualities the loved one possesses that nobody else has in the same way or degree. Aristotle noted this when he criticized Plato's suggestion in the *Republic* that selfishness could be abolished by eradicating private property and replacing the parent-child relationship with a "community of wives and children." That way, Plato claimed, all adults would regard all children as equally theirs, and love them equally. Aristotle considered this dangerously absurd, because without *special and unequal* attachment, adults would have no reason to take genuine care of the children.

A world in which special attachment and preference were obliterated would be devoid of love. But as North Korean defector Yeonmi Park attests, Plato's idea of eradicating the inherent inequality of love is not entirely a matter of theory:

"In North Korea," she writes, "the only kind of 'love' you can describe is for the Leader. We had heard the 'love' word used in different ways in smuggled TV shows and movies, but there was no way to apply it in daily life in North Korea—not with your family, friends, husband, or wife."

Love Is Personal

Another special quality about love is that it takes place entirely within the lover's mind. Actions, behaviors, habits, can all be seen from outside, but love is internal. That makes it inherently personal and impossible to fake. You can pantomime the outward signs of love—you can kiss, hug, or have sex with someone you don't love—but it's never possible to *actually* fake love, as an internal assessment and judgment. That's also why you can conceal love, or love from afar. To love someone means to appraise that person yourself, and find her worthy, even glorious. But internal judgment and appraisal cannot be manufactured or forced, only counterfeited.

We exercise this judgment toward ourselves, also. In her essay, "Thinking and Moral Considerations," political philosopher Hannah Arendt described the individual conscience as an internal dialogue in which a person constantly evaluates herself. A person of conscience does right because she cannot abide the idea of living with someone (herself) who does wrong. Introspection helps make us better people because that internal conversation serves as a judge of our own character— as a psychological mirror. "What makes a man fear this conscience," Arendt writes, "is the anticipation of the presence of a witness who awaits him only *if* and when he goes home."

What's true of self-love is true also of the love of others: as an internal appraisal, it can be mimicked and even evaded, but cannot be created on demand. That's significant because it means that there is a genuinely *untouchable* thing inside us— something which is not a tangible object or law of physics, but which is nevertheless impervious to any outside will. Love is inherently and inextricably *of the self*. It's what the American Declaration of Independence calls "unalienable."

These two factors—its *inequality* and *inalienability*—have always made love a challenge for tyrants, and the history and literature of tyranny is riddled with stories in which love and tyranny collide, from Sophocles's *Antigone* to the *Hunger Games* trilogy. One of the most interesting and revealing political writers on this point is Niccolò Machiavelli. In *The Prince*, he asks whether it is better for a ruler to strive to be loved by his subjects, or to see to it that they fear him, instead.

It's sometimes said that he concludes in favor of fear, but what Machiavelli actually says is that fear is *safer* for rulers than love, because love "is preserved by the link of obligation," which means it is always possible that the subject might "turn against" the ruler who depends on love. Love is not wholly in the ruler's power. Fear is: it is simple for him to make subjects fear him. Therefore, "men love according to their own will," but "fear according to that of the prince." The prince should therefore "establish himself on that which is in his own control"— fear. Machiavelli reinforces this conclusion later in the book when he discusses how the prince should deal with unpredictable fortune. Fortune, he writes, "is a woman, and if you wish to keep her under it is necessary to beat and ill-use her."

We will come back to Machiavelli's rape metaphor later. For now, note that he is actually wrong about fear being safer than love. While a ruler can more easily *inspire* fear than love, fear is not *safer* for the ruler, nor does it lead to a better society. The tyrant who lives *by* fear must also live *in* fear: he must keep a wary eye on his subjects at all times, because he knows they will rebel if given the chance. Nor are citizens more productive in a society built on fear: they will likely do the minimum necessary to avoid punishment, instead of looking for new and innovative ways to make society better, which is what people do when they love their societies.

Be that as it may, what Orwell recognized in *1984* was that totalitarianism had a different approach to the interaction between love and political control than any previous form of tyranny. Whereas kings and dictators in the past had always seen love as a challenge, and had struggled to obliterate or subjugate the power of love, totalitarian rulers like Big Brother try instead to force subjects to love them.

Totalitarianism as Total Rule

The term "totalitarian" was adopted by the fascist dictator Mussolini. He meant that the state should control every aspect of the individual's life—that there should be no dividing line between personal and political, between social and self. Thus Arendt considered totalitarianism more like a religious cult than a political party. A totalitarian movement, she argued, stands above politics (or claims to) and uses the state as a tool to achieve total social revolution. That movement demands the totality of each person—and thus it is fundamentally opposed to privacy, self-interest, independence, and dissent.

That is why censorship, collective ownership, the eradication of privacy, and, especially, hostility to sex (and, incidentally, to humor), are essential to the totalitarian ruler. Free speech and private property are obviously obstacles to his power. But privacy, humor, and sex are also distractions that divert the citizen's attention away from total and constant devotion. They encourage the citizen to think independently and foster interests outside of the circuit that connects him to the ruler.

Political philosopher Anthony de Jasay explained the origins of Stalin-style totalitarianism especially well: a society in which economic production is controlled by the government must first establish "detailed instructions concerning factor inputs, product outputs, incomes, and prices." Yet while such a system is "necessarily rigid," it is always subject to "random shocks," such as unexpected shortages or crop failures—and any factor of production that does not follow the instructions will disrupt the dictated production system. So the ruler must establish more instructions, and more, dictating production in ever finer detail. Yet "the more exacting are their orders and the greater is their complexity, the stronger will be the likelihood of laxism in execution and dissimulation of failures."

Enforcement of these rules is costly, which creates an even greater likelihood that random factors will throw the system off. "The need for severe enforcement," Jasay concludes, "brings into being an authoritarian political system that must make heavy exertions to legitimate itself and leaves little room for democratic trappings. Political relaxation is quickly translated into a worsening economic performance that may degenerate into uncontrolled rout."

In a free society, people can better resolve unexpected crises because they are free to choose how to act, and—to take economics as an example—will seek profit by meeting demand with supply. If a storm destroys the orange crop, the price of oranges will rise, and farmers in a neighboring state will ship oranges to meet demand and make money. The decentralized nature of the economy allows for the efficient allocation of resources. The same is true in a non-economic context. Which citizens should marry which? In a free society, each decides for him- or herself. Those who choose well "profit" by obtaining a happy, loving family—while those who choose poorly pay the price of unhappiness or divorce. But in the totalitarian society, these one-on-one decisions are forbidden in order to impose the "right" answer in the form of instructions backed not by desire for profit but fear of punishment.

The obvious challenge is that people who don't stand to profit, literally or metaphorically, aren't likely to work hard. They'll do just enough to avoid punishment. But the totalitarian's answer is to use love as a tool of discipline and compulsion: if the citizens are committed *enough*—if they *love* the ruler—then they will exert themselves even in the absence of personal gain. That requires transforming their consciousness—re-educating them. That is the source of the totalitarian impulse toward thought-control. Winston must adore Big Brother so that he will serve without hope of gain.

Totalitarianism as Compulsory Love

To be a good citizen of Oceania means loving Big Brother so fully as to lose yourself. In the actual totalitarian states on which Orwell based his novel, this form of love was manufactured by relentless propaganda backed by terror.

The propagandizing and persecution in which Big Brother and his real-life counterparts engage are necessary because, if love is fundamentally anti-egalitarian and self-directed, and thus impossible to manufacture on demand, the totalitarian who attempts such a thing must control the whole reality that surrounds the individual. That is what totalitarianism seeks to do.

The consequence, as Martin Amis puts it, is that the totalitarian ruler compels the citizen "to collude in a fiction." Because manufacturing love is not truly possible, citizens must instead constantly *pretend* they love the ruler—and this risks blurring the line between fiction and reality in their own souls. "When an ideologically totalitarian society makes its people live a lie," writes scholar Trudy Glover, "more than politics is compromised. The very social fibre is ruptured: people . . . cannot say what they think, must hide many aspects of themselves from others, and cannot fully develop relationships or even their own thoughts or emotions. . . . There is no way reality and appearance can coincide and be comfortable."

The line between fiction and reality is critical to understanding totalitarianism because totalitarian rule is ultimately an expression of the ruler's (or "the people's") *will*—a will that is supposed to control not just politics, but even physical nature itself. The reason for this is that the totalitarian seeks to remold society to suit his ideology, but society is built partly on certain natural differences—including inequalities of wealth, status, skills, intelligence, physical strength, or desire—and these must also be eliminated if the totalitarian's new civilization is to exist. That's why Plato sought to eliminate the affection between parents and children: to create a new society where all will be equal, even nature, which is unequal, must be overcome. And overcoming nature requires an effort, not of reason, but of will.

Orwell emphasizes throughout *1984* that Big Brother's rule rests fundamentally on forcing reality to fit his will. This is best embodied in the Party's self-contradictory slogans—peace is strength; war is peace; freedom is slavery—and Winston at last accepts that $2 + 2 = 5$.

These contradictions help break down the independent judgment, and thus the autonomy, of the citizens. If they accept such blatant lies as truth, they will accept anything. Big Brother's anti-reality slogans take this effort to the greatest extreme: Oceania's existence is premised on the idea that *reality itself* is a social construct.

Is Reality a Social Construct?

If reality is a social construct, there's no role for individual judgment—including the appreciation on which love depends—because the difference between "true" and "false" or between "this" and "that" is transformed from a determination of reality to a function of the ruler's will. This reconfiguration of reality takes place largely within language—that's the

purpose of Newspeak—because language is the most important gateway between the mind and the natural world. Control
it, and the individual is utterly vulnerable. Big Brother uses
Newspeak—which allows no speck of nature to reach the mind
unfiltered—to subject the citizen's mind to a sort of sensory
deprivation—what O'Brien calls "collective solipsism."

If there is no difference between this or that, then—perhaps ironically—there can be no difference between love or
hate. When "collective solipsism" reaches its most extreme
point, it becomes something like what physicists call a "singularity": a point where gravity is infinite and physical laws no
longer apply. Just as the indiscriminate and equal love of all
people would really mean not loving anyone, so the difference
between love and hate becomes merely semantic when Big
Brother's methods are pushed to their greatest point, in Room
101. Thus O'Brien tells Winston that "Obedience is not
enough." Unless the person you rule is suffering,

> how can you be sure that he is obeying your will and not his own?
> Power is in inflicting pain and humiliation. Power is in tearing human
> minds to pieces and putting them together again in new shapes of
> your own choosing. Do you begin to see, then, what kind of world we
> are creating? It is the exact opposite of the stupid hedonistic Utopias
> that the old reformers imagined. A world of fear and treachery is tor-
> ment, a world of trampling and being trampled upon, a world which
> will grow not less but more merciless as it refines itself. Progress in
> our world will be progress towards more pain. The old civilizations
> claimed that they were founded on love or justice. Ours is founded
> upon hatred. . . . There will be no love, except the love of Big Brother.

When reading this passage, we can substitute "love" for the
words "suffering," "power," or "torment," and the meaning
remains the same. In Room 101, there is no such thing as reality, and therefore no such thing as a connection between the
individual and the real world, or the things or people in it.
That means there can be no such thing as love, only power—
labeled as "love" or "hate" as Big Brother arbitrarily chooses.

"The world we are preparing," says O'Brien, is "an endless
pressing, pressing, pressing upon the nerve of power." When
Winston feebly protests, O'Brien explains, "You are imagining
that there is something called human nature which will be

outraged by what we do and will turn against us. But we create human nature. Men are infinitely malleable."

When Winston breaks at last—when he has been tortured to the point where he loses the strength to exercise judgment or self-generated desire, and has therefore lost the ability to love—he realizes not only that "the so-called laws of Nature" are "nonsense," but that he is also capable of bending backwards intellectually and loving Big Brother.

At the close of the novel, he regards his loving of Big Brother as a triumph: as if he is running and "cheering himself deaf," because he believes he has overcome himself. He truly has "won victory over himself," in the sense of a man who has managed to break his own legs by sheer force of will. He has accomplished something truly difficult: he has obliterated his own soul.

Love and Rape

I've said that love is inherently personal and unequal. The philosopher Ayn Rand called it "selfish" because "one gains a profoundly personal, selfish joy from the mere existence of the person one loves." This is why Big Brother persecutes sex so thoroughly, eradicating all privacy and policing sexual mores via the Anti-Sex League.

Big Brother seeks to ban sex in part because it is natural and biological—and therefore not a constructed social reality—and partly because it is spontaneous and unplanned, which is intolerable to the totalitarian. (When Julia first takes off her clothes in front of Winston, it is "with that same magnificent gesture by which a whole civilization seemed to be annihilated.")

More importantly, sex is not so much forbidden in Oceania as it is channeled in a politically correct direction. Big Brother uses sex for his own purposes, especially during the Two Minutes Hate, when he allows people to engage in officially sanctioned ecstasy, directed toward himself. At the climax of the Hate, the people experience "a deliberate drowning of consciousness by means of rhythmic noise"—an orgasm—designed to reinforce the people's "love" for Big Brother.

Once again, this horrific moment is not entirely fantasy. It has been observed that public funerals are among the few occasions in the Islamic Republic of Iran in which men and women can commingle and express emotion. Consequently, they are often scenes of terrific frenzies, even riots, as participants release passions that have long been submerged.

In her book *Reading Lolita in Tehran,* Azar Nafisi describes the scene at the Ayatollah Khomeini's funeral as "oddly sexual"; a "frenzy of beating chests and fainting" in which countless Iranians surged forward and, in the climax, tore the body from its bearers and stripped off its funeral shroud.

A similar scene occurred at Stalin's funeral, when an unknown number of people—estimates exceed one hundred—were trampled and asphyxiated by the crowds. These episodes reveal what Christopher Hitchens called "the latent connection between sexual repression and orgiastic vicarious collectivized release." Systematized sexual repression enables the rulers to direct otherwise disruptive passions into a path that reinforces their rule.

Love and Sex: Political Acts

Big Brother is essentially trying to confiscate love. And it is when Winston and Julia reject that, and have sex simply because they want to, and enjoy it themselves, that Winston feels liberated—precisely because it is antisocial: "anything that hinted at corruption always filled him with a wild hope," Orwell writes. "the simple undifferentiated desire: that was the force that would tear the Party to pieces." Their climax is "a victory . . . a blow struck against the Party. It was a political act." That is because it is personal, spontaneous, natural, and their *own*. Sex asserts, even if in only a rudimentary way, the value of the individual as against the collective.

Sex is often a political act, whether it be publishing *Madame Bovary* or *Fanny Hill*—subjects of famous censorship cases—or kissing in public in Saudi Arabia, Dubai, or Morocco, or marrying outside one's race, as Frederick Douglass and Mildred Loving did. Sex is an assertion of free will, personal choice, and the individual's right to exist for her own sake. This assertion may sometimes possibly be self-destructive, as with the main character in Dostoyevsky's *Notes from Underground*, who acts self-destructively as a means of asserting his own free will. The difference is that where Winston asserts his free will by an act contrary to the artificiality of Big Brother's rule—to assert the primacy of nature—Dostoyevsky's Underground Man does the reverse: his self-assertion consists of *defying* nature to assert that he is free of its bonds. The Underground Man *embraces* the idea that $2 + 2 = 5$ as proof of his intellectual independence—as opposed to seeing it, as Orwell does, as ultimately a path to submission.

Winston's and Julia's choice to have sex is thus essentially a statement of "I am," independent of political authority. The *New York Times Book Review*'s claim that *1984* represented "a whole new discovery of the beauty of love between man and woman," has often been ridiculed, but in this sense, at least, it's accurate.

When Winston is broken at last, it is because his feelings for Julia have rendered him uniquely vulnerable. She is the only thing that truly *belongs* to him. To betray her at the nadir of his panic—"Do it to Julia! Not me!"—is to surrender the one thing that has kept him a defined individual. The fact that it is surrendered, not merely taken, makes it particularly cruel. But it is also logical, because love, being inalienable, can never actually be taken away, only given up. What breaks Winston isn't that he's tortured, but the knowledge that he has renounced the only thing that ever mattered.

Love cannot be compelled, but of course you can be compelled into the outward signs of love. The most obvious example of this is rape. Sexual love—willing union—is differentiated from rape by one essential quality—consent, or the lack thereof—which, like love, is inalienably personal. Rape is wrong because it violates the victim's right of ownership over herself. But in a tyranny, where the ruler claims to own the individual, he might as well take what he likes. Big Brother goes further: he wants not mere obedience, but love. So, what Winston endures in Room 101 is analogous not to rape but to the internal abandonment of any distinction between love and rape. Winston must not merely *say* he loves Big Brother, but *actually* love him. This explains Orwell's otherwise oddly transcendent description of Winston's collapse: "He had fallen through the floor, through the walls of the building, through the atmosphere, into the gulfs between the stars." Such phrases might decorate a teenager's love poem, but they appear here because Winston has been deprived of a connection with reality. He has reached the singularity where will replaces reason, and the laws of reality no longer apply.

Happily Ever After

1984 actually has a "happy ending" of sorts: the appendix explaining Newspeak is written in the past-tense, which indicates that at some point, Big Brother's rule came to an end, and civilization prevailed before the year 2050. Presumably this was because human nature cannot fundamentally change, and love, being inalienable, is always possible so long as humans exist.

It appears that by the time the note on Newspeak is composed, language and literature have revived. But so has love, for the author of the appendix tells us that Newspeak was intended to eradicate love along with other thoughtcrime. Had the Party succeeded, the appendix says, a person's sex life would have been reducible to "two Newspeak words: *sexcrime* (sexual immorality) and *goodsex* (chastity)." The former would have included not only adultery and fornication, but also "normal intercourse practiced for its own sake," while the latter would have referred to marital sex "for the sole purpose of begetting children, and without physical pleasure on the part of the woman."

More importantly, it would have become impossible—literally unimaginable—to articulate the sentence "I love you" in Newspeak, at least as meaning

> I love thee to the depth and breadth and height
> My soul can reach, when feeling out of sight
> For the ends of being and ideal grace.
> I love thee to the level of every day's
> Most quiet need, by sun and candle-light.
> I love thee freely, as men strive for right.
> I love thee purely, as they turn from praise. (Elizabeth Barrett
>   Browning)

"Doubleplusgood" doesn't exactly do that justice.

11
When Cruelty Is Not Enough

DANIEL CONWAY

Orwell's readers tend to trace their most profound experiences of horror, disgust, and outrage to the extended torture scene depicted in the third and final section of *1984*. O'Brien's coldly efficient assault on Winston is literally the stuff of nightmares.

Psychological and physical torment, humiliation, betrayal, isolation, deprivation, Doublethink, Room 101, electrodes, hungry rats, and O'Brien's dispassionately clinical narration: all are now firmly entrenched in the *Zeitgeist* as metonyms for the cruelty we have come to identify with the excesses of authoritarian rule and totalitarian control. Orwell is rightly hailed, sixty years on, for facing his readers with their worst fears of a political experiment gone dangerously awry.

To be sure, this is gruesome stuff, tailor-made to scare the daylights out of anyone who even pauses to consider the supposed advantages of a scheme to "control life . . . at all its levels" (p. 222). To my way of thinking, however, Orwell's depiction of torture in *1984* is both anticlimactic and tedious. Once it is stipulated that O'Brien is in total, unchallenged control of the situation, the rest follows naturally. *Of course* he compels Winston's betrayal of Julia, unleashing the accursed rats just as Winston reaches his breaking point. *Of course* Winston comes to love Big Brother (and hate basic arithmetic) as he welcomes the arrival of the bullet speeding his way. How else could this cautionary tale have possibly ended? With the rebellion-*cum*-victory of "human nature" (p. 222), led perhaps by the singing proles? Not a chance.

None of this surprises us. We expect nothing less from O'Brien than what we (and Winston) in fact receive. If anything, we learn that O'Brien too is captive to the program of torture he directs on behalf of the Party. Were he to deviate from the prescribed regimen, granting the mitigation or reprieve that Winston hoped he would receive, the Party would not be as formidable (and frightening) as Orwell meant it to be. I dare to suggest, in fact, that these decisive chapters are almost perfunctory in their plodding elaboration of what we have long understood to be a *fait accompli*. As O'Brien remarks to Winston, "Nothing has happened that you did not foresee" (p. 225). The same may be said of Orwell's readers.

The genuine nightmare of *1984* unfolds several chapters earlier, as Winston and Julia suddenly realize what they should have known all along: their grimy love nest is equipped with the dreaded telescreen. O'Brien and his team have been watching them all along, carefully recording the details of their illicit (and treasonous) affair. In this decisive moment, the lovers (and Orwell's unwitting readers) are obliged to confront the sheer, comprehensive totality of O'Brien's betrayal.

It's not simply that he has surveilled them, documented their transgressions, and thoroughly invaded the privacy they had labored so resourcefully, if naively, to secure. The crowning horror of the book dawns as we realize that Winston and Julia were already known to be thoughtcriminals, even as they were recruited (= entrapped) by O'Brien. He could have apprehended them on the spot and remanded them without delay to Room 101. But he did not.

Instead, O'Brien cleverly urged them to pursue their conspiracy against Big Brother. He encouraged them to believe that he and they belonged to the mysterious Brotherhood, which, he further encouraged them to believe, would prevail in its efforts to overthrow the Party. He abetted their clandestine meetings above Charrington's shop, where, *he knew*, they would imbibe the teachings of Emmanuel Goldstein and rekindle their hopes for the future. *Only then*, as they foolishly pledged to champion the doomed cause of the proles, did he finally end the subterfuge and apprehend the criminals.

Cruelty: What's Up with That?

Richard Rorty's influential reading of *1984* galvanized philosophical interest in the nature and practice of cruelty. Boldly declaring that "cruelty is the worst thing we do" (*Contingency, Irony, and Solidarity*, p. xv), Rorty advanced a persuasive case for a program of liberal education grounded in those works of literature, like *1984*, which acquaint thoughtful readers with the full extent of their unacknowledged complicity in sprawling regimes of cruelty.

A particularly instructive element of Rorty's interpretation of *1984* is his account of the displacement of the book's central character in its final section. Orwell's enduring contribution, Rorty allows, lies not in his account of the failed rebellion staged by Winston and Julia, but in his portrait of O'Brien as the embodiment of the cruelty that we may expect from a hyper-educated intellectual who has lost his faith in liberal causes and progressive ideals (p. 183).

Accustomed as we are to the cruelty dispensed by rednecks and ruffians drawn to the flame of top-down authoritarian control, we are understandably disturbed to discover the depth of the cruelty administered by post-liberal intellectuals like O'Brien. Orwell's point, as illuminated by Rorty, is that a love of reason, books, science, and ideas offers no guarantee of a principled opposition to illiberal political institutions and regimes (pp. 175–76). Cruelty is, or can become, the coin of any realm, from the most intellectual to the least.

Drawing appreciatively on the landmark research of Elaine Scarry, Rorty interprets O'Brien as intent upon the complete humiliation of Winston:

> The only point in making Winston believe that two and two equal five is to break him. Getting somebody to deny a belief for no reason is a first step toward making her incapable of having a self because she becomes incapable of weaving a coherent web of belief and desire. (p. 178)

This point is important to Rorty, for he ascribes to Orwell the view that "a coherent web of belief and desire" is *all* that anyone ever is. Once this web is undone, there remains no residual self, and certainly no autonomous, timeless, character-laden self, which might be expected to maintain its core integrity in the face of O'Brien's torture (p. 185). As profiled by Rorty, O'Brien thus appears to be bent on the "social death," as Lisa Guenther puts it, of selves and worlds, and only, as an afterthought, on snuffing out those lives his program of torture has rendered meaningless.

Rorty's attention to O'Brien is both illuminating and insightful. Ever keen, as Rorty puts it, to "tear human minds to pieces and put them together again in new shapes of his own choosing," (p. 177) O'Brien skillfully deploys invasive techniques of physical and psychological torture, all of which are meant, just as Rorty explains, to invalidate Winston's claim to selfhood. O'Brien thus appears as the *Doppelgänger* (or evil twin) of those liberal heroes whom we reflexively applaud for taking a principled stand against the excesses of illiberal political regimes. When cruelty is not enough, O'Brien is the man for the job.

Understandably concerned to track O'Brien's efforts to unmake the world that Winston and Julia have fashioned for themselves, Rorty is less attentive to O'Brien's role in nurturing their intimacy and coaxing into existence the crescent world he subsequently undermines. Rorty's interpretation of *1984* thus fails to capture what I take to be the most terrifying element of O'Brien's administrative sadism: *the selves he undoes and the worlds he destroys are of his own making.* He specializes in humiliating "criminals" and dismantling worlds into which (or whom) he has poured his own energy, his own passion, and his own humanity. And although he certainly is pretending as he plays matchmaker for Winston and Julia, he is convincing in this role only because he is not *simply* pretending. If the Party is as truly frightening as Orwell wishes it to be, O'Brien must be understood to be genuinely invested in those very selves and worlds that he has marked for destruction.

On my reading of *1984*, the true horror exemplified by supposedly cold-blooded sadists like O'Brien is that they are in fact warm-blooded, situationally sympathetic creatures, equally proficient at cultivating the selves and worlds they are obliged to dismantle. Simply put, O'Brien is not to be confused with central casting criminal masterminds, Bond villains, Dr. Evil, or other representatives of the cartoon Right or Left. He represents a new and frightening type of sadist, a type we would do well to study, understand, anticipate, and disempower.

As we see in Section Two of *1984*, O'Brien displays genuine talent for helping fugitive souls find one another, trust in one another, and work together to build a world in which they once again may place their hopes for their future. Orwell's vaulting aspiration is to invest O'Brien with sufficient humanity that readers of *1984* may understand him to excel, sincerely and credibly, at the tender business of *worldmaking*. It is entirely understandable, in other words, that Winston initially suspected O'Brien of being a double agent: playing both sides is both his job description and his métier. Presumably, he was groomed for the office he holds precisely because he can summon genuine human feelings that he can then banish on cue.

Family Values

Those critics who sought to ban or burn *1984* for its explicit sexual content should have read further. What begins as a lurid account of a reckless carnal liaison soon morphs into a conventionally wholesome paean to traditional family values. While the graphic sex scenes were no doubt intended to scandalize Orwell's neo-Victorian readership, they yield soon enough to scenes of tenderness, commitment, domesticity, monogamy, and futurity. All of these scenes, as well as their sequential progression, attest to the handiwork of O'Brien. He is both a breaker *and* a builder of hopes and dreams.

When initially "recruited" by O'Brien, Winston and Julia declared that they would not separate, especially if doing so meant that they would never again see one another (p. 143). Unbeknownst to them at the time, this brave disclosure alerted O'Brien to their signal weakness, which prompted him to design the specific program of torture that would eventuate in their undoing. Rather than proceed directly to compel their betrayal of one another, however, O'Brien granted them the time and opportunity to deepen their bond. His motive for doing so was particularly despicable: Confident that he could break them in any event and at any time, he manipulated them into forging the kind and quality of bond that would buoy their dormant hopes for the future. The destruction of *this* bond, he reasoned, would strike a blow from which they would not recover.

Cognizant that a license to engage in naughty sex would not suffice to rekindle their hopes for the future, O'Brien engineered the conditions under which they would develop the kind of bond he was determined to explode. He actively encouraged their budding intimacy, displaying in the process a deft and gentle touch that we typically do not associate with sadists. (For all we know, in fact, he made it possible for them to acquire the black market goodies that injected accents of conviviality into their otherwise grim assignations.) The retreat he arranged for them above Charrington's shop soon became a quasi-Edenic paradise, wherein "the last man in Europe" and his mate plotted a brighter future for the human race.

Interested at first only in their *verboten* lovemaking (p. 105), Winston and Julia gradually fashioned for themselves the uxorious framework of what can only be called a *home*, wherein they bravely joined their fates and futures. As their illicit passion yielded to the creaturely routines of homemaking, they shared their respective stories and became an actual couple. Treating one another to purloined delicacies, they laid a foundation of intimacy and trust.

In preparation for what would be their initial tryst above Charrington's shop, Julia uncharacteristically paused to apply the makeup and perfume she had acquired (p. 118). Up to this point, of course, she had been the equal of Winston, every bit as brave, rebellious, and sexually aggressive as he. Now, however, everything changes between them. Julia's simple gesture of masquerade not only marks their graduation from the unvarnished carnality of their early days together, but also announces her decision to submit, voluntarily, to a traditional, unbalanced division of gendered household labor. (Winston does not offer to scrub up for her, and she neither asks nor expects him to do so.) No longer live-for-the-moment outlaws, much less equal partners in crime, they surrender to the primal law of hearth and home.

Just prior to pledging to bring about the future they now behold, Winston and Julia contemplate the meaning of the birdsong to which they were treated during their inaugural *rendezvous*. Each holding true to form, Julia explains that the bird outside their window sang (and sings) for no one, and certainly not for them, while Winston insists that *singing*, whether by birds or humans, represents the limits of the Party's power and influence (p. 182). The inspiration for this interpretation is the unnamed woman who sings in the nearby

yard as she hangs and collects her laundry. Previously unap-
preciative of the magnitude of her labors, Winston pronounces
her *beautiful* (pp. 180–81).

In sharp contrast to the Party's efforts to narrow, coarsen,
empty, and flatten the world, Winston has discovered beauty
where he never before had encountered it. Before his very eyes,
the world he and Julia have fashioned for themselves is growing,
expanding, and, as a result, reviving their hopes for the future.
This sudden and unexpected upsurge of beauty inspires him to
interpret the woman's singing as evidence of a potentially global
rebellion against the Party: Led by the shadowy Brotherhood, he
enthused, the singing proles would prevail in the end.

Julia does not agree with Winston's assessment of the
woman, noting that "she's a meter across the hips, easily" (p.
181), but she joins him in beholding their crescent new world.
Not unlike first-time parents gazing on the new life they have
created, they share a tender (albeit fleeting) moment ripe with
love, hope, and futurity. Although they will have no children of
their own, other children, perhaps even the conjectured children and grandchildren of the singing washerwoman, will
inherit from them a brighter, more hopeful future. They will be
as procreative in their own way—"by word of mouth, from mind
to mind" (p. 181)—as the fertile woman next door.

We Are the Dead

We thus arrive at the moment of their betrayal. Before considering this moment, we should note that O'Brien has guided
(and in fact orchestrated) their passage from nihilistic rebellion to hopeful fecundity. As they revel in the giddy exhilara-
tion that accompanies (what they take to be) pure freedom,
well beyond the panoptic gaze of Big Brother, O'Brien adroitly
manipulates the stimuli to which they unwittingly respond.
Even love itself, that most mysterious and elusive of human
emotions, falls under the purview of his technical expertise.

In the beginning, Winston and Julia soberly counted themselves among "the dead," reciting together the macabre motto
that was emblematic of their foolhardy rebellion against Big
Brother. In pursuit of nothing greater or nobler than the satisfaction of their carnal desires, these rebels without a cause
knew their days to be numbered.

As their relationship deepened, however, and especially as their trysts gave way to cozy routines of homemaking and worldmaking, they came to adopt a far less cynical view of their prospects together. While continuing to count themselves among "the dead" (p. 182), they increasingly found meaning and purpose in their deathbound existence. They will die, of course, but no longer in vain, especially if they succeed in "passing on the secret doctrine that two plus two make four" (p. 182). On the strength of their efforts, others, most notably the singing proles, will inherit the hopeful future they now envision.

Goldstein's secret, which in fact reprises the not-so-secret teachings of Marx and Lenin, is that the future belongs to the proles (p. 181). As idealized by Winston, the proles will persist in their singing, which he now regards as emblematic of their individuality and freedom, even under the duress of excruciating, back-breaking labor. (He apparently believes that the woman working next door will continue to sing even as she is whisked away to the Gulag.) The Party may break him and Julia (and other rebels), but it will not succeed in depriving the proles of their futurity. According to Goldstein and now Winston, the proles will prevail not only on the strength of their overwhelming numbers, but also by virtue of their inherent goodness, their indomitable will, and their indefatigable singing.

In a solemn declaration of their togetherness, and of their mutual commitment to the future they have glimpsed, Winston and Julia rehearse for the last time a familiar line that has taken on new significance:

"We are the dead," he said.

"We are the dead," echoed Julia dutifully. (p. 182)

And then, the shocking confirmation of their betrayal, the inevitable echo they somehow had convinced themselves they would not hear:

"You are the dead," said an iron voice behind them.

In this fateful moment, the world they had fashioned for themselves and their envisioned progeny vanishes into thin air. They *are* the dead.

But why now, especially if the telescreen concealed in their love nest has been operational all along? O'Brien has waited patiently for Winston and Julia to build a world together. Now they are not simply traitors. At long last, they are *hopeful* traitors, who have dared to project themselves beyond the horizon of their forbidden love. Thus emerges the real enemy of the Inner Party and the target of its cruelest methods: not Emmanuel Goldstein or the tenebrous Brotherhood, *but hope itself*. Here, too, we appreciate the urgency of Orwell's profile of the techno-sadist O'Brien, who is tasked with elevating the hopes and dreams he later will demolish.

The Object of Torture

The torture depicted in Section Three of *1984* is methodical, time-consuming, and wildly inefficient. It elicits no actionable intelligence; nor was it intended to do so. O'Brien's program of torture does nothing to further the geopolitical aspirations of the Inner Party, which, for all we know, favors the *status quo* of perpetual warfare, be it real or illusory. Why, then, is Winston subjected to this narrated regimen of soul-crushing, world-deranging torture? What does the Party hope to gain?

O'Brien famously informs Winston that "the object of torture is torture" (p. 217), which Rorty, among others, takes to be a key insight into the Party's *modus operandi*. According to me, however, O'Brien's disclosure is best appreciated as ingredient to, rather than revelatory of, the program of interrogation it is supposed to explain. O'Brien favors this account of torture not because it's true, but because Winston will unravel if he *believes* it to be true. Which, of course, he does.

According to Rorty, the torture of nobodies like Winston is pursued for the sole purpose of causing pain, the outward expression of which brings pleasure to members of the Party, including O'Brien (pp. 179–180). There is obvious merit to this interpretation. As we know from the notoriously viral Abu Ghraib photos, especially those of Specialist Lynndie England posing with humiliated prisoners, torturers may take pleasure in their assertion of total control of their captives, independent of the quality of the intelligence their cruelty elicits. As Nietzsche was fond of pointing out, even "civilized" human beings are loath to disavow the sublimated pleasures available

to them through their participation in state-sponsored spectacles of cruelty (pp. 65–67).

But O'Brien is not Lynndie England. A patient, serious, but-
toned-down intellectual, he takes no obvious delight in the
humiliation of Winston Smith. And why would he? Nothing in
the text of *1984* suggests that Winston is an alpha criminal, or
that his "rebellion" against Big Brother is somehow unique or
unprecedented. And although we may be tempted to figure
Winston as a worthy adversary, in whom O'Brien very nearly
met his match, a more plausible account of their interaction
would acknowledge that O'Brien has vanquished hundreds,
perhaps thousands, of inconsequential "rebels" just like
Winston. For O'Brien, the breaking of Winston was nothing
special, just another day at the office.

Far from gratuitous, meretricious, or playful, the torture
O'Brien inflicts is carefully calibrated to produce a result spec-
ified by the Party: the unmaking of Winston's self and world.
Any pleasure O'Brien derives from torturing Winston must
therefore remain fully consistent with (and supplementary to)
his service to the Party. As such, the pleasure he derives is
more closely related to the satisfaction experienced by a scientist or scholar who solves a vexing problem, interprets a for-
bidding text, or cracks a stubborn code. To O'Brien and his ilk,
Winston is just another puzzle to be solved, a Rubik's cube to
be twisted and contorted toward a final resolution.

To Rorty's emphasis on pleasure I thus add two friendly
amendments. The first is attributable to Hannah Arendt, who
understood before anyone else that totalitarian regimes flourish by weaponizing technocrats and bureaucrats who display
no rigid allegiance to the prevailing ideology of the party or
regime they serve (pp. 287–88). All that is required of these
recruits is that they function efficiently under conditions of
what Arendt preferred to call *thoughtlessness*, which, she
insisted, should not be confused with *stupidity* (pp. 287–88).
Arendt's paradigmatic example of bureaucratic thoughtlessness, Adolf Eichmann, was notable for his persistent failure to
imagine the plight of his victims (p. 276). Untroubled by self-
recrimination, and insulated by the Nazi regime from all external sources of rebuke, Eichmann did as he was told and basked
in the positive recognition he received from his superiors
("Banality, Again," pp. 81–84).

Orwell's presentation of O'Brien is similar in important respects to Arendt's profile of Eichmann. Both are functionaries within a Party on which they are utterly reliant for recognition, and both achieve a measure of success by remaining reliably thoughtless. In O'Brien's case, two assumptions are crucial: first, that he has lost all faith in those liberal ideals that previously may have guided his intellectual curiosity; and second, that he is ensconced in a well-defined setting—an office, role, or station—in which he is affirmed for his intellectual gifts and technical acumen.

What O'Brien needs (and receives) from the Party is actually quite simple: he must be affirmed as a *bona fide* intellectual, and he must be insulated from objections arising either from his own conscience or from his peers. He can live with himself as a torturer, Arendt thus suggests, because there are no viable alternatives to the ideals of the Party—here we recall his clinical dissection of Winston's various appeals to "human nature," justice, goodness, and so on— and because he is good at what he does. The goodness of *what* he does, which in another context would be debatable (or even risible), is vouchsafed by the Party he faithfully serves. The Party determines that Winston must be broken, and O'Brien happily designs the most efficient means of achieving this particular objective.

The second friendly amendment is drawn from the critical theory elaborated by Max Horkheimer and Theodor Adorno, who warned that the rise of technical rationality has elevated science to the status of a secular religion (pp. 76–86). As other forms and sources of cultural authority have dwindled, science now presides without serious challenge, in part because science determines what will count as a serious challenge to its authority. Like religion before it, science is permitted (and even encouraged) to validate its own agenda, irrespective of extramural objections to its methods and techniques (pp. 35–47).

As in the case of O'Brien's Ministry of Truth, science has become the official sponsor of programs of cruelty that otherwise would not be tolerated. Whereas an ordinary citizen (such as a lion-killing dentist) who tortures animals for sport and pleasure may be subject to public shaming, a credentialed scientist who "experiments" on animals may expect to receive praise, fame, tenure, prizes, and government-sponsored research grants. And although O'Brien's work on human subjects places him beyond the acknowledged pale of contemporary scientific research, the enthusiasm among government types for clandestine experiments on unwitting human subjects (for example, the Tuskegee Study) suggests that lab-coated sadists may be more common than we care to believe.

The worry voiced by Horkheimer and Adorno is that civilized humanity has become increasingly captive to the runaway momentum of technical rationality (pp. 94–101). Under its sway, skilled technicians like O'Brien are authorized to undertake various projects and experiments *simply because they are able to do so* (pp. 66–74). In this respect, Orwell's signal achievement in conjuring O'Brien was to provide his readers with an initial, accurate profile of the kind of sadist who takes cover behind the unchallenged, quasi-religious authority of science. At one point, in fact, O'Brien refers to himself and his fellow torturers as "the priests of power" (p. 217). Enough said.

O'Brien's Legacy

That O'Brien could excel at matchmaking, while failing to develop any lasting attachment to the lovers he has joined, is downright terrifying. We *know* that he could devote his considerable talents to the civilizing aims of Eros—nurturing stable selves, healthy relationships, and sturdy worlds—because we see him do precisely that for Winston and Julia. Under other circumstances, we suppose, he might have found happiness as the avuncular mentor whom Winston and Julia initially took him to be.

As we now understand, however, his allegiance to Eros, though very much real, is only ever provisional, for it is trumped by his allegiance to the Party. Enjoined by the Party not simply to torture Winston, but also to obliterate his tenuous claim on selfhood, O'Brien instinctively turns on the charm, baits the trap, and launches a lethal confidence game. In doing so, he substantiates the fear voiced by Freud ten years earlier, as he observed the dark cloud of National Socialism gathering over Europe: The desired, civilization-sustaining priority of Eros is by no means assured, and it certainly is not woven into the fabric of the cosmos.

O'Brien defies this priority, moreover, on purely (or technically) rational grounds, in the service of the "higher" ideals espoused by the Party. From his coldly clinical perspective, the world he has prompted Winston and Julia to create is simply collateral damage in a much larger campaign to secure the desired end of unchallenged, rebellion-proof Party rule. As Rorty notes, we cannot excuse O'Brien on the grounds that he is ignorant, confused, or mistaken. He knows exactly what he is doing, even as he dispatches the rats to deliver the prescribed *coup de grâce*, and he is unflinchingly convinced of the merit of his course of action.

Of all those whom we meet as we traverse Orwell's dystopian hellscape, O'Brien may be the most likely to sleep soundly at night, untroubled by self-doubt or moral recrimination. He is a true believer, the likes of which are arrayed, Orwell warns, across the political spectrum. That he is an intellectual, a man of reason and science, is no guarantee of his unwavering commitment to progressive ideals. When you're entrenched on the right side of history, or when you're persuaded that there is no right or wrong side, no sacrifice is too great.[1]

---

[1] This chapter is dedicated, in love and admiration, to my daughter Olivia, who revived my interest in Orwell and prompted me to revisit *1984*. May she never suffer trauma or betrayal.

12
No Crack in the Wall?

OSHRAT C. SILBERBUSCH

"If you want a picture of the future, imagine a boot stamping on a human face—for ever" (*Complete Novels*, p. 898)

That devastating one-liner—courtesy of O'Brien—just about sums up not only life (and death) in Oceania, but also the feeling any reasonably sensitive reader walks away with after getting a short glimpse of it. Said boot hovers over Winston throughout the book, long before he (and we the readers) know just how inescapable it is. Even before the last section, which reviewer Orville Prescott rightly called "unspeakably dreadful," Orwell methodically crushes every hope of a way out of the wretchedness: Winston and Julia's little love nest turns out to be a wired trap, its owner, the old whimsical Charrington, not just a proletarian snitch, but a member of the Thought Police. O'Brien meanwhile, imaginary accomplice of Winston's crimethink during the first two parts of the book, reveals himself in due time as one of the Party's most accomplished torturers.

And for those who were hoping that at least Winston would somehow withstand it all, lone beacon of light in a world of darkness, the ending comes to thoroughly crush that illusion. SMASH! The last man in Europe (*The Last Man in Europe* was an alternative title Orwell considered) goes with a bang—or rather, in tearful bliss—and there is literally nothing left to hold on to.

1984 gives us no simple answer, no uplifting inspiration, no hero to emulate, just merciless bleakness. It's almost too much gloom to handle. We're only human after all—we need something to hold onto, be it but a tiny glimmer, something that leaves open the possibility of another ending. *1984*, at least at first sight, has none of that—it leaves us utterly stunned.

Too Much Gloom?

It's fair to assume that Orwell, who named "political purpose" as one of his main reasons for writing, had no intention to send us moping in a corner. So why the descent into utter hopelessness? Doesn't it defeat that very same political purpose? What *1984* depicts, we could argue, is so over the top that we can smugly shelve it as an entertaining literary dystopia that has nothing to do with us and our world. And there is something paralyzing about so much gloom: with no crack in the wall for resistance to take hold, *1984* could appear to discourage rather than inspire action.

Let's leave aside for the moment the question of whether there really is no crack in the wall and instead dive a little deeper into *1984*'s bleakness. What can be said to the objections I just raised?

There's at least one twentieth-century philosopher who would have thoroughly approved of Orwell's refusal to mitigate the darkness of his novel: Theodor W. Adorno, prominent member of the Frankfurt School and one of the founding fathers of Critical Theory. First of all, because he would have agreed with Orwell that even if things were maybe not quite as bad (yet, or anymore) in post-war Europe as in *1984*'s Oceania, they were rotten enough, with the bad lurking much closer under the surface than the average contemporary of Adorno and Orwell would have cared to admit (or even see).

And there's no better way to rip off the veil that covers the rot than to exaggerate a little—or rather, to take the worst that has been (and hence could be again), and present it as the essence that has to be grappled with. As Adorno wrote, in characteristically stark wording, "only exaggeration is true. The essential nature" of history "is the appearance of utmost horror in the particular. A statistical compilation of those slaughtered in a pogrom that also includes the mercifully shot, conceals its essence, which emerges only in an exact description of the exception, the worst torture" (Horkheimer and Adorno, *Dialectic of Enlightenment*, p. 92).

The worst is not a freak excess—it reveals an essential truth. In that reading, the essence of Nazism lies in the babies ripped out of their mothers' arms and thrown alive into the flames so as to not waste gas on them. The essence of Stalinism lies in the starved peasants eating their own children during the man-made Ukrainian famine. With such truths looming large in the recent past, how could the description of *any* atrocity be discarded as a mere fiction, an inconsequential exaggeration?

Orwell certainly never retreated into that kind of false sense of security. Like Adorno, he was acutely aware that the authoritarian tendencies that had brought about three fascist regimes in Western Europe, and a totalitarian colossus in the East, continued to exist, even where the regimes no longer did. The very worst was no longer just a nightmare of a hypothetical future, but a historical fact of the past, the ever threatening possibility lurking in the bad that things had since reverted to.

For Adorno, Auschwitz was the end of the world that the world had somehow survived—not necessarily to its credit—and the post-Auschwitz reality was one where moral certainties had irreversibly been unmasked as the self-satisfied delusions they always were. "This will never happen" just doesn't hold anymore when the unthinkable has already occurred. In this new reality, every philosopher, every artist, every writer, has the obligation to 'exaggerate'—to bring out into the light the trends that can make us, at any moment, stumble back into the darkness that lurks just under the surface.

"The authentic artists of the present are those in whose works the utter horror trembles" (*Critical Models*, p. 48)—because not to look away is the first and most important step on the path to resistance. "There is no beauty left and no consolation except in the gaze that faces the horror, withstands it, and, *in unreduced awareness of the negativity, holds on to the possibility of a better [world]*" (*Minima Moralia*, p. 25). In order to keep alive the possibility of a better world, we first have to have unreduced awareness of the horrors around us. Being bleak, in this reading, is being faithful to the beauty that could be, rather than betraying it by offering a cheap ersatz. By portraying a world that is all grey, Orwell saves the colors. The dystopia, in other words, hides a utopia. Negatively, the bleakness of *1984* stands for the paradise that is lost—or that we will lose if we don't defend it—the possibility of a better world.

Had Orwell offered a different ending—say if, for example, Winston had died with his love for Julia, or his disgust for Big

Brother intact—it would have softened the horror just enough to allow the reader to heave a big sigh of relief and pick up the sports section. The fact that Orwell refuses to relieve the tension until the bitter end—finishing, as it were, with a kick in the guts—makes that kind of escape harder. Which basically turns the earlier objections onto their head: *1984* is a powerful call to action precisely *because* in it, all action is stultified.

The hopelessness it inflicts on us is for the sake of hope—hope for *us*, who still *can* act. "Where everything is bad it must be good to know the worst," the British philosopher Francis H. Bradley once said (and Adorno loved to quote). The very worst *1984* depicts shines a stark light on the bad that is happening now (in Orwell's now, and in ours), the shock it produces a wake-up call to stand up and fight before it is too late.

True, shocks can paralyze—but they can also have the opposite effect: just like exaggerations, they can shake our numbed minds out of their torpor, make us see things that we couldn't see, and push us to do things that we thought we couldn't do. Adorno considered it every public thinker's obligation to deliver shocks, as a kind of radical version of Socrates's questions, with the same goal: to make us think. Sometimes we have to swap the pastel colors for the glaring ones, focusing, to use Adorno's words, on the "worst torture" rather than on the "mercifully shot," because it is the former that will make clear to us what there really is to fear.

1984 is not a gratuitous flight of fancy of a particularly pessimistic author—rather, it "extends into the future with remorseless clarity trends that are already apparent in the present," as the 1949 *New York Times* review put it. It is, to quote the same reviewer, "convincing madness. Knowing what has happened already in this century, one believes Orwell's madmen." It's the exaggeration that shines a glaring light on our normalcy.

In a letter to an American enquirer, Orwell wrote: "I do not believe that the kind of society I describe *will* arrive, but I believe that something resembling it *could* arrive . . . Totalitarianism, *if not fought against*, could triumph anywhere" ("Letter to Henson," p. 564). And that possibility alone is ample justification for Orwell showing no mercy with his protagonists, and his readers. The danger is too real. We just cannot afford to sigh a sigh of relief.

The Cracks in the Wall

Now that I've vindicated *1984*'s bleakness, it's time to mitigate it a little. I have no intention of changing the big picture, nor could I—*1984* is an utterly devastating read. And yet. Let's have a closer look and ask ourselves again whether there really is no crack in that wall.

The *New York Times* reviewer that I quoted earlier called the third and last part of the book "unspeakably dreadful." There's no arguing with that—except that the dread really starts in the very first pages. In place of the psychological and physical torture of the last part, the first two parts deliver unspeakable dreariness. "The truly characteristic thing about modern life was not its cruelty and insecurity, but simply its bareness, its dinginess, its listlessness" (p. 786). A dinginess so heavy it's literally suffocating. The first breath of fresh air comes at the beginning of the second part, in the form of three words written on a scrap of paper: "I love you" (p. 806). The words, the feeling they express, seem so out of place in the universe Orwell describes that the reader is about as stunned as Winston. It's as if life suddenly broke into a world ruled by lifelessness.

The same thing happens just a few pages later, when Winston takes the train to the countryside and makes his way to his first private encounter with Julia: "Winston picked his way up the lane through dappled light and shade, stepping into pools of gold wherever the boughs parted. Under the trees to the left of him the ground was misty with bluebells. The air seemed to kiss one's skin. It was the second of May. From somewhere deeper in the heart of the wood came the droning of ring-doves" (p. 812).

Ring-doves? Bluebells? Air that kisses one's skin, pools of golden light? Are we in a different book? The contrast is stark, to say the least, to the dreary, depressing scenery that has so far set the tone in *1984*. Again, what breaks in is life—life unsubjugated. It reminds us—and that's what makes the description of the blooming, chirping woods so eerily moving—that even within a terrifyingly totalitarian system, there remain things that elude Big Brother's all-powerful grip. At first sight, nature's peaceful babbling and Julia's impromptu declaration seem to be two very different things. Yet as I already hinted, they are in fact closely related. Both Julia's spontaneous love, which pays no heed to the Party's strict rules on promiscuity, and the unorchestrated droning of the ring-doves, represent the other that enrages the totalitarian mind and trips up its aspiration to uniformity.

The fact that it's a description of nature that brings that other most starkly to the fore is far from coincidental. It is indeed nature, in the broadest sense, that is totalitarian reason's biggest enemy—in the form of human emotions and feelings, and in the form of the nature that surrounds us and that belies the pretense of total control. In their scathing post-war analysis *Dialectic of Enlightenment*, Adorno and his friend Max Horkheimer present totalitarianism as an extreme consequence of the one human drive that shaped Western enlightened civilization and made science the new God: to subjugate nature within and without and to strip reason of everything that is not strictly 'rational': emotions, feelings, impulses, intuitions—everything that is not narrowly predictable in a framework of logic in which every step A is followed by a step B known in advance.

Oceania fits well into that picture. Any natural urges are suppressed: parental and filial love is thwarted as children are alienated from and turned against their parents, compassion is nipped in the bud as hate rituals and public executions fuel aggressivity and coldness, erotic love is made obsolete as people are matched with mates according to the party's breeding plan ("We have cut the links between child and parent, and between man and man, and between man and woman," p. 898), intuitions are stifled as the Party enthrones its own logic over and above everything else (the Party's "final, most essential command" is to "reject the evidence of your eyes and ears," p. 790).

The fact that the Party has created its own logic where 2 + 2 may well make 5 and where the past is infinitely malleable does not contradict Adorno's claim that at totalitarianism's core lies rationality, not irrationality. True, in a sense, the party's truth is irrational—by constantly rewriting the past and forcing its subjects to *doublethink*, it tramples some of the basic rules of logic. Yet in just as important a sense, it is profoundly rational. It does not reject the sovereignty of reason—rather, it takes it to an absurd paroxysm, where calculation, planification, and homogenization take over every nook and cranny of society, and where the human mind is so omnipotent that it can freely change its own rules.

More than irrationality, it is megalomaniac rationality, or as Adorno would have put it, "insanity that is anything but unreasonable" (*Negative Dialectics*, p. 225). Anything outside of reason that could mitigate its lone mastery, any corrective, has been silenced. For the Party, "the heresy of heresies was common sense" (p. 790)—gut feelings, intuitions, "the evidence of your eyes and ears," the objectivity that belies the subjective deceit. "The terrible thing that the party had done was to persuade you that mere impulses, mere feelings were of no account" (p. 841)—and because it has largely succeeded, its rationality has become truth, even though to us, it seems a lie.

Without any input from the outside, no world against which its claims are tested—as O'Brien's says: "Nothing exists except through human consciousness" (p. 897)—reason will only tautologically reaffirm itself, even if it says that $2 + 2 = 5$. It becomes a mere tool, an empty vessel, literally disembodied and as such recruitable for any cause. "If the sort of world that I am afraid of arrives, . . . two and two could become five if the fuehrer wished it" Orwell wrote in 1944 in a letter to a friend.

For the Party, rationality equals efficiency—efficiency in the service of one single goal: the consolidation of its own power. Anything that fails the test—*oldspeak* with its "useless shades of meaning" (p. 773), the "ineffectual" and therefore "meaningless" love Winston's mother gives to her dying child (p. 841)—must be eliminated. What's left is bare instrumental reason in which the goal determines the rules. "The totalitarian power has granted unlimited rights to calculating thought . . . Its canon is its own brutal efficiency," as Adorno writes in *Dialectic of Enlightenment* (p. 106).

Julia's love, the ring-doves, the bluebells—they are simply there, they don't fit into any equation, they don't serve an obvious purpose. In the framework of calculating thought, they are useless—they are the antithesis of what the Party stands for. Not only do they contradict its logic, but as we will see, they seriously endanger it.

The Nonidentical

Adorno called the ungraspable other that doesn't fit into the rational equation "the nonidentical." The nonidentical is unique, unpredictable, non-rational. It eludes the conceptual framework of reason, where everything is labeled according to the category which it falls under (a tree is *a* tree, a black man is *a* black man) even if there is no other exactly like it in the entire world.

Adorno called our mind's urge, not to say need, to do away with the nonidentical and make everything the same "identity thinking." We are all identity thinkers, inescapably. Our mind needs a conceptual framework into which to channel the innumerable phenomena that assail our senses at any given moment. We subsume ("this thing falls into the category old white man, this thing falls into the category bird, this things falls into the category black woman," and so forth) in order to make the overwhelming richness of the universe more graspable. In itself, this doesn't need to be a problem, but it can become one—if you're no longer aware that you are losing something along the way and simply stop seeing the unique, if a category suddenly becomes a value judgment (as it does in racism and sexism), or if making everything the same becomes an end in itself—that is, if erasing the unique, the non-graspable, the difference, turns from an inevitable necessity of reasoning into an ideal.

In totalitarianism, making everything the same is an end in itself. For Adorno, totalitarianism is identity thinking gone mad, homogenization for the purpose of total control. The totalitarian dictator knows he cannot control the nonidentical, all that messy nature with its singularities, unpredictabilities, contingencies, and therefore focuses all his power on eliminating it. The goal is complete uniformity, as made glaringly visible in the last century in the Nazi regime's brown masses, its Aryan ideal, and not least, its systematic annihilation of the perceived other.

In Oceania, identity thinking rules. Everything is done to make people think, act, fear, hate the same. Everything is a collective exercise. You cheer collectively, you fear collectively, you execute collectively, you exercise collectively, you even hate collectively—collectively and identically. To be alone, "even to go for a walk by yourself" ("ownlife," p. 791), is a grave transgression. Because thought is closely linked to language, the party has invented Newspeak, a kind of textbook parody of what Adorno fought against when he warned of the dangers of identity thinking. In Newspeak, meanings are "rigidly defined," "all ambiguities and shades of meaning" (p. 918)—in other words, all latitude for individual expression, independent thinking, for taking singularity into account—are purged.

Designed to "diminish the range of thought" (p. 918) and "rouse the minimum of echoes" (p. 922), Newspeak creates a uniformity of speech that helps to achieve the Party's goals: an inability "to think deeply on any subject whatever" (p. 864), and eventually a "complete uniformity of opinion on all subjects" (p. 862).

In Oceania, *difference* itself is abolished. Past and present are identical. If politics change, if the enemy is suddenly no longer the same, then the past has to be rewritten to erase that change. If someone is made to disappear, then records are 'corrected' to prove that he never was. And of course, it is completely out of the question that *people* are different, as Winston wistfully notes in his diary message "from the age of uniformity" "to the future or to the past . . . when men are different from one another" (p. 758). Difference is in fact a crime. The seven-year-old Parson girl has somebody arrested because "he was wearing a funny kind of shoe—said she'd never seen anyone wearing shoes like that before" (p. 776). You either look, dress, act, speak the same as everybody else, or you vanish.

In the light of all this, is there really any significance to a lone declaration of love, or some ring-doves and bluebells that do as they please? I want to claim that there is, because they show us not only that despite all efforts to the contrary, the nonidentical persists, but also where to look for it—and therefore what needs to be saved at all costs. The serene placidity of nature that Orwell so much insists on is as significant as Winston and Julia's forbidden love, even if it is watched. With the nonidentical, Adorno wrote, "freedom breaks into experience"—and freedom is precisely what these short flickers of respite feel like. The fact that they exist, that the thrust not only still sings, uninvited, but that its song moves Winston, shows that Big Brother's grip is not total. Things could be different than what they are—that is the essential truth of the nonidentical. What we are made to believe and experience, be it by our necessarily limited conceptual ability, be it by the manipulation of a power, totalitarian or not, that further mutilates that ability—is not everything.

The Mute Protest in Your Bones

Throughout *1984*, there are moments where the other, the unsubjugated, raises its battered head. Beyond the two passages we have seen, many of them are linked to the body, which again points back to totalitarianism's archenemy nature. Repeatedly, Winston remarks on a certain somatic unease with Oceania's reality. Eating in the crowded canteen, he notes that "always in your stomach and in skin there was a sort of protest, a feeling that you had been cheated of something that you had a right to" (p. 777). And he reflects:

> And though, of course, it got worse as one's body aged, was it not a sign that this was *not* the natural order of things, if one's heart sickened at the discomfort and the scarcity, the interminable winters, the stickiness of one's socks, the lifts that never worked, the cold water, the gritty soap, the cigarettes that came to pieces, the food with its strange evil taste? Why should one feel it to be intolerable unless one had *some kind of ancestral memory that things had once been different?* (p. 778)

The body protests against what the mind is trying to convince you to accept as normal. You can't quite express what is wrong because you don't have the words for it (maybe because they've been taken from you), but it's as if against your mind's 'better judgment', your body was screaming NO!

Elsewhere, Winston calls it "the mute protest in your bones, the instinctive feeling that the conditions you lived in were intolerable and that at some other time they must have been different" (p. 786). Over and over again, the same feeling: things were once different, they could be again—the grey of the here and now is not everything. This is what makes the bluebells, the singing thrush, and Julia and Winston's love so important. They are the utopian glimpse that unmasks reality as the lie that it is, they vindicate the gut feeling that life in Oceania is one big fraud. Out in nature, Winston's Golden Country briefly steps out of his dreams to become a real place, as a living, chirping, blooming proof that things could be different.

In Oceania, everything is done to silence the mute protest in your bones. The Party craftily manipulates the somatic by channeling it into orgiastic outbursts of fear and hate that are but an ugly shadow of what human emotions could be. Because it is acutely aware that the biggest threat against its reign comes from the body—the ancestral memory, the gut feeling, eros—it focuses all its might on mutilating it.

If This Is a Man

As O'Brien demonstrates, the Party's powerful not only know exactly where the danger lies, they also pretend to have it under control. When Winston tells O'Brien that "life will defeat you," O'Brien sarcastically responds (and it sounds like a refutation of all I have just said): "You are imagining that there is something called human nature which will be outraged by what we do and will turn against us. But we create human nature. Men are infinitely malleable." (p. 899).

Knowing that Winston puts some hope in the less closely controlled proles, O'Brien calls them helpless animals, echoing the verdict in Goldstein's book (which again sounds like a direct response to what I've just raised) that "the proles are without any impulse to rebel, without the power of grasping *that the world could be other than it is*" (p. 863). If O'Brien (and Goldstein, or whoever poses as him) is right, then of course everything I've just written about the power of the nonidentical, about the cracks in the wall, is wrong. But I want to persist, like Winston, who carries on undaunted: "I *know* that you will fail. There is something in the universe—I don't know, some spirit, some principle—that you will never overcome." He calls the principle "the spirit of man" (p. 899).

O'Brien again is dismissive: "If you are a man, Winston, you are the last man." He forces Winston to look at a mirror and face the "bowed, grey-coloured, skeleton-like thing" that stares back at him, and concludes: "If you are human, that is humanity" (p. 901). O'Brien's words eerily echo with a voice that has reached us from what is arguably the worst man-made hell of human history. The Italian Jewish writer Primo Levi called his 1947 memoir about his year as a prisoner in Auschwitz *If This Is a Man*. The question hovers over the entire book, most importantly in its description of what the camp inmates called the "Muselmänner", who remind us of the Winston in O'Brien's mirror:

> Their body already in decay . . . Their life is short, but their number is endless; they, the Muselmänner, the drowned . . . an anonymous mass, continually renewed and always identical, of non-men who march and labor in silence, the divine spark dead within them, already too empty to really suffer. One hesitates to call them living: one hesitates to call their death death. (p. 103)

If this is a man, Primo Levi muses—and answers himself by calling them non-men. The echo with Orwell is important, because Levi not only shows that *1984*'s worst nightmares have already become reality, but also, if we look at his book as a whole, that O'Brien is wrong. Yes, man can be broken. Yes, the numbers of the drowned are endless. But Levi's memoir testifies that even in absolute hell, humanity, the human and the humane, survived. Barely, but it did. Winston's "spirit of man" could be found even in Auschwitz. And if it existed there, doesn't that mean that it can never be overcome?

Of course, O'Brien has an answer to that too. So fine, it survives, it may occasionally raise its head, but it's ultimately irrelevant. It's just the face to be stamped on: "The heretic, the enemy of society, will always be there, so that he can be defeated and humiliated over again" (p. 898). Who cares about the nonidentical scratching the surface a little bit if identity always comes out victorious?

But truth is, we do care—and so does O'Brien. As long as the nonidentical persists, the ruling identity hasn't won, even if it claims to have done so. It is constantly proven to be a lie. Despite O'Brien's ostentatious triumphalism, he is very aware of it, as he indirectly concedes himself: "It is intolerable to us that an erroneous thought should exist anywhere in the world, however secret and powerless it may be" (p. 890). Words that echo Adorno's observation that "the slightest trace of the non-identical is as unbearable [to identity thinking] as is to the fascist the other in the remotest corner of the world" (*Jargon of Authenticity,* p. 140).

As unbearable as it may be, it can be found in many places in Oceania. Not just in the heretic, but everywhere where Big Brother's control falters. In the birds and the trees and the streams, in Julia's love and the "scores" she has slept with (despite the Party's efforts to kill the sex instinct), in the proles who, as Winston notes, "have stayed human" (p. 842), and sing spontaneously, managing somehow to put feeling even into the most artificially versified song. There is such a thing as human spirit, there is such a thing as life, and it's because the Party knows it and knows of its threat that it has turned Oceania into one big prison. The powerless may be scared, but so are the powerful.

Yes, things look bleak in *1984*. And any change of that state of affairs may seem like a long shot. But Big Brother has not won. Even if Winston and Julia are broken, their truth is not, and as O'Brien himself admits, it never will be. Oceania's identity is a lie, and there will always be someone whose bones will protest, whose ancestral memory is awakened by droning ring-doves.

Orwell made his book radically bleak, delivering the shock necessary to shake us out of our torpor, and yet he left a glimmer of hope. By allowing infinitely small reprieves in the suffocating uniformity, he shows us where the cracks are, where the potential for resistance slumbers, and most importantly, what we, in our nominally free world where Big Brother is not yet all-powerful, must more than anything protect and strengthen: nonidentity, difference, diversity, and the ability and will to fight for a different ending.

13
Hangings, Shootings, and Other Funny Stuff in *1984*

JARNO HIETALAHTI

Danish philosopher Søren Kierkegaard famously claimed that the comic always lies in a contradiction. If this were true, catch-phrases like "War is peace!", Freedom is slavery!", and "Ignorance is strength!" would sound remarkably funny. However, for the people living in the imaginary London of Oceania in George Orwell's *1984*, there is nothing humorous about these slogans. On the contrary, they are dead serious.

1984 is widely acknowledged as a satirical masterpiece, but it's not a particularly funny book. There is only one joke in the whole book (see below). However, the book contains humorous contradictions like those mentioned above. It's rather amusing when a character called O'Brien argues that nineteenth-century biologists have actually invented fossils of different kinds of extinct animals, and how stars are bits of fire just a couple of kilometers away from the Earth—even though the very same lights can be used to navigate oceans as if they were actual stars in the universe.

Despite these potential seeds of comedy, the reader rarely laughs with the book, because Oceania is a gloomy, gray and agonizing place. In this dystopian London there's little room for independent thought, high culture, or—as the main character Winston Smith puts it—dignity of emotion, because there are no deep or complex sorrows. However, humor and laughter have not disappeared altogether in this world.

Humor is such a central feature of human life that even the most dystopian societies can't erase it. In Aldous Huxley's *Brave New World*, people use a special kind of drug, called soma, to make entertainment and fun more intense. For characters intoxicated by this drug, even rather dull jokes trigger amusement. In *1984* people don't need additional chemical substances to enjoy mirth but instead, their source of humor is more natural, so to speak: the socially shared hatred against enemies feeds their amusement and laughter.

This is surprising, because nowadays we see humor and laughter as positive phenomena. By default, smiling is considered to express pleasure, amusement, joy, or sociability, and not by any means hostility. It's often stated that laughter prolongs life, and that possessing a good sense of humor makes you more attractive to potential romantic partners. Hatred and loathing don't fit well within this conception of humor. However, Orwell's book proves otherwise. In certain respects, his dystopian portrayal comes quite close to Plato's thoughts on the subject. Plato claimed that laughter should be chained by laws. In his view, it's utterly dangerous to let people laugh whenever they happen to feel like it.

Plato argues that humor is based on mixed feelings; it's a form of malice, and on closer inspection a mixture of pain and pleasure. Laughter gives you pleasure but when you laugh at your friends' (or foes') misfortune, there's always at least some degree of hostility involved. For a noble philosopher, this kind of malignant attitude corrodes the soul, and for this reason you should be very wary of the devious pleasures offered by humor. Unfortunately, most often we are generally blind to how our own sense of humor involves deriving pleasure from laughing at other people's misfortunes. Even though Orwell rarely handles humor in a straightforward manner in *1984*, there's one example from the book which illustrates this problem. In this excerpt, Winston writes in his secret journal:

> Last night to the flicks. All war films. One very good one of a ship full of refugees being bombed somewhere in the Mediterranean. Audience much amused by shots of a great huge fat man trying to swim away with a helicopter after him wallowing along in the water like a porpoise, then you saw him through helicopters gunsights, then he was full of holes and the sea round him turned pink and he sank as suddenly as though the holes let in the water, audience shouting with laughter when he sank.

It would be easy for us to judge and criticize the reactions of the audience, to yell that there is nothing funny about refugees—even fat ones—being shot in the water. Unfortunately, taking this view would require that we neglect the range of human experience; clearly, according to Winston's description, there *is* something funny about this scene for the cinema audience. Instead of denying that anything could be deemed humorous about such an occasion, we should ask, what the logical continuum behind all this fun is. How is it possible that people can be so vicious with their sense of humor?

Society Determines Humor

Orwell offers a social-philosophical answer to the previous problem. Humor in Oceania is alive, and although its characteristics are somewhat different from ours, there is something familiar about the phenomena of humor and laughter. You may notice that the philosophical core of humor is still the same: as Kierkegaard claims, humor is triggered when we perceive paradoxes; that is, things appear funny when they violate or contradict what we conceive to be normal. Normally, foreigners are a great source of amusement in comedies, and *1984* follows this idea in its own twisted way. Refugees are foreigners and also a potential threat to Oceania. Therefore, they do not belong to "us," and thanks to the malicious nature of the people, it is highly amusing to see refugees dying. Misfortune is funny, it seems.

The idea that humor is dependent on the prevailing cultural conceptions also explains why there is nothing funny in a statement like "War is peace", even though it is obviously ridiculous to a modern Western reader. To understand humor (or a lack of it), you need to have a grasp on the cultural norms. Generally speaking, we develop within a certain culture and adopt the conceptualizations within that culture. So, when we observe a deviation from our own cultural norms, we find it funny and laugh at that oddity.

For example, in Western culture there still are certain dress codes and norms expected of different genders. This is why a man dressing as a woman—or even vice versa—is, or at least has been, a textbook example of humor. But, in a culture where men and women dress alike, there is nothing particularly funny about a man wearing a frock. Similarly, there is nothing contradictory in a statement like "Freedom is slavery!" for a citizen of Oceania, because it's repeated constantly and pervasively. People grow up with these truths, and learn to accept them at face value. There's no need, or even the possibility, to challenge these founding principles. The root of this thought system can be traced to so-called *Doublethink*.

In *1984*, Doublethink refers to the psychological capacity to hold two contradictory beliefs simultaneously. This, of course, is in a striking conflict with classical logic which states that a thing is what it is, and nothing else. To put it in a more formal manner, philosophers in their analytical enthusiasm have extracted three central features of this logic: the law of identity (A = A), the law of contradiction (A ≠ non-A) and the law of the excluded middle (A can't be both A and not-A, or neither A nor not-A).

Roughly put, a logical contradiction is an impossibility, and that's it. Despite the annoying formality, it's hard to argue against logical insights. We all share them even if we don't realize it, and they are self-evident in the modern world. However, these logics don't hold in Oceania. In Orwell's imaginary world, it's entirely possible and even normal to tell lies while believing in them, and to deny the existence of objective reality and at the same time acknowledge the reality which you deny. This all sounds silly in relation to our own logical formulations, but Doublethink is alive and well in *1984* nonetheless.

Because of it, it's logical to have, for instance, the Ministry of Peace which oversees wars, the Ministry of Truth which focuses on creating new lies, the Ministry of Love which devises and enacts methods of torture, and the Ministry of Plenty which furthers starvation. When Doublethink pervades social life, it becomes rooted in people's behavior, and for this reason it guides their actions and thoughts, including their sense of humor. Orwell's *1984* shows clearly how laughter echoes the standards of the surrounding society. Thus, if we want to grasp the social significance of humor and laughter, that which is deemed funny must be analyzed in its cultural context. Society governs our conceptions of humor in a most covert manner.

Humor researchers, and probably all of us in our everyday lives, have noticed that humor brings together like-minded people while at the same time excluding from the cultural inner circle those who do not share a similar sense of humor. This is clearly present in what we might call the guiding principles of ethnic humor: foreigners are funny, and they themselves don't have a sense of humor.

Laughter is in principle universal but, nevertheless, it's always the laughter of a specific social group. This is the founding idea by a Nobel Prize–winning philosopher Henri Bergson, who combines some of the central features of Plato's and Kierkegaard's ideas about humor: laughter is actually a form of social punishment. If an individual behaves in an odd way, laughter will be used to punish that person. This is the general function of laughter: it intimidates by threat of humiliation. If there were no spitefulness in laughter, it could not perform its social function; laughter can't offer sympathy, but instead demands a certain kind of anesthesia of the heart. Bergson claims that humor is always addressed to the intellect, not to the emotions.

Humor Full of Hatred

Bergson's suggestion about intellect and emotions is a bit problematic, but he does suggest elsewhere that empathy is the enemy of laughter. If you feel for someone, it's much harder to laugh at him or her mockingly. However, it can't be concluded that there would be no room at all for emotions in humor. By contrast, the way we relate to humor and amusement is highly dependent on the current social character—that is, socially shared and emotionally-based attitudes.

As it happens, in Oceania the prevailing moods are fear and hatred accompanied by adulation and orgiastic triumph. Naturally, these are the emotional compasses for laughter, too. Humor, then, is a tool that helps to preserve a given culture's moral and political standards, which are habituated through psycho-social routines. In Orwell's world, all habits, tastes, and mental attitudes are designed to sustain the power of the prevailing Party, and this is evident in how people relate to humor and laughter.

What else do the people of Oceania find funny besides refugees being shot in the water? Orwell isn't explicit about this, but you can find clues here and there throughout *1984*.

For instance, in the book people yearn to see public hangings, and these popular spectacles are organized on a regular basis. At least for Winston's neighbors' children, being denied a chance to see the enemies of Oceania hanged is a grave disappointment. His co-worker, Syme, in addition, praises a particular hanging and gleefully recounts how those hanged kicked about in the air, their blue tongues sticking out. Apparently, these kinds of details appeal to him.

Based on these pieces of information, it's reasonable to assume that for at least some part of the population, these occasions are rather amusing. In other parts of the book, Oceania's archenemy, Emmanuel Goldstein, is described to be senile and silly looking, his theories are constantly ridiculed. In addition, during Hate Weeks, everyone shouts insults at Goldstein who, like a false carnival king in medieval festivities, is burned in effigy. As unusual as it may sound, it's clear that this dystopian society is not humorless. The state clearly considers entertainment such an important mechanism of control that the Ministry of Truth promotes an amusement industry to keep the masses in line. The Party offers its citizens, among other things, cartoons and films—both genres presumably involving humor. For instance, a caricaturist called Rutherford draws brutal cartoons which inflame the popular opinion, and these pictures appear in a popular news magazine frequently— well, at least until he is terminated.

When humor is a form of malice and a tool for social punishment, it lets you trample on people. This can be done in subtler or harsher ways. For example, the only explicit joke in *1984* sounds somewhat innocent but it, nevertheless, contains a hint of aggression. This happens when Winston enters a shady bar searching for people who could remember the days before the Party. There, men discuss the difference between pints used in previous times and liters used in the present day:

"You could'a drawed me off a pint easy enough. We didn't 'ave these bleeding liters when I was a young man."

"When you were a young man we were all living in the treetops", said the barman, with a glance at the other customers.

There was a shout of laughter, and the uneasiness caused by Winston's entry seemed to disappear.

The old fellow is put on his place with a roar of laughter. He is humiliated, and others enjoy this. They feel superior to the ridiculous senile runt, whose days are well past. There is vile pleasure in beating those who don't belong to the same group in this never-ending social wrestling match called human life. Bursting out in laughter indicates that you're the successor, and that the other has failed miserably. In this setting, humor is based on selfishness and hostility towards others, where there is no need to consider the poor bastard's feelings.

This is very much in line with the political ideals of Oceania; the Party yearns for a perfect future society where the only emotions are fear, rage, triumph, and self-abasement. The latter term might sound odd at first sight, but this negativity towards the self is an essential individual characteristic in Oceania; the Party must always be greater than all the individuals together. The social wrestling match between individuals is also realized at a collective level. Individuals of Oceania must abase themselves so that they do not question the supremacy of the Party.

As O'Brien sees it, in the perfect Oceania the only laughter will be laughs of triumph over a defeated enemy. Humor, then, becomes very one-sided. In addition, the general logic of Orwell's dystopia dictates that comedy's counterpart, tragedy, does not exist in Oceania. It belongs to social systems where people value privacy, friendship, and love. In *1984*, these values are replaced by fear, hatred, and pain. In this societal setting of emotions, there's no need for complexity as every emotion is based on deep hostility towards enemies. Other kinds of feelings are unnecessary, and therefore basically non-existent and incomprehensible. This holds for humor, too. Things that don't go in line with the general atmosphere of Oceania, are considered to be silly, and silliness is a sign of difference. In this light, it's easy to understand why foreigners are perceived as strange, unsympathetic animals. There's no reason to spare such beasts.

Judge Them and Yourself

So, what about the moral of the story? Even though the dystopian sense of humor in *1984* appears to be vulgar and loathsome, it's a fully logical possibility. Orwell shows how twisted a shared sense of humor can be. His book highlights the fact that we can be blind to the uglier sides of how we have fun. In this respect, it would be too simple to merely criticize and judge the shared sense of humor in Oceania; instead, Orwell calls into question the hidden premises of our own sense of humor.

What is implicitly present in *1984* is that we should be ever more critical towards our own cultural forms of humor. Humor isn't always innocent or positive, even though laughter feels deceptively pleasant. Nowadays, living in an era marked by fun and amusement, being a killjoy is one of the greatest sins. Orwell's implied suggestion, however, is that despite the current ideological optimism around humor, we should always turn a critical eye towards what we consider comic, even if we're afraid of what we might find behind our sense of amusement. A blind commitment to optimism in humor is one form of fanatic fundamentalism, especially if we're not willing to listen counter-arguments.

This criticism is directed not only towards hateful humor, but can also be applied to the fashionable argument that everything should be ridiculed all the time. Simple slogans like "humor gives freedom, and freedom gives humor" are as ideological as Big Brother's manifestos about war and peace, freedom and slavery as well as ignorance and strength. Nonetheless, a significant number of contemporary comedians and laymen claim that political correctness kills humor. For them, humor is the last bastion of freedom which should not be restricted under any circumstances; a right to offend is much more important than another's right not to be offended.

However, as Orwell's book demonstrates, freedom can easily turn into unfreedom, if it is used to oppress or to diminish independent thought. Humor makes no exception here, and it's always intertwined with wider societal values; it can't be understood in isolation. Of course, this does not mean that we should ban certain topics from humor, because this would lead to a modern version of Newspeak.

1984 reminds us that the evaluation of humor must be based on how it treats other human beings—not merely on which words may be used, nor on how funny something happens to be. Appalling things like hangings and shootings may be amusing to some, but that hardly makes them praiseworthy. As Winston so touchingly reminds us, we are not simple creatures but complex beings with dignified emotions, even if society says otherwise.

14

The Seduction of Winston Smith

MARK ALFANO

On the first page of *1984*, Winston Smith is confronted with several posters featuring the face of Big Brother and the famous sentence, "BIG BROTHER IS WATCHING YOU." This may not seem like a promising way to seduce someone, but the seduction of Winston Smith by Big Brother in *1984* is a most unusual love story.

I call it a seduction because Winston's mind and heart are slowly won over in the aptly-named Ministry of Love. Moreover, in the final scene of the novel, Winston gazes, with tears in his eyes, up at Big Brother on the telescreen. The last sentence of the book states, simply, "He loved Big Brother."

How does Big Brother seduce Winston Smith? He certainly does not employ stereotypical methods. Big Brother is not particularly sexy, and his incessant angry shouting does not seem calculated to foster adoration. On top of that, Winston never meets Big Brother in person. His only access is through media: posters, stories, and the telescreen. We all know that it's hard to maintain a long-distance relationship. Long-distance seduction is even more challenging. So how does Big Brother manage it?

What Is Seduction?

To answer this question, I use the theory of seduction first articulated by the philosopher John Forrester, who argues that "the first step in a seductive maneuver could be summed up as, 'I know what you're thinking" (p. 42). By 'thinking', Forrester here means not just calm contemplation but the whole of some-

one's inner life: their beliefs, desires, values, emotions, sentiments, and so on. Thus, to say to someone, "I know what you're
thinking" is to assert authority over their inner life.

Ordinarily, we assume that our minds are our own to
know and express, that there are things about our inner life
that no one else has access to, that we are able to keep some
things private. A seducer attempts to break down that
boundary, to insist that he, too, knows what's going on inside
your head.

The authority that a seducer claims for himself is different from the authority of brute force and coercion. A seducer
doesn't command, "Do what I say because I say so, whether
you like it or not." Instead, a seducer asks, "When you think
about it, isn't this really what you want to do?" Only an
enthusiastic affirmation to that question counts as a successful seduction. A seducer thus aims at, requires, even
fetishizes consent.

The seducer insists that he is better-placed to know what
the seducee thinks than the seducee himself is. Such a maneuver cajoles its target: if only you would stop and reflect on it,
the seducer suggests, you'd realize that this is what you think.
This is precisely the realization that Winston Smith arrives at
in the closing scene of *1984*:

> O cruel, needless misunderstanding! O stubborn, self-willed exile
> from the loving breast! Two gin-scented tears trickled down the sides
> of his nose. But it was all right, everything was all right, the struggle
> was finished. He had won the victory over himself.

Winston's struggle is to be the person that Big Brother insists
he already is, to shape his own mind to the pattern Big Brother
suggests when he says, "I know what you're thinking."

In addition, saying, "I know what you're thinking" presupposes or establishes an intimate bond. Nothing is more bound
up with personal identity than someone's inner life—their
thoughts, feelings, emotions, and values. The seducer's insistence that he knows what the seducee is thinking thus brings
the two into close connection.

Beyond that, saying, "I know what you're thinking" blurs
the line between description and prescription, between asser-

tion and imperative. It can function as a self-fulfilling prophecy: I know what you're thinking, but only because I've told you that that's what you're thinking—and you accepted what I told you. This sort of self-fulfilling prophecy can work because human agency and cognition are often built up through dialogue and conversation. We find out what we think by expressing it and hearing it echoed back in a way we can accept; we also find out what we think by having thoughts attributed to us and agreeing with those attributions.

But how, exactly, does Big Brother manage to seduce Winston Smith in the narrative of *1984*? To answer this further question, we need to pay attention to the ways in which knowledge, trust, ignorance, and doubt are structured in the story— how Big Brother can say "I know what you're thinking" and Winston Smith will respond, "Yes, you do." We need what philosophers call an *epistemology* of seduction.

The Epistemology of Seduction

In the previous section, I asked how Big Brother was able to get inside Winston Smith's head to such an extent that Winston— who had been tortured by Big Brother's agents—was seduced into loving Big Brother. I count four methods.

Watchers, Watchers Everywhere

First, Big Brother relies on an extensive network of telescreens, bugs, informants, and Thought Police to learn about almost every detail of Winston's life. These devices record not only someone's spoken words but also their facial expression, posture, and other "tells," which the psychological inquisitors read and interpret.

O'Brien, an expert in these methods, puts them to work during his torture of Winston. At one point, Winston thinks to himself, "Then why bother to torture me?" As he does, O'Brien "checked his step as though Winston had uttered the thought aloud," then says to Winston, "You are thinking that since we intend to destroy you utterly, so that nothing that you say or do can make the smallest difference—in that case, why do we go to the trouble of interrogating you first? That is what you were thinking, was it not?" Winston, betrayed by his own subtle emotional expressions, confesses, "Yes."

In addition, some surveillance devices are openly displayed, like the telescreen in Winston's apartment. This helps to create the illusion that there is a distinction between moments when Winston is being surveilled and moments when he can express his private thoughts. For instance, Winston labors under the misapprehension that he can keep a private diary so long as he hides it from the telescreen in his room. He thinks that his trysts with Julia are not recorded, allowing him to disclose his most intimate feelings and hopes. And he thinks that O'Brien is capable of turning off the telescreen to ensure that their words are not overhead and recorded.

In fact, however, even when Winston thinks that he can finally express himself candidly, he is being surveilled. In this way, he is bamboozled into disclosing his innermost secrets, which makes it all too easy for Big Brother and his agents to insist that they know what he's thinking. In many cases, they *do* know, as they know about Winston's murophobia.

The Annihilation of History

Second, the bureaucracy of the Ministry of Truth operates with the aim of destroying people's trust in externalized memories. By constantly revising the official record of documents, photographs, and other artifacts that serve as epistemic touchstones, the Ministry of Truth undermines collective trust in these artifacts. Think of the monuments, memorials, gravestones, and other artifacts we use to remind ourselves of what we think, what we value, and who we are. If these objects are subject to continuous revision to fit the whims of the Party, they cease to serve their function. They no longer stand as objective, publicly-verifiable reminders.

This is why Winston is so overwhelmed when he thinks he finds an original, unaltered photograph of Jones, Aaronson, and Rutherford. As Orwell puts it, "this was concrete evidence; it was a fragment of the abolished past, like a fossil bone which turns up in the wrong stratum and destroys a geological theory." Winston is so terrified of his discovery that he drops the photograph into the memory hole. He thus participates in the destruction of history and the undermining of trust that later

enable Big Brother to seduce him. A copy of the same photograph re-emerges in the torture chamber of the Ministry of
Love. After glimpsing it, Winston cries out, "It exists!" But
O'Brien, who has by that point already tossed the copy down
another memory hole, responds:

> "Ashes," he said. "Not even identifiable ashes. Dust. It does not exist.
> It never existed."
>
> "But it did exist! It does exist! It exists in memory. I remember it.
> You remember it."
>
> "I do not remember it," said O'Brien.
>
> Winston's heart sank. That was doublethink. He had a feeling of
> deadly helplessness. If he could have been certain that O'Brien was
> lying, it would not have seemed to matter. But it was perfectly possi-
> ble that O'Brien had really forgotten the photograph. And if so, then
> already he would have forgotten his denial of remembering it, and for-
> gotten the act of forgetting. How could one be sure that it was simple
> trickery? Perhaps that lunatic dislocation in the mind could really hap-
> pen: that was the thought that defeated him.

Undermining Self-Trust

This brings me to the third method employed in the seduction
of Winston Smith.

Destruction and faking of official records leads people to
doubt both the common knowledge base and each other. It
destroys social trust. It also destroys self-trust, as we see in the
quotation above. Winston is "defeated" by the fact that he cannot be certain about O'Brien's lying. If O'Brien really has no
memory of the photograph, and no memory of intentionally forgetting about the photograph, maybe the photograph never
really existed. In that case, Winston's own memory must be
faulty in some way.

And if Winston's memory is faulty, then perhaps his other
cognitive capacities are also defective. To the extent that he
takes this worry seriously, he loses trust in himself. Winston
considers this problem while looking at a history book embla-
zoned with a portrait of Big Brother:

> It was as though some huge force were pressing down upon you—
> something that penetrated inside your skull, battering against your

brain, frightening you out of your beliefs, persuading you, almost, to deny the evidence of your senses. In the end the Party would announce that two and two made five, and you would have to believe it. It was inevitable that they should make that claim sooner or later: the logic of their position demanded it. Not merely the validity of experience, but the very existence of external reality, was tacitly denied by their philosophy. The heresy of heresies was common sense. And what was terrifying was not that they would kill you for thinking otherwise, but that they might be right. For, after all, how do we know that two and two make four?

During his torture in the Ministry of Love, Winston faces this question again. O'Brien shocks him for saying—truly—that he is holding up four fingers. He wants Winston to say that there are five. But he also shocks Winston for merely mouthing the words when it's clear that he is lying. While turning the lever that sends shocks into Winston's body, O'Brien again holds up four fingers and asks,

"How many fingers, Winston?"

"Four. I suppose there are four. I would see five if I could. I am trying to see five."

"Which do you wish: to persuade me that you see five, or really to see them?"

"Really to see them."

As I pointed out above, the seducer—here embodied by O'Brien—aims for enthusiastic consent.

After several more moments of torture, O'Brien again asks how many fingers Winston sees. This time, Winston responds, "I don't know. I don't know. You will kill me if you do that again. Four, five, six—in all honesty I don't know." O'Brien retorts, simply, "Better."

Isolation

Living in a world in which your thoughts can be extracted at will by surveillance and psychological interpretation, in which neither objective records nor your own inner life can be trusted, is a lonely existence. We humans thrive only when we feel that there is something or someone we can trust. A life devoid of that—in which it's impossible to share a secret without worrying that your confidence will be betrayed—is hardly worth living. This brings us to the final method used in the seduction of Winston Smith: isolation.

Consider the case of Tom Parsons. Tom is not very bright, but he is as committed to the Party as anyone in Oceania. Nevertheless, Tom's children are educated to suspect their own parents and be prepared to inform on them. And that is precisely what they do. Poor Tom Parsons should not trust even his own family, but he is so indoctrinated that, when he is arrested, he cries, "Of course I'm guilty! You don't think the Party would arrest an innocent man, do you?" Parsons has lost his trust in himself to such an extent that, when his daughter accuses him of saying, "Down with Big Brother!" in his sleep, he believes her and regards that as a serious indictment.

By breaking down bonds of attachment and trust between intimates and replacing them with suspicion, Big Brother eliminates one of the few remaining objects of trust. But the insidious intervention goes further. In addition to destroying interpersonal trust, Big Brother's representatives insert themselves between people as gatekeepers. Tom Parsons's daughter did not keep her father's somnambulism to herself, bring it up with him directly, or consult her mother about what to do. No, she went straight to the Thought Police.

To understand the importance of this, it's helpful to think about the structure of trust in a community. In network science, it's common to model communities as sets of nodes that represent agents. These nodes are then connected by edges that represent some kind of relation; in our case, the relation is trust. A very simple network is shown in Figure 1.

Figure 1: Simple Dyadic Network

This network represents a small community in which A trusts B but B does not trust A.

Adding a reflexive loop indicates that the agent trusts himself, as in Figure 2.

Figure 2: Reflexive Dyadic Network

This network represents a small community in which A trusts B, B trusts A, and both A and B trust themselves.

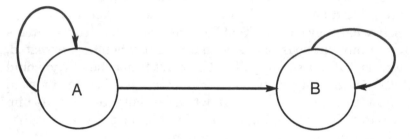

In the plot of *1984*, the method of isolation is combined with surveillance and the undermining of self-trust to transform healthy communities like the one pictured in Figure 2 into unhealthy communities like the one pictured in Figure 3.

Figure 3: The Community in the Ministry of Love after Winston's and Julia's Arrest

Note that Winston no longer trusts either himself or Julia, and Julia no longer trusts herself or Winston.

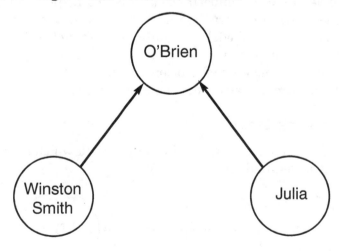

One of the few things that makes Winston Smith's life tolerable during the first half of the story is his intimate bond with

Julia. By isolating them from each other, torturing them into informing on and betraying each other, and undermining their self-trust, O'Brien strips Winston (and Julia) of a precious good. Near the end of the novel, they both confess to having betrayed each other, after which Julia says that sometimes

> they threaten you with something you can't stand up to, can't even think about. And then you say, 'Don't do it to me, do it to somebody else, do it to so-and-so.' And perhaps you might pretend, afterwards, that it was only a trick and that you just said it to make them stop and didn't really mean it. But that isn't true. At the time when it happens you do mean it. You think there's no other way of saving yourself, and you're quite ready to save yourself that way. You WANT it to happen to the other person. You don't give a damn what they suffer. All you care about is yourself.

Having done precisely this himself when threatened with the voracious rats, Winston echoes her sentiment, then Julia says, "And after that, you don't feel the same towards the other person any longer."

From *1984* to the Twenty-First Century

What can we learn from *1984*? Is Orwell's dystopia something we managed to avoid, or does contemporary society stand on the brink of a new dystopia? Are we, like Winston Smith, being seduced at a distance by a loathsome monster? To shed light on this question, we can ask to what extent the four methods employed in the seduction of Winston Smith are also being employed today.

The answer is scary. I will use recent developments in the United States to make my case. The United States is just one country, of course, but what's happened there could happen in many other places.

First, consider surveillance. After the 9/11 attacks on New York City and the Pentagon, the United States government set up a massive surveillance system that taps phone and email communications both within the country and abroad. This sort of system has also been implemented in Britain, China, Russia, and to some extent the European continent as a whole. Moreover, sometimes we know we're being observed and recorded, but in many cases we think that we're enjoying a private moment when we are actually being surveilled.

Second, consider the annihilation of history and official documentation more generally. After being inaugurated, Donald Trump directed his administration to impose a gag rule on scientists working in the Environmental Protection Agency and elsewhere. In addition, reports produced by these scientists were quashed, and the website of the Environmental Protection Agency was scrubbed of all mention of "climate change."

Third, people are being invited to distrust their own perceptions. For example, despite losing the popular vote by approximately three million ballots in 2016, Trump continues to insist that he actually won the popular vote and was somehow defrauded by millions of illegally cast ballots. Only a handful of such illegal ballots have been discovered, however, and many of them were cast for Trump himself. While this isn't exactly the same as insisting that two and two make five, it is insisting that 62,984,825 is greater than 65,853,516.

Likewise, Trump has insisted that the crowd at his inauguration was the largest in history; photographs of the event show otherwise, but Trump's supporters—when surveyed by psychologists—often follow his lead rather than trusting their own eyes.

Fourth, by hurling the epithet of 'fake news' at everything that shows him in a bad light, Trump is undermining trust in the media. Indeed, he recently bragged about this on his Twitter feed, saying. "It is finally sinking through. 46% OF PEOPLE BELIEVE MAJOR NATIONAL NEWS ORGS FABRICATE STORIES ABOUT ME. FAKE NEWS, even worse! Lost cred." While this is not exactly the same as the interpersonal isolation that O'Brien imposes between Winston Smith and Julia, it has a similar effect: Trump is essentially telling people, "Don't trust each other or your own eyes—trust me instead!"

The good news is that the resistance to Trump and those like him is much stronger and more organized than the resistance to Big Brother in Orwell's novel. The bad news is that there is no guarantee the resistance will win.

15
Happy in Oceania?

JOSIP ĆIRIĆ AND BRUNO ĆURKO

> Nothing was your own except the few cubic centimeters inside your skull.
>
> —GEORGE ORWELL, *Nineteen Eighty-Four*, p. 26

Orwell's novel presents a bleak outlook on life under a totalitarian regime: inhabitants of Airstrip One are confronted with total control, coerced into blind obedience toward Big Brother, and have learned to hate Oceania's enemies.

Security is not to be found neither at home nor within family—every room contains a two-way TV screen and you may never know when you're being watched; kids are members of the Spies, a youth organization created to watch over their parents and report if they stray from the Party's policy. Two Minutes Hate, destruction of language and thought, sexuality allowed for procreation purposes only . . . it's dehumanization and depersonalization on an industrial scale. Thus, Winston's end fits neatly into the distorted society he lives in—in the final moment, when he learns how to love the Big Brother, a bullet hits him; he has lost the only part of authentic self, truly becoming a party drone and his meaningful life ends.

So, what could philosophy possibly do for poor Winston? Wise men across cultures like Socrates, Epicurus, Spinoza or Siddhartha Gautama teach us how to avoid losing dignity under unfortunate circumstances. Their lessons include: the unexamined life is not worth living, there are paths to eliminating suffering, we may be both free-from and free-to. Such lessons provide a person with a form of power that reveals the emptiness of Ingsoc threats. Winston may be confronted with a violent regime which brutally eliminates its discontents, but the regime's power is based on obedience. When Winston denies it, the Party is no longer the master. Despite the book's bleak ending, a promise of freedom in the face of terror is not ruled out.

What does "doing philosophy" mean? Unfortunately, inside the philosophical community there is no agreement about what philosophy is, how it should be properly done, or even what makes good philosophy. There is a special branch of philosophy dealing with those disputes, called, surprise—metaphilosophy. For non-philosophers, doing philosophy is a highly intellectual task and mostly focused on some minute aspects of the world without much care for practical application. Alternatively, philosophers are considered to be in possession of some particular wisdom that provides them with serenity and calmness when coping with the challenges life throws at them.

We present two solutions to Winston's ordeals, emerging from philosophy: the first is the link with psychotherapies (the philosophical counseling approach) and the second deals with critical thinking skills.

Tweaking Airstrip One

Certainly, *Nineteen Eighty-Four* presents a life we never want to wake up into. Orwell's disgust with the totalitarian regimes of the twentieth century led to writing Winston's and Julia's tale. Autobiographies of numerous dissidents from Communist regimes reveal similar disregard for identity, liberty, and humanity, as well as a focus on blind obedience, no matter how absurd the consequences. Even worse, the book was used as a blueprint for Jim Jones's Peoples Temple, claims Philip Zimbardo (pp. 144–46), and who knows better about totalitarian institutions?

But what if we tweak Orwell's plot just a little bit? After all, not every Communist fate was a tragic one. There was some opposition and, although life was hard, a certain space for creative expression existed. So let us suppose the Party did not purge all inappropriate books, and that some, an inconspicuous few, remained. There may have been a dusty cardboard box that contained a couple of those in Winston's rented room.

While he was waiting for Julia, Winston could have browsed one, say, a collection of letters by Sir Horace Walpole. Besides writing the first gothic novel, *The Castle of Otranto*, Walpole's letters reflect a certain philosophy, although he was not a philosopher, at least not officially. In one of the letters (1769) he wrote "I have often said, and oftener think, that this world is a comedy to those that think, a tragedy to those that feel—a solution of why Democritus laughed and Heraclitus wept."

You may excuse Winston's confusion when he came upon this passage—it was something so different from his perspective of how the world worked. He knew very well about various fears—rats, pain, Room 101. Although Winston kept some rebellious thoughts, fear was the major force in his life. And there was someone claiming that you could have a completely different perspective and a completely different experience of life. There was also Julia. She presented him with another perspective. If only he had recognized its potential! She did not focus on fear, she was about small, instant pleasures instead, avoiding the Party's steel fist for as long as possible. She did not have any interest in rebellion either.

Worldview

So, what's philosophical about it? First, a general point of view you have about your life is called, in philosophy, a worldview (or as philosophy nerds prefer it, *Weltanschauung*). The term was first used by Kant, made popular by Hegel, and it may now be found in other related areas such as linguistics, cultural anthropology, sociology, and religion.

Kant's philosophy lays the foundations of later inquiry into worldviews. In very short and simple terms (we know of at least a few dozen philosophers who will be pulling their hair because of this statement, and of at least half a dozen who will recommend us to Room 101), Kant asks what the limits of our knowledge, ethics and purpose are.

Kant is one of the most influential philosophers of all time. If you analyze an authoritative source in philosophy, such as the *Routledge Encyclopedia of Philosophy*, you find that Immanuel Kant is both the second most out-linked and the second most in-linked person. Imagine the Facebook for philosophers—out-links are people you know, in-links are people who follow you. The higher the numbers, the more central you are, and Kant is a very popular fellow. In more technical terms, out-links represent how many other philosophers Kant's encyclo-pedia article points to (meaning he is a good starting point for browsing through the encyclopedia), the in-links represents how many other encyclopedia articles point to Kant (a measure of his relevance in the philosophers' network).

Kant's stroke of genius (How else should you call a philoso-pher who also devised a physical theory on the formation of galaxies, now called the Kant-Laplace theory?) is to turn the problem upside down—the one thing we may know is our states of mind, not the world outside. This approach implies several important innovations in philosophy, which we will mostly skip before this turns into a lecture. The most interest-ing one for us is a shift in philosophy towards the personal. It resulted in various theories: those about the functioning of the mind which later developed into the philosophy of mind, others using perception as fundaments which developed into phenom-enology, and the third dealing with the meaning of . . . well—life (sorry, "42" is not the valid answer), which branched into various existentialisms. If there are limits to what we may know of the world and how our minds work, then what we per-ceive is a sort of theory. Such a theory may work in favor of our well being or against it if we ignore wisdom.

Secondly, worldviews have psychological consequences too. Or to put it another way, psychological interventions start from certain philosophical assumptions. Here's a little exercise—you may identify some portions of your worldview when you fill in the blanks in the following sentences:

Everyone is _____.   All men are _____.

All women are _____.   The world is _____.

Good person never _____.   You should always _____.

Finally, pick one: unexpected experiences present more of a) challenge or b) threat.

So, you get the general idea. There are a few issues with these sentences. For starters, not everyone shares the same set. Even worse, just a couple of people in your network do. If you ever wondered why it's hard to make new friends, maintain long-term relationships or make a world a better place, part of the answer lies there. There is no philosophical system without psychological implications and no clinical psychology without philosophical assumptions.

Another tricky issue is that some of the answers are . . . there's no way to put it nicely—irrational and dysfunctional. You may expect everyone to like you or to get along with everyone you meet, that consequences will fit the intentions, that you have to be perfect, that evil people deserve the harshest punishment, or that true lovers never argue . . . the list goes on and on. Unreal expectations only give birth to frustration. And yes, there's more—the set of your most precious beliefs may be logically inconsistent, which both makes it bad philosophy, and makes you more neurotic. If you want to check inconsistencies in some of your basic philosophical attitudes, you may try an online questionnaire available at Philosophical Health Check (Stangroom 2017).

This is all nice in theory, but what use is it for Winston? If he had given more thought to Julia's approach to life as meaningful, to reflect on his own, he might have found there was room to redefine parts of his own worldview which did nothing but hurt him—he might have started to undervalue fear and shift the focus from impending doom, or he might have started a revolution he knows he may not finish, or he might not have cared about Big Brother's love. He might have used Walpole's sentence to render his world anew. Imagine this—we are presented with a description of collective madness at the rally (pp. 188–190) when Oceania's enemy and ally switch in the middle of the speech.

People yell sabotage and treason, develop elaborate conspiracy theories without a shred of critical reasoning. If you focus on emotions, you may feel their panic, madness, fear of being swallowed by the frantic crowd. If Walpole's words are worth anything, then you could switch to reason and perceive it in a different light—you may find the scene utterly absurd, akin to a Monty Python sketch. The Party's attempt to shrink the vocabulary to the minimum is a method of oppression, but it is also the opposite of itself—there is a significant cognitive effort invested in destroying cognition, a sort of linguistic chasing of their own tail.

Psychotherapies and Philosophy

Let's tweak Winston's story even more—the book ends with news of Oceania's victory and the war is over. What if the end was more like real history—the oppression ran out of steam, and life could return to normal?

Perhaps this is the most debatable assumption in Orwell's novel. O'Brien claims that the Party is forever, no matter how individual life is spent. Hatred is no more exhaustive than love, he claims, therefore civilization would not commit suicide as Winston believes (p. 281). History and psychology beg to differ—there are examples of cults and regimes who wielded tremendous power over their subjects, but only for a short while. On the other hand, it seems our evolution favored co-operation and social support, not an opportunistic collective grab for power. If we agree with Pinker's analysis in *The Better Angels of Our Nature*, there is another argument against the Party's endurance: the long-term trend to fewer violent conflicts.

Winston could seek professional help—he could choose among the four hundred (and counting) psychotherapy approaches available today. Some of them are not shy to point out their philosophical inspiration: existentialist therapists build on Heidegger's work, Freud's psychoanalysis rests on a medical approach, as well as on classical empiricism, which is also the founding bed for behaviorism. Additionally, Ellis's rational-emotive behavior therapy (REBT) is inspired by Greek stoicism, while Rogers's client-centered therapy draws inspiration from both existentialism and romanticism (Jones and Butman 2011).

Philosophical counseling is another approach to providing well-being by means of philosophy: using its history and literature as a repository of questions and possible solutions to problems of living applicable to its skills such as, logic and critical thinking to solve, or at least, define life's issues.

Since philosophy and psychotherapy are intertwined, we may use both to observe what philosophy has to offer to make you happy . . . or happier. Early philosophy argued that it might provide comfort for the soul. Seeking wisdom was a search for spiritual calmness, a lack of strong passions, as ancient Greeks called it—*ataraxia*. The Epicureans and skeptics considered it a basic ingredient of happiness.

Similarities may be found with the Buddhist teaching of the four noble truths and the eightfold path of escaping the circle of rebirths and suffering. Various existentialisms provided plenty of opposing answers on how to live a meaningful life: from religion to atheism, from pessimism and reflection on suicide to Buber's I-Thou interpersonal relationship or various applications of Socratic dialogue in psychotherapy. The Kantian distinction between freedom-to and freedom-of is also reflected in Glasser's control theory.

On the other hand, if we start with psychotherapy, we soon discover that Stoic philosophy contains certain proto-cognitive therapy techniques for the cognitive rearrangement of situationa, bridging (such as Seneca's task to imagine the worst possible outcome to prevent frustration), to Frankl's logotherapy as a golden mean of finding meaning in one's experience—not enough meaning leads to depression, too much to paranoia. The formula is simple, whatever the direction—you create meaning, you choose how to act, your emotions are coupled with attitudes and behaviors and there is no valid ideology which could sell you the only way to live. We empower ourselves when we know about the constructive nature of our experiences. As far as acquiring worldviews goes, do you remember sticks-and-stones?

So You Want to Build a Totalitarian State . . .

There is only one truth and it is ours!" is a central motif of political systems which seek to impose maximum control over their citizens. To establish government's opinion as the only correct one is a basic dictatorial principle. Incapacitating people's natural drive to think and reflect on everything that happens around them enables a dictator/overseer/Big Brother to dominate and exercise absolute control. There is an indicative passage in Goldstein's book:

> The two aims of the Party are to conquer the whole surface of the Earth and to extinguish once and for all the possibility of independent thought. There are therefore two great problems which the Party is concerned to solve. One is how to discover, against his will, what another human being is thinking, and the other is how to kill several hundred million people in a few seconds without giving warning beforehand. In so far as scientific research still continues, this is its subject matter. (p. 201)

Thus, the Party's holy duty is to destroy any thought, making the physical conquest of the world the only task of similar importance. This is the very reason why critical thinking is utterly unacceptable to any ruler who seeks total government control.

Critical thinking is a mode of thinking "in which the thinker improves the quality of his or her thinking by skillfully taking charge of the structures inherent in thinking and imposing intellectual standards upon them" (Paul and Elder). You may call it light philosophy, we won't mind. For John Dewey, the main educational goals should be developing thinking skills in children:

> No one doubts, theoretically, the importance of fostering in school good habits of thinking. But apart from the fact that the acknowledgment is not so great in practice as in theory, there is no adequate theoretical recognition that everything the school can or needs to do for pupils, so far as their minds are concerned (that is, leaving out certain specialized muscular abilities), is to develop their ability to think. (p. 226)

Being exposed to various attempts at manipulation on a daily basis through commercials, click-bait, political propaganda, or inauthentic relationships makes critical thinking even more important. On the psychological side, we have to be aware of biases in inference our minds make (such as, basic attribution error, illusory correlation, hindsight bias, magical thinking . . . the list goes on) and how to compensate them. On the philosophical side, it leads to interesting new concepts such as bullshit. Yes, you read that right. And no, no self-respecting Party would allow a single copy of Frankfurt's book *On Bullshit* to survive.

We should ask ourselves if we are on a path similar to Oceania's, forgetting how to think, search, and stick to our attitudes. There are similarities: cheap entertainment for the masses is a sort of Fremen "mind killer," directed use of our leisure time directly limits our capabilities to think things through. Moreover, there is aggressive promotion of what to think and how to behave. It is of little importance who is in charge of the manipulation, in Syme's words it means that "there will be no thought, as we understand it now. Orthodoxy

means not thinking—not needing to think. Orthodoxy is unconsciousness" (p. 56). Becoming a small cog in a soulless machine,
deprived of any knowledge of a better life, obedient to authority, whether it is called Big Brother, the Wizard of Oz, or
Weyland-Yutani Corporation, is what may be in store for us.

Orwell provides insights into techniques of achieving such
obliteration of the critical mind: destroying language and con-
verting it into a simple signaling system thus destroying
thought, acquiring doublethink, an ability to hold two logically
opposite thoughts in the mind at the same time, *crimestop*, a
protective stupidity, and *duckspeak*—mindlessly quacking
orthodoxies. Using such confusing messages may be recognized
as the psychological technique of double binding, a communication pattern where any response of a participant is treated as
inappropriate or wrong. When such a pattern is established
between a mother and a child, it may trigger a schizophrenic
disorder.

There are less subtle techniques, of course—power is nothing without the possibility to humiliate, O'Brien reminds us. As
Zimbardo points out (p. 128), Orwell seems to focus the entire
mechanism of control on aversive emotional conditioning, a
new approach in clinical psychology at the time the book was
written. Social control may be achieved by brutal coercion or by
the pleasure principle. Orwell chose the first approach, but the
second may be thoroughly destructive as well, as in Huxley's
Brave New World (1932). Projects of thought control are not
just science fiction, as Zimbardo points out—the CIA's MK-
ULTRA program, Jim Jones's Peoples Temple, as well as
numerous totalitarian regimes of the twentieth century used
those techniques. In fact, avoiding social isolation is one of the
most important prevention factors to mental illness. "Each of
Nineteen Eighty-Four's technologies of mind control is aimed at
either undermining or overwhelming some personal attribute
central to the human spirit" (Zimbardo, p. 129) such as freedoms of action, association and interpersonal trust, independence of one's thought, reality-based perceptions and decisions,
human pride, use of language to convey and focus cognitive
functions, personal privacy and solitude, individuality, eccen-
tricity and diversity, a sense of Self based on one's experience.

In the world of Oceania no philosophy or critical thinking
should ever be allowed. When you compare totalitarian

regimes of the twentieth century, not only will you find state-controlled philosophy, but also sociology. If we want to avoid similar scenarios, developing critical thought at the youngest possible age should be paramount. The history of philosophy is full of appeals to develop our thinking skills—from Socrates onward, philosophy is both the source of and the incentive to critical thinking. And this is barely enough—we have to embrace critical thinking for the rest of our lives. As Kant puts it: "Have the courage to use your own understanding—is therefore the motto of the Enlightenment."

There may yet come a time when freedom may be found only in the couple of cubic centimeters inside your head, but such freedom is yours to maintain and nourish. The very weapon the Party wields against its own members is the same weapon by which it may be defeated. Philosophy has found itself under the oppressor's boot more than a few times, but it is still alive and kicking.

III

Ignorance Is Strength

16
Bad Faith and Make-Believe

ISKRA FILEVA

Professors teaching philosophy classes sometimes ask students to imagine being offered several million dollars to acquire the belief that two plus two equals five, or some other randomly chosen number. Can you come to believe that two plus two equals five? Probably not. Not even if the reward is attractive enough to make you really want to.

This thought experiment is used to illustrate something important about the nature of belief: our beliefs are not under our own voluntary control. This is because as rational beings, we respond to evidence, and we cannot induce in ourselves beliefs that blatantly contradict the evidence or rational principles.

We're not perfectly rational: we sometimes form wishful beliefs or self-deceptive beliefs, as when a mediocre painter believes himself to be a misunderstood genius or a mother of a drug-addict succeeds in explaining away the evidence of her daughter's addiction. But these are distortions at the margin. By and large, we know that there's an objectively existing reality—a world that does not depend on what we think about it—and for the most part, our beliefs aim to match that world. This is why we cannot mold our beliefs to our liking.

Or can we? What if instead of being offered several million dollars, you are threatened with torture or actually tortured? Made to confront your very worst fear? Have your sanity questioned? This is what happens with the protagonist of *1984*, Winston Smith. The whole novel can be seen as one rational person's journey on the way to adopting the belief that two plus two equals five or that anything else Big Brother wants him to believe is true.

How do Winston and other Oceania residents bring their beliefs into conformity with the Party line? And what exactly do they believe? We might suppose that Orwell's claims about the beliefs of Oceanians are simply implausible: after all, as the little thought experiment I started with demonstrates, we cannot just make ourselves believe on command. However, I will suggest that Orwell's description of the psychology of believers must not be dismissed as an artistic exaggeration intended for dramatic effect. Rather, reflection on *1984* can offer insights into the nature of belief. If I'm right, the message of Orwell's book is at once more chilling and, as we will see at the end, more hopeful than it might, at first, appear.

Obedience without Understanding and Limited Disobedience

Dictators typically know that in order to stay in power, they must control not only actions, but beliefs. Techniques such as censorship, propaganda, restrictions on free discussion, war, and instilling hatred of the enemy are totalitarian regimes' stock-in-trade. Oceania's ruling Party makes use of all these techniques—its propaganda is blasted all day long from big telescreens, and free discussion is out of the question.

Oceania is perpetually at war without any real interest in winning—with the sole purpose of creating uniformity and patriotic sentiments among citizens. To the same end, the Party has citizens practice the Two Minutes Hate daily—a combination of rituals and propaganda, meant to channel hatred away from the Party and toward the enemy.

But Oceania goes further than most dictatorial regimes. The Party forges historical records and expects citizens to bring their beliefs in accord with the amended records *even when they have vivid memories of the actual history*. On one occasion, the Party line regarding who the current enemy is changes abruptly, and a speaker addressing a big crowd must switch course in mid-sentence, to reflect the new reality: the enemy is no longer Eurasia, it is Eastasia. Not only that, but citizens must come to believe that the enemy has *always* been Eastasia. The current enemy should be seen as a perpetual enemy—otherwise, attitudes toward the hostile nation may become nuanced and deviate from Party orthodoxy. This is true even when the war with the current enemy actually began only a minute ago.

Perhaps most striking of all, the Party expects citizens to bring not only their conscious thoughts but their unconscious processes and instincts into conformity with the ideology: Oceanians can be charged with thoughtcrimes committed while asleep. It would seem that such a degree of control over your beliefs is impossible to attain, and yet, according to Orwell, many people do attain it. How?

The proletariat, or "the proles"—comprising about eighty-five percent of the general population—for the most part, do not need thought control, at least not according to *The Theory and Practice of Oligarchical Collectivism*, a book by the purported founder of the secret Party opposition, The Brotherhood: "What opinions the masses hold, or do not hold, is looked on as a matter of indifference. They can be granted intellectual liberty because they have no intellect" (*1984*, Signet edition, p. 210). Those among them who are gifted and ambitious and who might possibly "become nuclei of discontent, are simply marked down by the Thought Police and eliminated" (p. 209).

Then there are people like Winston's lover, Julia, who rebel in their actions only, not in their wider political beliefs. Julia has a series of lovers, something not tolerated in Oceania: the Party attempts to stifle sexuality since sexual drives may lead citizens to pursue their own pleasure at the expense of Party objectives. All sexual intercourse must be in the service of Party goals, such as procreation with the aim of bringing about Party loyalists.

In addition to breaking the rules by being sexually promiscuous, Julia buys forbidden items such as good coffee on the black market, another crime. She attempts to divert attention from her unlicensed activities with an exaggerated display of conformity. For instance, she's a member of the "Junior Anti-Sex League"—an organization whose purpose is to discourage hedonic sexual pleasure and to encourage the view that sex must be put in service of Big Brother's goals.

Julia works for the League regularly, handing out flyers and doing other activist work. But she has no interest in objective reality beyond the way it has an impact on her personal life.

Sometimes, Winston talks to her about the forgeries he's had to commit while working at the Records Department—an agency in charge of reconciling public records with Party claims and doctrines, and a branch of the ironically labeled "Ministry of Truth." Julia seems not to understand why Winston cares that he has had to amend historical records:

> Such things did not appear to horrify her. She did not feel the abyss opening beneath her feet at the thought of lies becoming truths . . . In the ramifications of party doctrine she had not the faintest interest. (p. 154)

Orwell then goes on to say that the Party can successfully impose its ideology on those who, like the proles or Julia, lack either interest or the ability to understand what they have been asked to believe, since:

> They could be made to accept the most flagrant violations of reality, because they never fully grasped the enormity of what was demanded of them, and were not sufficiently interested in public events to notice what was happening. By lack of understanding they remained sane. They simply swallowed everything, and what they swallowed did them no harm, because it left no residue behind, just as a grain of corn will pass undigested through the body of a bird. (p. 156)

Not all Oceanians, however, are like the apathetic among proles or like Julia with her strictly limited rebellion. There are some reflective people, for instance among those working at the Ministry of Truth, where employees correct historical records. Some of these people find it difficult to adopt the beliefs expected of them. What about them?

Thought Contortionists or Who Is Mad?

The first step is to get people to *commit* to attempting to form the sorts of beliefs expected of them. The Party does this mainly by using fear. It instills in the citizenry the sense that they are being constantly watched. In the very first scene, Winston looks at a poster that says, "Big Brother Is Watching You." The poster is a preview of what's to come. What we learn later is that citizens can be monitored in every house and in every room.

In addition, the Party makes use of children as "junior spies"—many children, naturally impressionable and easy to manipulate, spy on their own parents, and some betray their parents (thereby becoming Party heroes). Children are enticed to identify with the Party, to become the abuser and thereby escape the powerlessness of childhood.

Last but not least, the Party creates the impression that resistance is not simply futile but meaningless—if you persist in resisting Big Brother, you will be vaporized (as many have been), and historical records will be changed, so that it will look like *you never existed*. You won't become a heroic martyr who makes a sacrifice for a worthy cause—you will just vanish without a trace.

Once citizens have acquired the intent to mold their beliefs in accordance with orthodoxy, the government offers them techniques for keeping their own thoughts and beliefs within the boundaries of the permissible. These include, above all, Newspeak and crimestop. Newspeak is a revised version of English meant to take away people's power of independent thought. For instance, a person who has been vaporized for thought crimes is, in Newspeak, an "unperson." An "unperson" is not a deceased person, but rather, *nobody*. An "unperson" *never* existed, and must be completely forgotten even by family members. The name of an "unperson" can be neither mentioned nor thought (thinking it would be a thoughtcrime). Newspeak disempowers thought by taking away the words which thought can use as its tools.

Here, we have an insight into one way of controlling thought: controlling language. When you take away certain concepts, you undermine people's ability to think certain thoughts. But language is something that *can* be controlled, at least to a large extent.

Yet, what if an unlicensed thought nonetheless comes unbidden? Suppose you have a thought about a vaporized loved one. There is a technique meant to help nip such thoughts in the bud and arrest rational processes. The technique is called "crimestop." Orwell describes it thus:

> *Crimestop* means the faculty of stopping short, as though by instinct, at the threshold of any dangerous thought. It includes the power of not grasping analogies, of failing to perceive logical errors,

of misunderstanding the simplest arguments if they are inimical to
Ingsoc, and of being bored or repelled by any train of thought which
is capable of leading in a heretical direction. *Crimestop*, in short,
means protective stupidity. But stupidity is not enough. On the contrary, orthodoxy in the full sense demands a control over one's own
mental processes as complete as that of a contortionist over his
body. (p. 212)

This passage contains a key insight into the nature of belief:
being rational and staying rational require work, and rationality can be undermined both by a refusal to do the necessary
work—asking questions and engaging in critical examination,
or apathy, as we noted earlier in discussing the case of Julia
and the proles—and by deliberately undermining rationality,
for example, by systematically diverting one's attention away
from what seems questionable and unbelievable. Just as you
can intentionally try to *hone* your rational abilities by adopting
certain habits of mind, you can deliberately *blunt* your rational
abilities by adopting different mental habits, habits that mili-
tate against reason.

Still, we may have the nagging suspicion that Orwell is seriously exaggerating our ability to control beliefs, and that we
cannot get ourselves to sincerely assent to an obvious falsehood, try as we might.

Orwell's answer to this is that we do not have to fully
silence the beliefs that run counter to the orthodox ones we are
trying to induce in ourselves. The process of thought "contor-
tion" mentioned earlier is often a matter of holding *contradictory* beliefs. The technique is known as "doublethink":

Doublethink lies at the very heart of Ingsoc, since the essential act of
the Party is to use conscious deception while retaining the firmness
of purpose that goes with complete honesty. To tell deliberate lies
while genuinely believing in them, to forget any fact that has become
inconvenient, and then, when it becomes necessary again, to draw it
back from oblivion for just so long as it is needed, to deny the existence of objective reality and all the while to take account of the reality which one denies—all this is indispensably necessary. . . .
Ultimately it is by means of *doublethink* that the Party has been
able—and may, for all we know, continue to be able for thousands of
years—to arrest the course of history. (p. 215)

Doublethink resembles ordinary cases of self-deception, but there is a twist. The twist has to do with the role of self-awareness. Many instances of ordinary self-deception are a matter of motivated belief-formation, meaning that our *desires* influence our beliefs: we come to believe what we want to believe. Motivated belief-formation often proceeds unconsciously—our desires influence our beliefs without any deliberate attempt on our part to reach one or another conclusion.

Consider the so-called "optimism bias." It's well established that people believe they are less likely to experience adverse events such as crime or illness, compared to other people. This may lead to tension between beliefs, for example, a person may believe that four out of ten people will get cancer in their lifetime and yet estimate her own chance of getting cancer to be less than ten percent, without any evidence to support the belief that she is less likely than an average person to get the disease. Motivated belief-formation stands in need of an explanation, but it does not raise the sort of puzzle doublethink does, namely, how it is possible for a rational person to consciously and deliberately endorse a contradiction.

Other cases of motivated belief-formation involve something closer to a purposeful attempt on the believer's part to reach a certain conclusion, but result in no contradiction. The mother who wants to maintain the belief that her daughter is not a drug addict may deliberately look for alternative explanations of her daughter's spending and poor grades. The mother does not believe simultaneously that her daughter both is and is not a drug addict. She just believes—though not fully rationally and not with complete certainty—that her daughter is not dependent on drugs.

Doublethink—if it does exist and is not an artistic invention—is more puzzling than these garden varieties of self-deception. The citizens of Oceania have contradictory beliefs and often know they do. How, if at all, is that possible?

I believe the answer has to do with the always alive possibility of mistake on our part. Descartes once argued that even mathematical truths can be doubted, since it is possible that we have been induced to believe mathematical equations by an evil demon. Descartes's doubt was methodological, not psychological: Descartes did not actually doubt the truth of his beliefs about arithmetic, he simply showed that the truth of those beliefs is not fully and indisputably certain.

However, methodological doubt can turn into psychological doubt under peer pressure. Solomon Asch, in his famous experiments on conformity, demonstrated that people can be induced to doubt the evidence of their senses when everyone else present claims to see something different from what they see. While we have a natural disposition to trust ourselves, we also have a strong propensity to trust other people and to doubt ourselves in case no one else shares our view, no matter how compelling our evidence may be. Many of us tacitly assume that the overwhelming majority of people cannot be wrong.

When we experience a clash between what seems to us to be the case and what others say is the case—as happened to the subjects in the Asch experiments—we may come to doubt our own seemings. However, when our seemings are compelling, we often cannot simply disbelieve them, so the natural outcome of a clash between our seemings and the claims of others is a contradictory belief. If this is right, then the Party can induce contradictory beliefs in citizens by first getting each independent-minded person to believe that he or she is in a minority of one (a goal that can be achieved by restricting free discussion and exchange of ideas) and second, by reinforcing the idea that *sanity is statistical*—that when your judgment clashes with that of the overwhelming majority of people, you are at best wrong and at worst mad. Since almost everyone can be presumed to want to be sane, once a person is persuaded that sane people believe a proposition, he or she will attempt to convince himself or herself of the truth of that proposition.

There is a final detail to add to the picture: the Party, for its part, never wavers and never doubts. In this way, the Party resembles, curiously, psychopaths, who often succeed in getting others to believe the most outrageous lies by remaining confident and casting doubt on the others' rational abilities. Psychopaths can make a masterful use of our belief in our own fallibility. Thus, Paul Babiak and Robert Hare, who studied corporate psychopaths write that "even in the face of contrary evidence, the psychopath lies so well, that listeners doubt themselves first" (*Snakes in Suits*, p. 254).

When the Party succeeds in questioning citizens' rational abilities, it effectively swaps the places of sanity and insanity in citizens' minds, and it thereby creates what Orwell calls "controlled insanity"—a sort of collective trance that results, paradoxically, from citizens' desire to stay sane.

Jean-Paul Sartre once opposed a Freudian model of self-deception on which self-deception is a matter of conflict between different sub-agential systems. Sartre suggested, alternatively, that self-deception in general does not just *happen to us*. We are not its victims. It is something we *do* (*Being and Nothingness*, Chapter 2). If Sartre is right, then even garden variety self-deception involves control on our part: we form beliefs in bad faith when we could form them in good faith.

Sartre may be right, but we do not have to accept his account of self-deception in general in order to cede Orwell's point: whatever the role of agency in self-deception—whether or not garden variety self-deception is something that happens to us or something we do—we have enough control over our beliefs to become adept at doublethink. We can deliberately blunt our own rational capacities, motivated, ironically, by the desire to stay sane where sanity is understood as believing what everyone else believes. For a person in a totalitarian regime, then, it is crucial to resist the idea that sanity is statistical.

One man in *1984*, the protagonist Winston Smith, makes an attempt to resist that idea.

The Case of Winston

Before Orwell titled the novel *1984*, he considered the title "The Last Man in Europe." There is a sense throughout the book that Winston *is* the last man in Oceania. That he is humanity's last hope of stopping the loss of rationality and sanity. If he loses the battle, there is no hope.

Winston loses, though the Party has to use a number of tools from its toolbox in order to bring him to that point. Winston is a difficult case, and to deal with him, the Party employs its "heavy artillery"—O'Brien, an Inner Party intellectual who takes a personalized approach toward Winston. O'Brien first lays the foundation for the eventual breaking of Winston's spirit by giving him a book about Oceania's system of rule— *The Theory and Practice of Oligarchical Collectivism*. Winston has been hoping and perhaps wishfully believing that the book and its author, Brotherhood founder Emmanuel Goldstein, exist. But he had not known whether they do or do not. When he gets the book, he feels vindicated. Emmanuel Goldstein appears to see Oceania the way Winston does. The book makes explicit everything Winston himself has suspected. This makes Winston confess to O'Brien that he'd been committing both thoughtcrimes and real crimes. Winston desires nothing more strongly than to join the Brotherhood.

Shortly after, Winston and Julia are arrested. This is not yet a true turning point since Winston himself has, from the start, expected that he'd be arrested one day. He still has hope. Perhaps, members of the Brotherhood will find a way to slip him a razor, and he would be able to avoid being tortured and to end his life with dignity.

But O'Brien reappears and claims that there is no Brotherhood, that Emmanuel Goldstein does not exist, and that the book had been written by Inner Party members, including O'Brien himself. O'Brien suggests—and Winston accepts the suggestion—that Winston has always known O'Brien is a loyal Party member: Winston's hope to meet like-minded people had always been hope against hope. Hope in bad faith. Winston was self-deceived.

O'Brien goes on to make it a personal project to break Winston. O'Brien uses his own intellect. As a possible co-author of the book ascribed to Goldstein, O'Brien knows Winston's thoughts and doubts intimately. Orwell says of Winston:

> O'Brien was a being in all ways larger than himself. There was no idea that he ever had, or could have, that O'Brien had not long ago known, examined, and rejected. His mind *contained* Winston's mind. But in that case how could it be true that O'Brien was mad? It must be he, Winston, who was mad. (p. 256)

But this gets us only to doubt, not to the breaking point. In order to break Winston, O'Brien goes beyond arguments. He tortures Winston and makes him confront his worst fear—a fear of rats. As a consequence, Winston pleads that Julia be tortured instead of him. This is the beginning of the end of hope. Winston transgresses his own moral boundaries. Orwell here suggests that there is an important connection between sanity and morality: our own moral boundaries support our sanity and vice versa. We stay sane in part by never doing or wishing to do anything horrendous.

Maintaining our sanity thus requires work. Earlier, we saw that maintaining our rationality under pressure takes effort. So does maintaining our sanity more broadly. We must be willing to fight to stay on the right side of our own moral limits. If you break a person's fighting spirit, you win the fight. O'Brien breaks Winston's spirit when he gets Winston to plead that Julia be tortured instead of him. At that moment, Winston turns from the last man in Europe into a regular Oceania citizen. Now, he is ready to believe that two and two make five, if Big Brother says so. After all, if what you have always considered morally unthinkable suddenly seems permissible, then you were wrong about morality. So you were probably wrong about much else, including math.

What Does O'Brien Believe?

There is a final question I wish to address here: what does O'Brien believe? Does *he* believe that the amended historical records are true, for instance? Does he have contradictory beliefs?

O'Brien believes in the Party's ability to control reality by controlling people's thoughts. He thinks he can create reality by instilling in others the relevant beliefs. This is power over reality, not only over men. O'Brien is drunk on that power.

But does O'Brien believe with complete certainty that there is no objectively existing world, apart from people's memories and historical records? While interrogated by O'Brien, Winston thinks to himself:

> He is not pretending . . . he is not a hypocrite; he believes every word he says. (p. 256)

I suggested above that the Party is like a psychopath who preys on others' sense of fallibility by maintaining his own—the psychopath's—infallibility. Yet, while complete confidence is what the Party displays, we can argue that Oceania's Big Brother is like a psychopath secretly plagued by self-doubt. We can infer that from the zeal and determination with which O'Brien takes on the task of "curing" Winston of his beliefs. Why not simply kill Winston? After all, if there is no objectively existing reality, then Winston's thoughts and beliefs would be of absolutely no consequence once he was dead.

There are different answers to this question we can derive from the text. Perhaps O'Brien is perversely fond of Winston. Maybe, he too was a skeptic before the Party got to him, and he sees much of his younger self in Winston. Or perhaps, O'Brien likes to talk to intelligent people, or else enjoys the challenge of breaking a sane and rational person. All of these things may be true. But O'Brien also suggest that even when the Party has decided to kill a "thought criminal," Party members make sure to "cure" the person of his or her beliefs first:

> We do not destroy a heretic because he resists us; so long as he resists us we never destroy him. We convert him, we capture his inner mind, we reshape him. We burn all evil and all illusion out of him; we bring him over to our side, not in appearance, but genuinely, heart and soul. We make him one of ourselves before we kill him. It is intolerable to us that an erroneous thought should exist anywhere in the world, however secret and powerless it may be. (p. 255)

Why is an "erroneous" thought intolerable? I would argue that the heretical thoughts of those who are about to die are intolerable to the Party because of nagging self-doubt on the Party's part. A thought *truly believed* to be erroneous is rarely intolerable, particularly when the person who has the thought is about to be killed.

There's a hopeful message in this. Truth and reality are powerful foes, even for the government of Oceania. This is evidenced by the fact that the tiniest trace of truth surviving in the thoughts of even a single person sentenced to death is perceived by Big Brother as a threat. As something intolerable. This is because even Big Brother knows there is a limit to our control over our beliefs: truth is always ready to try and reassert itself.

The Party's victory cannot be permanently secured. There is, consequently, a limit to the Party's control. O'Brien claims that the future holds nothing but a full triumph of the Party over everything human: "If you want a picture of the future, imagine a boot stamping on a human face—forever."

The secret hopefulness of Orwell's message lies in the fact that O'Brien's vision itself seems wishful—and mad.

17
Through a Telescreen Darkly

Lavinia Marin

It was a peculiarly beautiful book. Its smooth creamy paper, a little yellowed by age, was of a kind that had not been manufactured for at least forty years past. . . . Even with nothing written in it, it was a compromising possession. The thing that he was about to do was to open a diary. This was not illegal (nothing was illegal, since there were no longer any laws), but if detected it was reasonably certain that it would be punished by death, or at least by twenty-five years in a forced-labour camp.

The Party fears blank paper. On every street corner, you can find newspapers printed with propaganda but blank paper, now that's nearly impossible to find. For nearly half a century no more notebooks were produced, no blank papers allowed to touch the hands of the masses. This restriction seems odd. Why is blank paper dangerous? What is treacherous about a nice leather-bound book with creamy pages?

The very act of writing on a blank paper is thoughtcrime and Winston knows it. The intriguing question for us is: what's at stake in the potential of a blank page? There is political potential in a blank page, it could contain a subversive message that could be passed on to others, yet blank paper to write on is much weaker than owning a manual printing press hidden in a basement. If Winston wanted to instigate rebellion against the Party, he would not handwrite manifestos, he should print them somehow.

There's something else going on with writing your thoughts in a notebook, and that is related to Newspeak. It's possible that, as long as people continue to write, Newspeak will never catch on. Here's why.

Newspeak for Everyday Life

Newspeak is an artificial language which needs to become the official language of Oceania by 2050. Quite an ambitious project, to say the least. There is a saying among linguists that every language is a dialect with an army and a navy. Oceania does not lack an army or a navy; however, is military power enough to make of Newspeak a proper language?

The main problem with Newspeak lies in its artificial nature. This is where the folly of the Party's project comes to the fore: the Oceanians are supposed to adopt an artificial language and use it as a natural one. Newspeak is not just another artificial language like Esperanto, it is an impoverished language which does not tolerate multiple meanings and this makes it harder to adopt. Yet Newspeak must be spoken if the Party wants to perpetuate its political system forever. Big Brother's well-being depends directly on the ability of his subjects to speak this cartoonish language which sounds so much like the quacking of the duck.

How can an artificial language like Newspeak effectively become the only language for everyday use? To clarify this, we must first understand what makes Newspeak special among artificial languages and what is the philosophical difficulty which confronts the proponents of Newspeak. The main purpose of Newspeak, as Syme tells Winston, is to "narrow the range of thought," to make certain thoughts impossible to think—especially what the Party classifies as "thoughtcrime." This narrowing is pursued by destroying words, "cutting the language down to the bone." However, no matter how talented the writers of Newspeak dictionaries are, no matter how great their language design is, they will hit an insurmountable difficulty when people will actually start using this language in everyday life.

Natural languages have a way of uncontrolled expansion, of forking words into multiple meanings, of becoming vague and slippery. For example, think of the expression "The Man." It started from a very banal noun, *man*, but now it means the established order, the oppressive group represented by a faceless noun; however, when not capitalized, it has the value of a compliment "You're the man!" Capitals and lower-case make it easier to see these two meanings apart, but it's ultimately the context which separates them.

In *1984*, the characters speak of the Party as "they." Just "they." In an actual conversation, the speakers know automatically when "they" means the Party and when it is a simple pronoun, referring to any ordinary group of people, without the negative connotations. Once a new word is released into the world, its meaning cannot be controlled or predicted. This is what makes natural language so poetic and complex: words have multiple meanings which cannot be exhausted by dictionary definitions.

Taming Natural Language with Rules

Already from the early twentieth century, the vagueness of natural language posed problems to philosophers such as Bertrand Russell who had tried to reduce philosophy to symbolic logic. The idea behind such an attempt was that, if you can reduce every proposition to its logical equivalent, then you can calculate its truth value and potentially decide every philosophical problem by logical computation. This was already a utopian project back then, because natural language, like a living being, twists and turns, develops new meanings as you study it, creates new uses for old words, as old words die, not to mention the appearance of ironic or sarcastic uses. Natural language is an untameable mess, so Russell gave up this project.

A few years after Bertrand Russell had given up the hope of taming natural language with logic, one of his students took up this project again. Ludwig Wittgenstein was the disciple who surpassed his master. Up to Wittgenstein, the dominant idea in philosophy of language was that each word should point to one thing from the real world. In his later philosophy, Wittgenstein described this misconception as the idea that "the words in language name objects" so, basically, for every word there is an object out there to which the word points. Hence, if we want to understand a sentence, we must decompose it into its words, look for the objects (or properties, relations, or whatnot) that correspond to each word, and then combine these all over again to understand the meaning of the sentence.

This naive picture of language prevailed in philosophy of language going back to thinkers like Augustine of Hippo. But if this picture of language were true, how would we know the meaning of sentences about fictional objects, vague words, or just words used ironically? All sorts of problems appear if we stick with this compositional view. In opposition to this philosophical tradition, Wittgenstein made a breakthrough in philosophy of language by advancing the idea that "meaning is use."

Instead of trying to reduce natural language to logical sentences, Wittgenstein made the reverse move and put natural language first. We first learn to speak, and only later do we come to analyze our words, breaking them into logical or grammatical rules. Logics, grammar, and philosophy come later, after the fact, after the speech is performed, to make an artificial separation out of the natural flow of speech. Language is just the abstract way in which we came to theorize the flow of speech.

Wittgenstein's idea of meaning as use was brilliantly simple: how do we know that we have learnt a word? When we can use it in multiple contexts and others understand us. Being able to hold a conversation which includes a certain word and being able to perform actions starting from that word is good enough proof that we know it. We don't even need the dictionary definition to "know" what the word means.

The traditional idea of language inherited from Augustine was that we learn the language one word at a time, usually by pointing at things: this is a telescreen, this is a piece of chocolate, this is Big Brother. But Wittgenstein came up with the idea that we learn the words always embedded in a complex of gestures and actions, even emotions. When a kid is told by his mother "This is Big Brother!", there is a pointing gesture at his picture, but there is also happiness on the parent's face. The kid not only learns what Big Brother is, but the correct attitude of happiness and respect towards this comrade. So, we never learn the meaning of a word neutrally, as if the word were isolated from other words in a void, we learn exactly at the same time what to do with that word: if it's Big Brother, you stand up and clap, you smile, you show love, and so forth.

We know what a "big brother" is when we know how to do the right actions around his image, and when others approve us for this. Even if we can't define Big Brother according to the dictionary definition, it's all right as long as we perform the correct actions with this word. The expression that Wittgenstein used for this complex of speaking while acting was "form of life." The idea was quite ingenious: you learn to speak in a certain way because you learn to live in a certain way. A way of life leads to a way of speaking and vice versa. We do not first learn to live and then to speak, as if these were separate stages. We learn how to act and speak at the same time, and this made things very complicated for philosophers of language who wanted to just analyze words separate from deeds.

However, if meaning is use for many words, what will the inventors of Newspeak do with their dictionary full of dead definitions? The language experts may define "goodthinkful" any way they like in the eleventh edition, they still need to find a way of making this definition stick to some practices. The inventors of Newspeak need to make it part of a way of life. This is where they will face another difficulty. Wittgenstein pointed out that there are many ways of living, hence many ways of speaking. The same words will be used differently as these occur in different forms of life. The problem with forms of life is that these are multiple, not just across cultures, but even inside the same culture. We live in so many ways, we do so many things, and words follow this multiplicity of living. Words need to have multiple meanings to be able to accommodate the many ways of usage. In order to impose Newspeak as the one way of speaking, the Party needs to impose one way of life, and then freeze it like this forever. Is this even possible?

Wittgenstein was aware that one of the major problems with his theory of meaning as use was the changeable nature of the forms of life. If people learn from their parents the right way to speak and to act, how does change even appear? Why are we not propagating the same way of life for eternity? Imagine a world where the children lived exactly the same life as their parents did, in which you could not tell the difference between the 1980s and the 1990s or the 2000s. This would be a very bizarre world indeed, for it would be a world where the past and the present blend together in the same indistinct strip of time. It would be a world without history, where the passage of time made no difference.

But wait, this world already exists; it's Oceania in 1984. Winston, one of the few Oceanians who actively tries to remember things, repeatedly has trouble with the timeline, he's not sure what year it is and when the things from his past actually happened. It looks as though the Party were halfway there in its quest to impose a unique way of life by erasing the past and, with it, the memory of other forms of life.

The Medium of Newspeak

In theory, the Party has all the force it needs to impose Newspeak. But is terror enough? If it were so simple to coerce everyone to the same form of life and hence to the same language, other historical conquerors would have done it already.

We only need to think of Poland's history under successive German, Russian, and Austrian occupations. Why was there still a Polish way of life and a Polish language despite so many centuries of occupations? Military powers come and go all the time, yet people live their lives indifferent to the historical catastrophes that surround them. Why should Oceania under Party ruling be any different? This is where Orwell's dystopian novel offers an interesting answer which eluded even Wittgenstein: the key lies in the dominant media used for communication.

People who remember words are not by themselves a problem for the Party. When Winston went to a proles' pub, he met an old man who could remember words from the old times, such as "pint" instead of half a litre, or "top hat" or "lackey." However, the old man cannot recollect how life was before, he cannot answer the fundamental question troubling Winston: was life before really worse? The old man remembers useless words, just floating residues in his memory which will be washed away with beer. The old man can't make sense of what these words meant, he cannot say anything about the way of life which included pints of beer and top hats because he cannot integrate his old life into a history, he cannot give it meaning. Perhaps he needed to write about it to remember.

When Winston first crouched with his notebook in the corner of his room, in that blind spot where the telescreen could not observe him, he knew that he was committing something unpardonable. To write your private thoughts in a notebook was an offense, unwritten in any law for "nothing was illegal, since there were no longer any laws." When Winston first wrote his words, it was a mess of disparate sentences, it had no meaning, just him 'recording' what he saw that day. But, as his writing progresses daily, Winston's thoughts become more coherent, he can say on paper what bothers him, he is starting to articulate the problem with the Oceanian way of life. He first needed to write about it in order to understand it.

Writing and Speech

There is a reason why Newspeak is not called Newlanguage. In Oceania, the favorite medium promoted by the Party is bound to orality (speech either in direct spoken form or as heard on the telescreen). Writing (and consequently print) is only secondary, kept more out of inertia because people like Winston still know how to read and you cannot unlearn that. The status of print in Oceania is shady at best. There are newspapers and books of dubious quality. News is "written" by dictating into the speakwrite machine. Books of fiction are composed by machines. Effectively, nobody puts pen to paper anymore. Writing seems like the activity most removed from the life of Oceania. Even though Newspeak is standardized in the form of a dictionary, even if it is an actual physical book—which may be sometimes used as a projectile against the image of Goldstein—Newspeak is all about orality and speech.

In the history of philosophy, little attention has been paid to the actual medium carrying the language—with a few exceptions and these exceptions were, remarkably, against writing. A philosophical distrust of the written language pervades the history of philosophy. It all starts with Plato who accused the new medium of writing of making memory weaker and humans dependent on stored records. If writing is about storing information on paper, why would we need to use our memory anymore?

This distrust of the writing technology continued until the twentieth century when we encounter it again in Wittgenstein—as J. C. Nyiri has shown. Nyiri points out a curious feature of Wittgenstein's philosophy which has been ignored by many commentators: Wittgenstein valued speech more than written language, for speech was clearer—embedded in a form of life through gestures, tone of voice, actions—whereas writing was ambiguous at best. Writing, with its fake way of separating words on paper as if each word is separate and means something distinct, was to blame for the major philosophical problems which led Russell and Whitehead to despair, because writing gives this impression of crispness and clarity—writing requires analysis (be it grammatical or logical) as if life itself were logical or grammatical in any way. Language is just a fiction that we posit when we try to analyze the continuous flow of speech. We would never have noticed that there is such a thing as language had it not been for the invention of writing. Philosophically, writing is to be blamed for the unrealistic striving for clarity in analytic philosophy of language.

In the dispute between writing and speech, many philosophers have favored speech—as being more authentic, more connected to a form of life. One notable exception was Vilém Flusser, the Czech-born philosopher who was very much influenced by Wittgenstein in his younger days. Flusser agreed that writing is a completely different thing from speech, but he also noticed that our dominant forms of life are quite immersed in writing. We cannot designate the speech-based forms of life as more "authentic" than the writerly forms of life since we are all literate beings and we live and breathe among written words. We learned to think while writing, and our thinking bears the traces of this writerly way of being.

The main feature of writing is its linearity (it always follows a direction, from left to right, from right to left, from top to bottom), so we came to think in a linear fashion: we analyze things in linear relations, as cause leading to effect, past to present, if this then that, our entire classical logic was born out of this linear striving for clarity. Also, for Flusser, writing created history with its record-keeping devices which allowed us to put events in order and say what happened before us. Before writing was invented, humans had no true history, just mythical stories of heroes and quests. Their collective past was hazy and hard to remember, much like Winston, struggling to remember something about Oceania's past in the absence of any written record.

Oceanians Reverting to Orality

We see the world of Oceania in 1984 through the eyes of Winston who is very much a literate creature of the old days. Winston finds it hard to believe that $2 + 2 = 5$ because he still clings to the rules of logic and mathematics, to the world of writing things down and looking for meanings in the symbols. It is much easier to believe the whisper "twoplustwoisfive" than to see the symbols written in front of you as "2 + 2 = 5" and assent to them.

The trouble with Winston is that he keeps imagining these written symbols, those pesky little things which require proof according to some universal law. Winston knows how to write and this doesn't help him in the oral-based world designed by the Party. The world of *1984* is dominated by the telescreens. Its official language, Newspeak, favors oral modes of communication which consist of repetitions and patterns of speech, emotions worn on your sleeve, memorization, and chanting. The Newspeak way of life rejects logical analysis, it requires only blind faith. At best, Newspeak sounds like the quacking of a duck. At its worst, it is a shout of hatred, an uncontrollable rage against the enemies of the Party. Newspeak defies logical analysis; its aim is to end thinking once and for all, and by this the Party means linear thinking.

All forms of life have a history, a past to which we can relate. In order to impose only one form of life and erase all others, history must be stopped. The citizens of Oceania live in a kind of post-history because all their records are tampered with while the telescreens create a virtual present for them all the time. They do not need to stop and think, for the tele-screens already tell them what to do and think. A post-historical world is immersed in streams of images and sounds. Nothing is linear there, hence logic can be surpassed. There are telescreens everywhere which keep on talking and flooding the atmosphere with music, news, whatever piece of information the Party wants you to know. The screens exist to interrupt thinking by asking for constant attention, making any withdrawal into the self impossible, abolishing private thoughts. How can you recollect your thoughts if the voice keeps on shouting and commending attention?

Writing has been, from the beginning, a way of taking distance from the flow of life. Writing was about arresting thoughts and speech on paper in order to look at them a second time, and think about them as if they were not your own. This was the beginning of what is usually called "objectivity"—to look at things as if these were objects separate from yourself, which makes analysis possible. You cannot think while you're shouting, marching, singing, hating. But you can start thinking once the words are written out and stand in front of your eyes ready to be scrutinized and analyzed.

Winston is writing private thoughts on paper. As he's doing this, he's clarifying his own thoughts and producing, without intending to, a form of history. Winston is keeping records of what happened. If Winston were to write down who Oceania is at war with today, or the amount of the chocolate ration, and if tomorrow all facts were changed, all newspapers modified to accommodate the new "truth," the information would remain as evidence in Winston's notebook. As if Winston were producing a witness who couldn't be bribed. Once he starts writing, the past is no longer mutable for Winston; he trespasses one of the sacred principles of Ingsoc.

Is Newspeak then a feasible project? If everybody forgets their past and starts living according to one form of life, then yes. The screens are the most important devices for imposing this unique form of life. The screens do not need to be rewritten like the newspapers. They can say in the news bulletins one thing and next day they can contradict it, for there are no records. Screens are just a flow of information, rendered as speech and images, which crosses the weary minds of people every day. Even if people might remember from one day to another what had been said in the news, they have no proof. If only they could keep a record on paper, then they could actually start making a history of the lies of the Party.

An Apparatus to Tame Another Apparatus

It seems that the only remedy against an artificial language such as Newspeak is another artificial device, writing itself. This technology, which imposes a certain linear structure on thinking, also immunizes thinking against the chants and the repetitions, the blind belief in anything Big Brother might say.

In the philosophy of language, writing has led many philosophers into temptation, making them seek clarity of meaning where perhaps there is none, just a form of life. Following Wittgenstein, this is how people live and speak, what more is there to analyze? Yet writing is what anchors Winston in the flux of time, writing with its strange logical rules that make propaganda hard to swallow.

Writing keeps Winston sane and, in the end, offers a way out of the madness of Newspeak. If many more people would jot down their thoughts and memories on paper, then the collective hallucination of a single possible form of life—the orthodox way of life—would fade away. In other words, spoken language is fundamental for how we live but our forms of life do change under the pressure of media so, at some point, we can't claim that one form of life is more "natural" or authentic than another.

We are writerly beings and this is why, as readers, we understand Winston's quest to find some piece of real history, to clarify the past. We take this form of being for granted; we see nothing wrong with it. But we would need to be in Winston's place, immersed in a world of audio-visual streams of information, to understand how strange our own way of life really is.

Flusser brings an interesting response to Wittgenstein's concern with natural language: once we had started writing, there was no going back to the oral mode of life, and then writing became nature, and language needed to be imagined as a logically separable unit. And this response is illustrated in a nice way by the literary experiment which is *1984*.

Orwell's *1984* sheds an interesting light on something that remained unsaid in Wittgenstein's later work: how mass media shape our forms of life and can indirectly change language. In theory, following Wittgenstein's approach of language as use, the publication of a new dictionary for Newspeak should not be able to influence the way in which language is spoken because one book in itself does not change forms of life. However, if we take a closer look at how Oceania's population is exposed to media, we notice that they are interacting with information mostly through the telescreens, which leaves the population permanently exposed to an endless audio-visual flux of words and songs.

The population of Oceania is reverting to the stage of orality because, in their case, the written word has no value insofar as it justifies nothing. In Oceania, the telescreens function as means of changing the forms of life of the population, because these screens are the main source of information and also because they can't be shut down.

In this chaos of audio-visual information, constantly filling everyone's attention span, only Winston manages to find a point of reference through his notebook. The notebook anchors Winston to his own past, to the events which he remembers, and to Oldspeak. As long as Winston has the notebook, his form of life cannot be changed without leaving traces. He will write even if nobody reads his diary; he will write for himself.

18
Thoughtcrime or Feelingcrime?

ALBA MONTES SÁNCHEZ

Why did Winston have to be tortured to insanity? What exactly did he do to deserve that? The first time I read *1984*— I must have been eighteen years old, perhaps a little younger— one of my central narrative expectations was thwarted. The initial descriptions of Winston's life, his clear critical perception of Ingsoc and of his own job, his small rebellious actions . . . it all led me to expect that he would be given a chance to fight, join the Brotherhood and meet others like him, blow up some printing machines, organize campaigns to mobilize the proles, what have you.

But all he does is have an affair? (And not a very romantic one, at that). And that takes him to the Ministry of Love? Well, perhaps that name, Ministry of Love, should have made my eighteen-year-old self think again . . . Because indeed, that name announces what the ultimate crime in Oceania is, and what the whole apparatus is geared to. It is geared to achieving that dreadful, despairing, bleak conclusion: "He loved Big Brother."

In Oceania obedience is not enough. The absence of resistance is not enough. Love is required. As this becomes clearer during Winston's captivity and torture, it also becomes less mysterious why loving someone other than Big Brother is the ultimate crime. But the reason why loving someone (or something!) other than him is criminal has nothing to do with Big Brother's intimate feelings: Big Brother (if he exists) is not personally jealous. Love is required for purposes of power and social control. But then the question resurfaces again: if it is all about control, why is obedience not enough?

In describing Oceania dominated by Ingsoc, Orwell puts a world in front of us where material things, natural resources, money, social structures, people's activities, everything, even truth, is under the firm grip of Ingsoc. But a regime that aims at perpetuating itself *infinitely* in power needs more than this. People's minds must also be controlled. A huge emphasis is placed on the control of thoughts and thoughtcrime. As the story reveals, however, there is a slightly different kind of crime that is never spoken of, but which constitutes the truly unpardonable crime, the one that lands people in the Ministry of Love: emotional crime, "feelingcrime" we could call it.

Winston, we are told, has been on O'Brien's radar for seven years. But when does he end up in the torturer's chamber? When he succeeds in establishing a romantic relationship with a woman and falls in love. He can be allowed to walk out in the world, among his neighbors and colleagues, for *eleven years* with the memory of having seen proof that the Party lies systematically and alters the records of the past. But he cannot be allowed to carry out a love affair for more than a few months: just the time that is needed for the purposes of the Ministry.

As Winston reads in Goldstein's book, for the regime to perpetuate itself it needs stability, predictability, control. Nothing innovative or spontaneous can ever happen: this would threaten the structure. Allowing different perspectives, different feelings, even small nuances of opinion on the same thing, is dangerous, because one of them might contain the germ of a movement that destabilizes and destroys the system. This is why even the nerdish linguistic imagination of a fanatic like Syme can't be tolerated for too long, and he too ends up in the torture chamber: nobody can love *anything but* Big Brother, not even word games.

Away with the Individual

Differences in intensity of feeling, style of thought, and interests are all dangerous: individuality must be eliminated, because individuality presupposes difference, and difference creates instability. The party seeks to cancel differences by filling up people's lives with things that uniform their thoughts and feelings: work, leisure, and political activities that leave no room for imagination or individual self-expression, and force people to become masses swayed by the same collective emotions. Newspeak is geared to depriving language of all its creative potential, so nobody has the resources to think outside the box. As O'Brien explains to Winston in Room 101, the goal of Ingsoc is to create a strong collective that encompasses, subjugates, and subsumes all individual differences.

However, there's an important obstacle to achieve this goal: individuality in one form or another is rather resistant. Some people care about truth and write diaries, like Winston; others care about words and poetry, like Syme; others want to be free to enjoy their bodily pleasures as they please, like Julia; even Parsons is betrayed in his sleep by unacknowledged idiosyncratic desires. As we will see in a moment, it's very difficult to pin down what personal individuality and selfhood amount to, what constitutes each person's uniqueness, and philosophers have grappled with this question for centuries. But as philosophers, sociologists, and social psychologists have begun to ascertain, it is at least as difficult to understand and specify what genuine collectivity is: is it enough to have complex coordination among people, like the one required for moving a large sofa, or one of the kaleidoscopes at the Fiction Department? Do we need shared emotions, like the rage and hatred of Goldstein that arises at an Ingsoc rally? Or is something like a hive-mind the only genuine form of collectivity (like the Borg in *Star Trek*)?

Many have recently tried to show that genuinely collective experiences are possible (see the works by Schmid, Szanto, and Sánchez Guerrero): the emotions that sway Oceanians during the Two Minutes Hate, the executions of war prisoners, or the Hate Week rallies would be good examples of that. Even Winston confesses to being swayed against his will by the emotions of the crowd. The main problem, however, is that individuality has a way of reasserting itself, because, where is the collective body, or the collective mind, that can have such experiences?

Ingsoc hasn't reached the level of a hive mind. Can humans possibly become one? And so it seems that, ultimately, we are left with individual bodies and individual minds that collectively undergo the same experience (probably with different nuances) at a specific moment, without losing the capacity to experience things individually. Perhaps experiences can be shared at a point in time given the right circumstances, but regardless of how collective our abhorrence of Goldstein is during the Two Minutes Hate, how identical our emotions are and how dependent they are on the mass phenomenon, on what everyone else at the rally is feeling and expressing, if you step on my toes, you won't feel my pain—we won't share that. It seems, therefore, that Ingsoc has an impossible obstacle to surmount on its way to its ultimate goal: humans are not ants, bees, or the Borg. But is this truly an obstacle?

The type of collectivity Ingsoc aspires to does not necessarily mean that everyone has to always do the same things and have the same experiences. My liver does not feel the pain in my toes, and yet they are both part of the same body. Ingsoc not only allows, but is actually based on a strict division of labor, on a social stratification that entails very different living conditions and experiences for the different social strata. This does not threaten the collectivity but strengthens it. For the collectivity to thrive, however, all organs have to work together towards the same larger goal of keeping the organism alive and flourishing. If one cell starts working towards its own interests at the expense of the others (as with cancer), a severe imbalance can ensue and the collectivity suffers or even dies. To keep this threat at bay, it is therefore important to ensure that this unity of a goal is kept without variations.

To do this, as O'Brien explains to Winston during their sessions at the Minstry of Love, it is essential to control people's perception of reality. Controlling material reality itself is ultimately unimportant, what matters are people's minds and motivations. This is why Ingsoc has such a gigantic propaganda machine, which offers an entirely biased view of the world, and is geared to eliminating critical thinking and making irrelevant the idea of truth and an outside reality. But in the end, beliefs and logical reasoning are sterile in a certain sense: they don't motivate action. Think about the problem of *akrasia* or weakness of the will, which has puzzled philosophers at least since Aristotle. *Akrasia* is actually a very familiar phenomenon: you know what you have to do and why, you understand this well, but you simply cannot bring yourself to do it. This is why many of us have trouble exercising as much as our doctor recommends, eating our greens, or flossing every day.

Dangerous Emotions

Knowing, understanding, believing or disbelieving things does not necessarily motivate us to act. What does, then? Desires, emotions, phenomena with an affective character. This begins to explain why, after seeing the picture of Jones, Aaronson, and Rutherford that proves the Party lies, Winston walks with his thoughts and knowledge for eleven years and does nothing: something motivationally stronger needs to happen to overrule his fear of the Party and his desire to avoid torture (or rather, postpone it as much as he can) and stay alive. When he sees Julia's love note, he acts: his desire for sex, affection, and human warmth does have the necessary motivational force.

This explains why emotions are more dangerous than thoughts. The paradox is that they are easier to manipulate (they don't require a Ministry of Truth, just some properly staged rallies), but at the same time much more fleeting and difficult to control. Emotions are more recalcitrant (they easily endure despite the evidence that there is no reason to feel them) and more subjective, more dependent on the individual's particular situation. Emotions are evaluative phenomena: they color the world, they present things (people, events . . .) to us as having certain values, as being threatening, inviting, offensive, attractive, and so on.

And in a sense, they individuate us. How? They always include a reference to yourself, to what you care about. If you don't care, you don't feel anything. You are indifferent. Julia doesn't care about history, and the information Winston gives her about how the Party lies and alters the records leaves her unmoved. For something to cause an emotion, it must be affecting us, impacting something we care about, therefore emotions manifest (some of) our values. Think about how Winston feels about Big Brother (hate, contempt, fear), about the coral paperweight he buys from Mr. Charrington (fascination, curiosity, nostalgia), about Julia (desire, love, tenderness, admiration for some of her attitudes, a little contempt for some others). All of these emotions reflect who Winston is.

However, this doesn't mean that all emotions reflect deep-seated values or respond to what individuates us or make us unique, to what is more characteristic of ourself as a person. There are degrees of caring: emotions have different intensities.

And many of our everyday cares are superficial, situational and fleeting: if I'm in a hurry, I may find the slow pace at which you are moving along the corridor in front of me annoying, while this would normally not bother me. This annoyance doesn't necessarily mean I am typically an impatient person, it simply reflects my current situation of being late for an appointment. So the care reflected by my annoyance is situational. Our emotions can also be ambivalent and contradictory, like those Winston recalls feeling towards his mother and little sister in the days of hunger and hiding, where love is mixed with envy, anger, and frustration.

Why Emotions Matter

Taking all this into account, are emotions then not too context-dependent and unstable to be what constitutes our individuality? Philosophers have proposed different theories of what is the essential factor that determines personal identity: it might be your character, which roughly consists on your core values and dispositions (this idea goes back to the ancient Greeks, Plato and Aristotle, among many others), or rationality and the capacity to make normative commitments (Kant, Hegel, Taylor, Korsgaard), or memory, the capacity to remember your past and connect it to your present (Locke), or narrative, the capacity to make sense of your life as a coherent life-history (Ricoeur, McIntyre, Schechtman, Goldie), or interpersonal and social recognition, the fact that others recognize your individuality, who you are, and treat you and interact with you accordingly (Hegel, Sartre, Fanon, Honneth, Cavell), or your freedom and your possibilities, the fact that as a person your identity is not static throughout your life, that you are open to change and will change, that human beings live projected towards the future (Kierkegaard, Heidegger, Sartre). All of these dimensions are important, and Ingsoc targets all of them for destruction through various weapons outside of the Ministry of Love, essentially by curtailing freedom, jeopardizing rationality, manipulating people's emotions and breaking any meaningful ties they may have to other human beings.

The powers of Ingsoc in this respect are absolutely overwhelming, but despite this, there is a stubborn residue of individuality in each Oceanian that requires even harsher and more targeted intervention. This is where the Ministry of Love comes into the picture. And their methods show that they think something fundamental about people's individuality is emotional: it depends on love. Why love specifically, of all emotions? Not all emotions are the same. Not all of them are fleeting, superficial and situational. And according to American philosopher Harry Frankfurt, love is the crucial one that individuates us, that consistently organizes our motivations, that expresses who we are.

When Frankfurt talks about love, he does not focus on romantic love, he thinks about it more broadly, as does Ingsoc. Recall how they intervene to prevent any kind of loving human relationship: between parents and children, between husband and wife, even among friends. Frankfurt analyzes love in the broad sense that can include love for a person, a child, a friend or a partner, or for a thing or activity, like a work of art, your job, or playing your favorite instrument. According to Frankfurt (*Taking Ourselves Seriously*, p. 40), loving means having "an involuntary, nonutilitarian, rigidly focused, and—as in any mode of caring—self-affirming concern for the existence and the good of what is loved." To love someone or something is to act wholeheartedly (according to my will) to foster what I take to be the good of my beloved.

It might be a bit difficult to recognize this as a description of an emotion: there is no mention of how the beloved catches our attention and occupies our thoughts, how it makes us feel overcome by tenderness or enthusiasm, or by pain and disappointment some times, how our hearts might race and so on and so forth. This is because Frankfurt is interested in understanding what love does to our will, how it organizes our actions and shapes our lives by determining what we do and don't do. Frankfurt is interested in what love does to ourselves even when we don't feel the palpitations or the enthusiasm. Because true, deep love doesn't go away when the palpitations are over, and it keeps shaping our lives even when we don't think about the beloved. That's at least what he thinks, and so do I. And so does Ingsoc, since they invest so many resources in making people love Big Brother!

Subversive Love

So what is love? What does it do to us? Why should we think it shapes our individuality? Let's go back to Frankfurt's definition.

It is involuntary: you don't willfully choose what you love, you are simply captivated, and love doesn't respond to reasons. Or rather, reasons are not enough to explain why we love. If Winston loved Julia simply because she is energetic, or daring, or a brunette, then why does he not love equally all energetic daring brunettes that cross his path?

Love is non-utilitarian: you don't love strategically, in order to achieve something else; if you love in the hopes that this love will get you social status, or money, then your love becomes suspect. We would say you don't really love.

Love is rigidly focused: once you love someone (or something) that individual can't be substituted by an equivalent one. If in the middle of their affair, Julia was vaporized, Winston wouldn't be able to simply replace her with an equally energetic, equally sensual brunette of the same age and body shape. This would feel outrageous to him: this is not Julia! He loves Julia, not someone else. Our objects of love are not exchangeable for "equivalent" ones. For love, there is no equivalent.

Love is self-affirming, "—as in any mode of caring—a self-affirming concern for the existence and the good of what is loved" (p. 40): what I care about reflects what I, personally, value. It reflects who I am as an individual. Frankfurt's basic idea is that our values, cares and concerns define who we are. But holding a value is not a matter of believing or saying you hold it. You must act according to it; otherwise, what can it mean to say you care about it?

Even in a context like Oceania under Ingsoc, where freedom is almost non-existent and people are under extreme coercion to act as the Party dictates, values, cares and concerns are still effective, they give people strong motivations to act. Take Winston's concern for truth. Winston is under extreme pressure not to reveal he knows the Party is lying, to do absolutely nothing about the picture he saw that proved it. He has other concerns aside from truth: he cares about his own life and well-being, about staying alive and avoiding torture for as long as possible. Most of the time this concern for self-preservation is stronger than his concern for truth. But eventually he buys the notebook and starts writing, in the insane hope that someone some time will be able to come to discover the truth through his testimony.

Caring has degrees. Winston also likes smoking, and despite the appalling quality of the cigarettes he can get, he still finds some comfort in smoking them. He cares to a certain extent about obtaining that "pleasure," but it's very unlikely he would do anything that risked landing him in the Ministry of Love just to get a cigarette (contrary to Julia, who is a much more pleasure-oriented person and is prepared to risk buying contraband coffee and make-up). Even those of us who don't live in stiflingly oppressive political regimes find ourselves having to constantly prioritize among our cares and concerns.

In our lives, then, we have a hierarchy of concerns with different degrees of priority. The context is always crucial and can make a usually lower priority trump a higher one on occasion, but as a general rule, the things we care about more deeply will be those that are more likely to determine our actions, especially those that have long-lasting consequences. My deep concern for my daughter's wellbeing won't have much of a role in deciding which blouse I'm going to wear today, but it probably will be very important when thinking about moving to a different city or a different part of town. Thus, over the years, our deepest concerns will shape the course of our lives in a relatively coherent way.

This is why Harry Frankfurt thinks that what we love is one of the main components of our individuality: because love is the deepest form of concern, the one that is most likely to have the higher priority, and so to shape our actions more or less consistently over time. But wait a moment: aren't oppressive circumstances, like the ones Winston lives under, *even more likely* to shape his actions *even more consistently* over time? This is certainly true, but such consistent shaping is coercive, external, and does not express his individuality. That is why all the other characteristics of love are crucial: love is self-affirming, it arises out of a spontaneous, involuntary but deeply personal interest or fancy, it is rigidly focused and felt for its own sake.

Winston and Julia love each other: they caught each other's fancy, nothing external compelled them to be together. They don't seek any strategic end with their love, just fulfilling it. And once in the Ministry of Love, they both feel that despite all the horrors and humiliations they are subjected to, despite all they are forced to do and confess, their deep core is not touched while they still love each other. O'Brien acknowledges this too in Room 101: all the previous torture sessions have been successful in changing Winston cognitively, but something essential in his emotional structure, in his values and priorities, remains untouched while he still loves Julia. Room 101 is designed specifically to destroy people's ultimate allegiances, to make them incapable to keep loving what they used to love.

Make War on Love

To completely destroy individuality, therefore, you must destroy people's love. To control people's will, you must control what they love. Two of the most iconic political science-fiction novels of the twentieth century, Orwell's *1984* and Huxley's *Brave New World* agree on this. They both agree that controlling people and their wills is controlling what they love, and their emotions more in general. But they disagree on which methods are most effective. Huxley proposes a model based on genetic engineering and pharmacological manipulation, together with coaxing, mesmerizing, and fascinating (and thus obliterating critical thought, creativity and innovation, leaving no room for them), to keep people "happy" and in line. To deprive them of any motivation to change the status quo.

Orwell, looking at Stalinist Russia, imagines an aggressive, decidedly destructive model, where fear keeps people under control and torture subjugates them. Since the ultimate aim, as O'Brien explains to Winston, is power for its own sake, subjugation and humiliation, the crushing of all individuality, it seems that everyone in Oceania eventually undergoes it. Even those Winston thought were perfect subjects of Ingsoc and incapable of thoughtcrime, like Parsons, end up at the Ministry of Love, betrayed by their emotions, because they love something other than Big Brother, and that can't be allowed.

There seems to be something of a paradox here, however: the Party can't use anyone after they come out of Room 101. They may walk out of it, but all the life energy is gone out of them. Orwell describes those who come out of it (Jones, Aaronson, and Rutherford, and Winston at the end) as gin-drinking zombies who can't do anything but look at the telescreens. There is no resistance in them that can be subjugated, but neither can they work as instruments of the apparatus of dominance, because they have no strength at all, no will. They can't act any more.

The paradox, then, is that the Party needs the willpower that comes out of people's cares and concerns: the willpower of an O'Brien to be torturer; the willpower of a Winston to resist and offer an appropriate target for torture and subjugation. That, perhaps, is the residual element that may hold some hope for Oceania: that out of those loves, something strange and unexpected enough will emerge to topple the system over. This might be why hope does lie in the proles, who are allowed to keep loving and feeling undisturbed.

What my eighteen-year-old self didn't understand back then is that, in Oceania under Ingsoc, loving someone other than Big Brother is the utmost act of rebellion, because it affirms your own individuality, it places above all else an intimate relation that can't be collectivized. Winston is given a chance to perform a truly rebellious act, much more rebellious and threatening for Ingsoc than violent action.

And we readers are shown an important insight: that revolutions are fed from the energy of meaningful intimate relations, whose motivational force can hardly be surpassed by anything else in human life.

19
Nineteen Eighty-Four's Religion

JAMES CROSSLEY AND CHRISTOPHER MARKOU

For most—if not all—of his life, George Orwell was an atheist who saw religion as a relic of the past that had become a weapon of the rich and powerful. As Orwell recalled in his autobiographical piece "Such, Such Were the Joys" (published posthumously), he grew up to hate the Christianity of his youth, where he saw God as a tyrant and even loathed Jesus. He identified closely with the baddies of the Bible from Cain to Judas, and even claimed a soft spot for Lucifer.

Yet as an adult he developed a fondness for the Church of England, its liturgy, language, and traditional hymns. We might call Orwell a kind of cultural Christian in the sense that he did not believe in God but could scarcely imagine the Church of England not having a central role in his life. Or indeed, death—his Will famously directed that his "body shall be buried (not cremated) according to the rites of the Church of England."

With this pool of knowledge and assumptions, Orwell reflected extensively on the role of religion in politics and society. Like much of his work, *Nineteen Eighty-Four* reveals his own political philosophy that views religion as both a resource for capitalism and an aspirational socialism. For Orwell, at the heart of such views were these sorts of questions: What is to be done with belief in something as unlikely as an afterlife? What is to be done with something as positive as shared communal values that are apparently integral to religion? What if religion becomes even worse than before? What if religion is a blueprint for a totalitarian regime?

The Slow Death of the Afterlife

Orwell believed that some forms of Christianity, particularly the Church of England, were benign. Others were thought to be quite the opposite, most notably the Roman Catholic Church. But Orwell thought that religious beliefs in general were in terminal decline and nothing better exemplified this than belief in the afterlife.

Few people, he claimed, *really* believed the afterlife was anything more than something they might pay lip service to on a Sunday. A few years before the publication of *Nineteen Eighty-Four* he made his point in stark terms in his "As I Please" series for the *Tribune* newspaper: "Have you ever met a Christian who seemed as afraid of Hell as he was of cancer?" (14th April, 1944).

To illustrate this terminal decline Orwell recounts a memorable anecdote in his essay "Notes on the Way" (1940) about a trick he played on a wasp. As the wasp was eating some jam, Orwell claims to have cut it in half. The wasp, however, merely continued eating the jam "while a tiny stream of jam trickled out of his severed œsophagus." It was only when the wasp tried to fly that it realized the reality of what had happened. And so it was with religion, not realizing it all along was the wasp.

Orwell may have liked to joke about religion but his humor was underpinned by serious convictions. He believed that the decline of religion was necessary. By the nineteenth century religious belief had become no more than a lie; a lie designed to help entrench the old social and economic hierarchies and allow the rich to keep the poor in their place—and the rich in theirs.

Orwell wrote about this classic socialist criticism of religion on a number of occasions even if the situation in *Nineteen Eighty-Four* is altogether murkier. The idea of religion being used to prey upon the weak and prop up the powerful is present in Goldstein's book, *The Theory and Practice of Oligarchical Collectivism*. Goldstein's book recounts how priests of bygone eras defended and promoted the hierarchical ordering of society and "softened by promises of compensation in an imaginary world beyond the grave" (p. 232).

Did Goldstein believe this? For all we know, O'Brien *might* have been telling the truth when he said he wrote Goldstein's book. Similarly, history books approved by the Party talk about "bishops in their lawn sleeves" complicit priests, and the practice of kissing the pope's toe (pp. 84, 103–04). These books *might* have been pointing to genuine practices of the oppressive capitalist system before the Revolution but can they be trusted any more than any other Party propaganda?

Winston certainly has every right to be skeptical, but the reader should not be let off so easily. Such readings were (and are) standard popular critiques of religion and so it is perhaps better to think that in *Nineteen Eighty-Four* the Party used this sort of critique of religion for its own authoritarian ends— just as Orwell himself expected of societies such as Nazi Germany or the Soviet Union.

The Power of Religion

For Orwell, the decline of religion may be necessary but it is what fills the gap left by its absence that is the real problem. With no belief in judgment in the afterlife, is there not a danger of losing ideas of right and wrong or losing a system of morality altogether? Orwell certainly thought this was a clear and present danger and one that could easily lead to the worship of power and deceitful promises of heaven on earth.

This is the gap filled by the Party in *Nineteen Eighty-Four*. One reaction to the Two Minutes Hate appears to be an utterance of "My Saviour!" and a prayer, no less, while Party members can be described as "zealous" (pp. 19, 63, 149). Whatever we make of the ultimate origins of Goldstein's book, there is presumably meant to be *some* inkling of truth in the idea that the Party learned lessons from the Catholic Church in terms of ensuring its long-term survival, as O'Brien later elaborates.

Like the Catholic Church, the Party advocates adherence to a "common doctrine" and practices the worship of a "semi-divine leader" (pp. 226, 239, 290). O'Brien claims that "We are the priests of power . . . We make the laws of Nature." From the perspective of O'Brien and the Party, God is—ultimately— power (pp. 303–04, 318). This development and replacement of religion is perversely and necessarily understood in biblical language. As O'Brien explains to Winston, the command of the old despotisms was "Thou shalt not," the latter-day totalitarians; was "Thou shalt," and the Party, concerned with deepest personal transformation, is *"Thou art . . .* everyone is washed clean" (p. 292; anyone interested in the biblical language might turn to biblical passages such as Isaiah 1:16; Ezekiel 36:25; Psalm 24:4; 51:2, 7; Matthew 23:25–26; James 4:8).

By replacing religion, the Party in *Nineteen Eighty-Four* can employ the language of apostasy. The arch-heretic Goldstein becomes the "the primal traitor, the earliest defiler of the Party's purity" and all "heresies" come from Goldstein (pp. 14, 17, 63). It is striking that rumors of his book—*"the book*," no less—say that it is "a compendium of all the heresies" and undesirable conduct against the Party is described in the language of "heresy," a point also made in Goldstein's book (pp. 53, 63, 242, 292, 307, 321, 323, 343, 349). Obviously political views deemed problematic by the Party must be deemed 'heresy' but, by the logic of a replacement for religion, anything else seen to be religious from previous times must likewise be deemed heretical. "God" should be removed from the definitive edition of Kipling's poems as much as confessing to be a religious believer is a crime alongside affirming capitalism, sexual perversion, or being in cahoots with Goldstein (pp. 265, 278).

Religion for the "Good"

Despite its numerous faults Orwell believed that there was *something* to be learned from religion. Socialism was a potential surrogate for religion but socialism needed to rethink and retain the positive aspects of religion to both challenge and escape the re-animation of the older form of religion terrifyingly updated as a totalitarian Inquisition for the hyper technical modern age. This—perhaps paradoxically—meant that as an alternative to totalitarianism a transcendent authority had to be put in place to ground morality and meaning in something or indeed *anything*.

People, Orwell elaborated in his "As I Please" column (3rd March 1944), need *some* reason to believe that what they do or what they believe is a cause worth dying for. A sense of good and evil had to be developed independently of outdated ideas about heaven and hell. In short, any aspirational socialism needed to keep the good bits of religion to promote its political agenda.

What might this involve? A sense of community and abstract values like patriotism, honor, duty, loyalty for a start, sure. This, for Orwell, might be shown in a general comradeship among human beings who are now a kind of secularized "children of God" or a "brotherhood" (to use one of Orwell's preferred terms). Orwell's non-existent deity was, of course, English (or British) and the communal values and language he admired were borrowed, partly, from the Church of England of his upbringing and even his everyday adult life.

But even more important for Orwell was the idea of the "common people," or the "proles" to use the preferred term in _Nineteen Eighty-Four_. In his essay, "The Lion and the Unicorn" (1941), Orwell claimed that these were people who enjoy the pleasures of gambling, swearing, drinking, and crude jokes without firm or clear religious belief but kept what Orwell thought to be a certain Christian-ish feeling or character, particularly fuzzy notions of equality and liberty.

This idea of a vague, tolerant, decent "Christianness" is why Orwell had such a penchant for highlighting churches as the nostalgic connection to pre-totalitarian England in _Nineteen Eighty-Four_. From the half-remembered rhyme, it is the churches of St Clement's and St Martin's in particular that provide the focal point of Winston's nostalgia for an England seemingly long gone. These were "the bells of a lost London" that "belonged to the vanished, romantic past" which in some ways provide an alternative vision to the totalitarian present (pp. 112–14, 130, 168, 198, 206). The difference, distance, and distinctiveness of such places in Winston's present world is highlighted by the description of the hiding-place known to Julia: "the belfry of a ruinous church in an almost-deserted stretch of country where an atomic bomb had fallen thirty years earlier."

Orwell's myth of an ethereal Christian England infused much of his work, including _Nineteen Eighty-Four_. That may seem too much like the soppy Christianity associated with popular understandings of the Church of England today and quite unlike the Orwell who fought fascists in Spain. However, in _Homage to Catalonia_ (1938) Orwell also saw the Spanish anarchists as not only heroic but retaining the virtuous aspects of religion in their combination of class struggle with self-determination and individual liberty. On a number of occasions Orwell also championed what we might think of as the tradition of English radical Christianity. This for Orwell was a stream of Christianity that not only emphasized tolerance, individual rights, intellectual integrity, and liberty (and was thus anti-totalitarian) but one that could bring about genuine social and economic change to a world of war, disease, poverty, and overwork, as he stressed in an article for the *Manchester Evening News* (31st January 1946).

This was for Orwell (and, incidentally, plenty of other twentieth-century British socialists) a tradition at odds with the idea of Original Sin, namely the idea that sin and human fallibility was introduced in the Garden of Eden. Instead radical socialist Christianity was deemed to be an optimistic tradition which looked to the potential of human beings to cultivate a better world. It was a utopian tradition that stretched back to the Bible and figures like Jesus and the prophet Daniel and one continued by medieval peasant revolts, the radical revolutionaries of the English Civil War like the Diggers and the Levellers, and later socialists such as William Morris.

But this is a tradition gone wrong in *Nineteen Eighty-Four*. The perverted fate of English Socialism is now Ingsoc. Goldstein's reading of the history of socialism, capitalism, and the Party explains that socialism is a theory that appeared in the nineteenth century and "was the last link in a chain of thought stretching back to the slave rebellions of antiquity . . . still deeply infected by the Utopianism of past ages." Goldstein's book adds that in the twentieth century, however, the "aim of establishing liberty and equality" was increasingly abandoned (p. 233). Without liberty and equality, we're back to where we were in Orwell's and Goldstein's logic: totalitarianism.

Pure Religion

Orwell assumed that there was both a pure or *purer* religion and a pure or *purer* socialism that were both close to being the same thing but both were corrupted by unworthy and power-hungry interpreters. Put another way, just as Jesus was misinterpreted by his closest followers, so this logic has it that Marx was too.

This was an analogy Orwell employed on different occasions in his essays and journalism. Both Jesus and Marx were into the radical redistribution of wealth, both were (or would have been) critical of the motives of millionaires, politicians, priests, judges, and the rest of the establishment, and neither would have supported founding a new order enforced by machine gun (compare Matthew 10:34). These emphases were lost on too many of their prominent interpreters, whether Christians or Marxists.

Like *Animal Farm, Nineteenth Eighty-Four* explains the fallout of a revolution that failed. This was a revolution that betrayed its purer origins and did so in language Orwell consistently used to describe both socialism and religion. Just as Ingsoc is a kind of perversion of English Socialism so, according to Goldstein's book, the Party, in the name of socialism, "rejects and vilifies every principle for which the Socialist movement originally stood" (pp. 42, 246). Crucially, the construction of a purer form of socialism, at least according to the portrayal of Goldstein and his proclamation of the betrayal of the Revolution, involves freedom of speech, freedom of the press, and freedom of thought. Similarly, Goldstein's book looks at how the Party diminishes "human liberty" (p. 222), a concept integral to Orwell's understanding of a purer form of religion as it was to his understanding of Marx.

As the figure of Goldstein might suggest, there is also the assumption of carrying out a correct interpretation of the ideas of the founder figure. But what Goldstein represents, is losing badly in *Nineteen Eighty-Four*, just like English Socialism, radical Christianity, Jesus, or Marx. This is what is lost if, as Orwell believed, we capitulate to totalitarian thought.

In this sense, *Nineteen Eighty-Four* is not only a warning about the possibility of totalitarianism but also about religion: be careful what you wish for because look what could happen once it's gone!

20
Wheat Can Become Rye!

WILLIAM GOODWIN

For Orwell, "science" in its broadest, most admirable sense meant a "rational, skeptical, experimental habit of mind" ("What Is Science?", p. 325). It was a way of looking at the world, and not a collection of facts drawn from the exact sciences.

A scientist in the narrow sense—"a specialist in one of the exact sciences"—needn't carry over their critical, experimental approach from the narrow domain of "graphs, test tubes, balances, Bunsen burners, and microscopes" (p. 324) to the larger political, social, and ethical issues involved in managing the world. Instead, in Orwell's experience, "mere training in one or more of the exact sciences, even combined with very high gifts, is no guarantee of a humane or skeptical outlook" (p. 325).

While writing *Nineteen Eighty-Four*, Orwell was particularly concerned with the role that scientists in the narrow sense were playing in undermining science in the broad sense. Perhaps drawn to the pro-science rhetoric of the Soviet Union, some influential scientists in Orwell's Britain found themselves supporting totalitarianism and, according to Orwell, thereby working against the notion of objective truth that formed the backbone of a broadly scientific approach to the world. As a result, he was keenly interested—while crafting his totalitarian dystopia—to establish that "any attack on intellectual liberty, and on the concept of objective truth, threatens in

---

"Wheat Can Become Rye" is a headline from a clipping describing Lysenko's work, pasted into Orwell's final literary notebook, dated 16th December 1949, one month before his death (*Complete Works*, XX, p. 214).

the long run every department of thought" ("The Prevention of Literature," p. 379).

Similarly, he wanted to understand why scientists who were, after all, in the business of inquiring should become conscious enemies of intellectual liberty, which is the necessary prerequisite for genuine inquiry. For such a scientist, this amounted to "demanding his own destruction". With *Nineteen Eighty-Four*, Orwell hoped to bring these scientists around (For Orwell's and *1984*'s sides in these debates, see Werskey1978 and Desmarais 2010.) to convince them that: "if he wants to safeguard the integrity of science, it is his job to develop some kind of solidarity with his literary colleagues and not regard it as a matter of indifference when writers are silenced or driven to suicide, and newspapers systematically falsified" (p. 380).

Syme

Orwell wrote a character into *Nineteen Eighty-Four* who was intended to reveal both the self-deceptive mechanisms behind some scientists' attacks on intellectual liberty and the fate of science under totalitarianism. This character plays a crucial role in creating and maintaining one mechanism of self-deception critical to Orwell's totalitarian future—Newspeak—while being a master at the other—Doublethink.

These mechanisms are extrapolations to end-stage totalitarianism of the mechanisms that Orwell found to be at work in the pro-Soviet scientists of his era. Newspeak was designed to enforce orthodoxy by facilitating abstract, mechanical, and unreflective reasoning similar to what Orwell had already found in some scientists' political writing. Doublethink, similarly, was the system of self-deception supported by a vague, idealistic doctrine about the nature of reality, playing a role much like Marxist Theory (Dialectical Materialism) did for these scientists. Ultimately, the fate of this character, in turn, reflects Orwell's prognosis for scientists serving the enemies of intellectual freedom—in late-stage totalitarianism, they would prove to be self-defeating.

Syme is a scientist. He is a philologist, an expert on Newspeak, who works in the Ministry of Truth with Winston and is his frequent lunch companion. His job is to prepare the definitive edition of the Newspeak dictionary, largely by eliminating words and thereby reducing the capacity for thought-crime. So rather than contributing to the degradation of writing, or ignoring the contributions of writers and supporting their repression (as Orwell might have accused the Communist scientists of his time of doing), Syme actively works to make literature and history impossible. Indeed, he does this by attempting to craft a language in which only duckspeak—unconscious articulate speech—is possible.

At that point, the hope is that "a Party member called upon to make a political or ethical judgment should be able to spray forth the correct opinions as automatically as a machine gun spraying forth bullets" (*1984*, Signet edition, p. 309). In spite of his goal of making conscious speech impossible, he is both passionate and reflective about his narrow area of expertise. Like many scientists in Orwell's experience, though, his insight doesn't extend to politics.

> In an intellectual way, Syme was venomously orthodox. He would talk with a disagreeable gloating satisfaction of helicopter raids on enemy villages, the trial and confessions of thought-criminals, the executions in the cellars of the Ministry of Love. (p. 49)

Syme has no problem accepting either moral outrages or obvious falsehoods promoted by the Party about current events or history. Winston speculates that he is a master of double-think—finding ways to consciously "deny the existence of objective reality and all the while to take account of the reality which one denies" (p. 214). Still, Winston anticipates Syme's demise, predicting: "One of these days . . . Syme will be vaporized" (p. 53). The reason is significant:

> There was something subtly wrong with Syme. There was something that he lacked: discretion, aloofness, a sort of saving stupidity. You could not say that he was unorthodox. He believed in the principles of Ingsoc, he venerated Big Brother, he rejoiced over victories, he hated heretics, not merely with sincerity but with a sort of restless zeal, an up-to-dateness of information, which the ordinary Party member did not approach . . . zeal was not enough. Orthodoxy was unconsciousness. (p. 55)

Syme was altogether too conscious of the workings of Newspeak, its goals, and the purposes of the innovations that he had worked to introduce. He was required to think, even if only in the service of the Party. But genuine inquiry, even in the service of the Party, requires intellectual integrity. And intellectual integrity, in the end, is the enemy of orthodoxy: "orthodoxy means not thinking—not needing to think. Orthodoxy is unconsciousness" (p. 53).

Syme ruined himself for life under the Party in the process of contributing to the Party's goals. To care about how things really work, to seek to find out not just what the Party now says, but rather what it should say to serve its own purposes, is to acknowledge the very chasm between how things are and how the Party says things are which it is crucial—for the Party member—never to recognize. The scientist is required to acknowledge objective reality and to be conscious of threats to the truth, while Party life requires its denial and unacknowledged compliance with the demands for self-deception. So being a scientist is ultimately incompatible with Party life—intellectual integrity anywhere is an enemy of self-deception everywhere. In the end, Winston's prediction for Syme's fate comes true: "Syme ceased to exist; he had never existed" (p. 147).

Pseudo-inquiry in *Nineteen Eighty-Four*

In *Nineteen Eighty-Four*, personified in the fate of Syme, Orwell tries to convince us that in late-stage totalitarianism virtually all inquiry will be pseudo-inquiry. Pseudo-inquiry is when a person pretends to themselves that they are trying to find out the truth about some matter. They aren't pretending to inquire for someone else's sake; instead, as Susan Haack explains, they want to think of themselves as trying to find out the truth while all the while undermining their own efforts to reach it in order to reach some predetermined conclusion.

Where adherence to ideology is centrally important, Orwell hopes to convince us, genuine inquiry—and thus science in either the broad nor narrow sense—cannot endure. This is ultimately why Syme must die, and why the scientific supporters of totalitarianism were, according to Orwell, undermining themselves.

The Appendix to *Nineteen Eighty-Four*, where Orwell describes the principles of Newspeak, makes Orwell's point particularly clear. There is a section of the Appendix devoted to a class of Newspeak words called the C vocabulary. The C vocabulary "consisted entirely of scientific and technical words," but the vocabulary contains no word for 'science' in Orwell's broad sense. Instead, the word 'Ingsoc', meaning roughly the sum total of Party doctrine, would cover all cases in which one might have been tempted, in Oldspeak, to refer to, "science as a habit of mind, or a method of thought, irrespective of its particular branches" (p. 310).

Inquiry has been replaced, in the most direct way possible, by Party doctrine. However, even in late-stage totalitarianism, in order to believe something people will have to think of themselves as believing it for a good reason, so instead of cultivating intellectual integrity such societies must instead promote and develop the opposite—mechanisms of self-deception. These facilitate the pseudo-inquiry required to ensure that Party doctrine can never be contradicted by allowing people to maintain the illusion that things are still believed for good reasons. Newspeak and Doublethink are the mechanisms of self-deception that Syme has mastered, and they are the extrapolated fictional counterparts of those mechanisms by which the Soviet-supporting scientists in Orwell's Britain ended up advocating against their own interests.

It is perhaps easy to appreciate why, in an end-stage totalitarian world like the one that Orwell describes, the Party would have an interest in controlling the population's understanding of the current state of the world, or even of history. If the Party's subjects were in a position to know that life under the Party was cruel or miserable, this would provide a basis for criticizing the policies and values of the Party. Similarly, knowledge of the past could form the basis for refuting claims of progress or rationalizations of current practices.

It is not as clear why the very concept of skeptical, empirical inquiry should not only be eliminated, but also replaced by the Party canons. After all, it seems that no matter what values or principles you subscribe to, skeptical, empirical investigation can only further your capacities to realize those values or live by those principles—knowing how things really work is the best way to empower yourself to craft the world according to your ideals. But finding out how things really work requires genuine inquiry, and genuine inquiry is not something that Orwell thinks late-stage total-itarianism can tolerate.

One obvious reason that a social or political ideology, taken as infallible, must make demands on our general capacity for empirical inquiry is that such ideologies have empirical pre-suppositions, sometimes about fundamental scientific issues. For instance, political and social systems based on fundamen-talist interpretations of religious texts might well be under-mined by results from geology about the age of the Earth or from biology about the evolution of man. Similarly, fascist ide-ologies may well make demands on theories of inheritance in order to support claims of racial superiority.

Thus allowing real inquiry in science is a threat to ideol-ogy—it leaves open the possibility that ideological canons can be shown to be wrong or misguided, which is exactly what, in a totalitarian context, cannot be tolerated. But even more funda-mentally, real inquiry cannot be allowed in a totalitarian con-text because such inquiry requires the cultivation of intellectual integrity. To cultivate intellectual integrity is to aspire to the truth and to attempt to avoid or uncover self-deception.

In the end, as James Conant has argued, totalitarianism cannot accept the idea of objective truth, which is the aspira-tional goal of genuine inquiry. To insist, for example, on the laws of nature in the face of the Party's denial of them is to "presuppose that somewhere or other, outside oneself, there was a 'real' world where 'real' things happened" (*1984*, p. 280) and if that is so, then it cannot be correct that—as the Party demands—"whatever happens in all minds, truly happens" (p. 280). Without the resources of Doublethink, it would not be possible to take yourself to have good reasons to believe things that are, in fact, believed simply because the Party demands it. It would not follow from the fact that the Party claims through all of its books and newspapers to have invented the airplane that the Party invented the airplane. The Party would no longer be able to control the past simply because it controls the present; but, according to Orwell, the mutability of the past is the central tenet of Ingsoc (p. 213). Basically, intellectual integrity, which is necessary for genuine inquiry, is the very opposite of Doublethink, or mechanisms of self-deception, which are necessary for totalitarianism.

Lysenko and *Nineteen Eighty-Four*

Orwell had good reasons for his belief that totalitarianism's constraining of social and political thought would extend to include scientific inquiry. Right before starting work on *Nineteen Eighty-Four*, Orwell learned of the Lysenko affair from a talk given by John Baker (*The Lost Orwell*, p. 130), where Baker cited the current state of Soviet genetics as "a vivid illustration of the degradation of science under a totalitarian regime" ("Science, Culture, and Freedom," p. 119).

Trofim Lysenko was the most prominent of a group of Soviet agrobiologists who gradually, by aligning themselves with Stalin and dialectical materialism, eradicated what had been the very proud tradition in Soviet genetics. Lysenko assumed the mantle of a peasant scientist, working in the interests of the people and maintaining that what made for "good" science was practical results. He championed a version of Lamarckism—the inheritance of acquired characteristics—that was explicitly contrary to the Mendelism then dominant among geneticists. Though Lysenko's theory was not scientifically supported and had few adherents outside of his fellow agrobiologists, Lysenko managed to convince the powers that be that it would allow for a revolution in agriculture because it would support rapid changes in the characteristics of plants—wheat could become rye.

Through a series of conferences, the Soviet political machine declared for Lysenko's theory, insisting that theories of inheritance accord with Dialectical Materialism and identifying Mendelism with fascist science. Mendelism was interpreted as holding that each person's nature was fixed and not the product of their place in the class system; and thus contrary to Marxist doctrine. Established Soviet biologists, skeptical of Lysenko's claims, became enemies of progress and, in a series of purges over the course of Lysenko's rise, many of them were killed. Orwell followed all of these developments, both while writing *Nineteen Eighty-Four* and after its publication.

For Orwell, the Lysenko affair represented the fate of science under totalitarianism. Beliefs about inheritance were no longer justified on the basis of scientific evidence. Instead, it was conformity with dialectical materialism and the dictates of the political establishment that determined what you should believe. Attempts to disagree were met with repression and alternative sources of knowledge (such as translations of Western science) were cut off; thus there were systematic attempts made to undermine traditional ways of supporting scientific beliefs.

Still, the rhetoric of science was important to Lysenko and the agrobiologists. The Soviet Union was, after all, a society founded on science where, contrary to fascist and capitalist alternatives, science was directed to meet the needs of the people. Thus a sort of doublethink was required: scientific standards had to be ignored in order to promote the new scientific society. And Marxist ideology provided the resources to justify the dismissal of any inconvenient dissenting arguments.

In the end, Lysenko's revolution in agriculture did not take place, but it wasn't until after the death of Stalin that his influence began to wane. Orwell described his intentions in *Nineteen Eighty-Four*, after its publication, as indicating "by parodying them the intellectual implications of totalitarianism." One of these implications was that, "the persecution of scientists in Russia is simply part of a logical process which should have been foreseeable 10–20 years ago" ("To Roger Senhouse," p. 488). And so, because Syme—like all true inquirers—required intellectual integrity in order to serve the party, he had to share the fate of inquiry in *Nineteen Eighty-Four*.

Scientism and Bernal

Orwell was not content to show that scientists contribute to their own eventual demise when they support totalitarianism, or to identify the mechanisms operating when they do so. He also wanted to bring out what might lead them into the absurd position of supporting political positions that were inimical to their own interests. Like Syme, they were working to support political entities that would eventually do away with them. Orwell's answer was *scientism*, or the fetishizing of science in the narrow sense.

Though an advocate for science in the broad sense, Orwell thought that a focus on the exact sciences, to the exclusion of "history or literature or the arts" could contribute to dangerous political naivety and moral bankruptcy. He resented the presumption that somehow "a chemist or a physicist, as such, is politically more intelligent than a poet or a lawyer, as such" ("What Is Science?", p. 324). To the contrary, training in the exact sciences to the exclusion of others would, he speculated, have the effect of narrowing the range of thought and generating contempt for these other branches of knowledge. The result, for the average man, would be that "his political reactions would probably be somewhat less intelligent than those of an illiterate peasant who retained a few historical memories and a fairly sound aesthetic sense" (p. 325). Instead, it was "the scientists themselves [who] would benefit by a little education" (p. 326). So, contrary to what many people at the time—including presumably the British scientists willing to ignore the persecution of journalists and historians in order to support the Soviet Regime—would maintain, Orwell did not feel that, "the world . . . would be a better place if the scientists were in control of it" (p. 324). To believe this would be a form of scientism and Orwell thought just the opposite: that the push for a scientific society and narrow scientific training would lead to moral and political outrages.

The scientist who best represented to Orwell the risks of scientism for the political mind was J.D. Bernal, the crystallographer and Communist, who played a leading role in Britain both advocating for a scientifically planned society and defending the Soviet Union. Orwell had written, midway through his work on *Nineteen Eighty-Four*, a scathing response to one of Bernal's pieces calling for co-operation with the Soviet Union in which he accused Bernal of maintaining that "nearly anything is right, if it is politically expedient" (Editorial in *Polemic*, p. 267). Additionally, he identified in Bernal's piece a connection between the "corruption of language" and the acceptance of totalitarian doctrines.

According to Orwell, Bernal was prone to the use of long, vague words that "blur the moral squalor of what is being said" and to "outright meaningless sentences" which were therefore no risk to his Marxist ideology. The intended effect of Bernal's vague and sometimes meaningless essay was to bring the reader around to support for the Soviet Union, in spite of the fact that this would require surrendering many moral standards and overlooking obvious falsehoods. Thus Bernal communicates in a real world, proto-Newspeak: his loose language facilitating the espousal of the Party line. Furthermore, according to Orwell, he invoked morality and honesty in the very process of arguing that they must be overlooked in order to reach the orthodox conclusion. He was a thus a real world counterpart to Syme—an accomplished scientist, innovator in the corruption of language, and a master of moral doublethink.

Of course Bernal did not live in a late-stage totalitarian society, and he was not vaporized like Syme or the Soviet geneticists who opposed Lysenko, still he did ultimately lose credibility and influence in political debates about the future of science because of his political commitment to Soviet Communism. His vision for a scientifically planned society serving the interests of the people and his credibility as a political voice were ultimately done in by the totalitarian regime that he had championed as a model.

Though Orwell died before he was able to witness it, Bernal was steadfast and public in his defense of Lysenko, long after almost all other non-Soviet scientists had recognized him for a fraud and enemy of science. He not only met with Lysenko, and defended him, but also publically promoted the Soviet model of science. He even penned a laudatory obituary of Stalin called "Stalin the Scientist," in which he praised the dictator's benevolent concern for "the advancement of oppressed peoples" (Andrew Brown, *J.D. Bernal*, p. 314). So whereas Syme was killed for his residual intellectual integrity, Bernal ended up surrendering whatever intellectual integrity he had, outside of his narrowly scientific pursuits, to his political commitments.

It's worth teasing out the extent to which Bernal's susceptibility to self-deception in the form of both corrupt language and Marxist doublethink might issue from his scientism. Scientism shows up, according to Orwell, as contempt for other departments of knowledge—the assumption that insofar as anything can be really known or taken seriously, it must be known scientifically (in a more or less narrow sense). When this is coupled with the old idea that there is an unbridgeable gap between scientifically accessible facts and values or moral judgments it leads to the thought that there aren't really facts at all in those vast domains of inquiry that are infused with human values. So morality and history, literature and art, are not anchored to the world in the satisfying way that an x-ray diffraction pattern is; they are matters of perspective, subject to reinterpretation, and can be manipulated in the interest of expediency. This can lead to a sort of callous, dismissive pragmatism in politics, of the sort shown by Bernal. As Orwell puts it:

> The friends of totalitarianism in this country usually tend to argue that since absolute truth is not obtainable, a big lie is no worse than a little lie. It is pointed out that all historical records are biased and inaccurate, or, on the other hand, that modern physics has proved that what seems to us the real world is an illusion, so that to believe in the evidence of one's senses is simply vulgar philistinism. (*Inside the Whale and Other Essays*, p. 165)

Without any unbiased truths to pursue, the historian and the poet, the journalist and the ethicist should be mere rhetorical servants to the scientifically planned classless society. Of course in Bernal's case, his willingness to reinterpret the facts to fit his own political agenda extended even to other domains of the exact sciences, such as genetics.

As suggested above, in rejecting scientific theories or moral principles that interfered with his politics, Bernal was aided by techniques of self-deception very much like those that Orwell described in *Nineteen Eighty-Four*. Marxism, for Bernal, was "the science of the laws governing the development of nature and society," which, in light of his scientism, justified taking it as the last word in matters of politics and society. It also, according to his biographer, provided Bernal with "a dogma that would not be refuted because it was all-encompassing, convoluted, and vague" (*J.D. Bernal*, p. 317). This allowed, in Bernal's mind, for the scientifically justified selective dismissal of inconvenient truths, such as the evidence for Mendelism.

Perhaps, as Thomas Kuhn once suggested, scientists like Bernal must be particularly adept at reconciling theories with recalcitrant facts, and so Bernal found ways to overlook the evidence for Mendelism in order to maintain his commitment to the correct science of society. So, just as Syme was a master of Doublethink, able to invoke the absence of objective reality in order to genuinely believe whatever absurdity the Party demanded of him, Bernal's scientistic dismissal of the legitimacy of other areas of inquiry, coupled with his vague appeals to Marxism, allowed him to continue to support the Soviet Regime in spite of its assaults on biological science. Moral outrages, in turn, could be evaded or ignored by the sort of vague

Marxist euphemisms and party line sloganeering that so outraged Orwell.

This is the real-world parallel of Newspeak, where the
degradation of language and writing contributed to the rise of
totalitarianism. Once scientism leads to the thought that there
is no such thing as honest inquiry in value-laden domains,
there is no longer a place for intellectual integrity in those
fields. And without a commitment to intellectual integrity,
wispy philosophical theory and degraded language were
enough to lubricate the descent into self-deception. So it is
Bernal's scientism, manifest in his willingness to dismiss the
legitimacy of historical or value-laden claims to knowledge and
his linguistic looseness that made it easy for him to end up
undermining himself.

Orwell, Science, and Society Today

Though society today does not much resemble the late-stage
totalitarianism that Orwell envisioned in *Nineteen Eighty-
Four*, his insights about the influence of ideology on science
should still concern us. Whatever pretense we once had that
science could remain above the fray of party politics has long
since disappeared with the emergence of partisan divisions in
the acceptance of, for example, climate change and evolution-
ary biology.

It would not have surprised Orwell that ideological differences in our news sources and history books would eventually
show up in our science as well. In the context of enforced orthodoxies, intellectual integrity is undermined, and when we
accept or expect self-deception in journalism or history, we
open the door to the complete loss of the distinction between
genuine inquiry and advocacy or pseudo-inquiry. Shouts of
"Fake News" eventually become shouts of "Junk Science" and
the prospects for basing our political decisions on honest
attempts to understand the world are lost in a political shouting match.

Employing the rhetoric of science is still useful, and so as
with Lysenko we can expect the absurd spectacle of party-line
hacks being appointed to run scientific agencies from which
they subsequently purge any vestiges of genuine inquiry.
Resisting the devolution of our politics into a state where it is

completely disengaged from the world it is intended to govern requires, according to Orwell, respect for inquiry in all its forms. The poet, the journalist and the historian, no less than the scientist, must all be supported in their efforts to get to the truth.

Orwell's concerns about scientism should also continue to resonate with us, albeit in new guises. Scientism is a version of the ancient human folly of supposing that because you're good with a hammer, everything must be a nail. In the mid-twentieth century, after science had helped to end World War II, the thought that science or scientists might solve all our problems if we would just put them in charge had some broad cultural appeal. Some of that is still with us, particularly among scientists, some of whom are still willing to blunder about in fields that they barely understand, content with their contempt for the subject matter.

It is commonplace, for instance, to cloak substantial, controversial ethical judgments under the guise of scientific cost-benefit analysis (Stephen Gardiner, *A Perfect Moral Storm*, Chapter 8). And the sad, Bernal-esque spectacle of scientists leveraging credibility gained in one domain of science (usually, like Bernal, physics) to attack other scientific fields in support of some grander political agenda is still with us. Examples are Freeman Dyson's dismissals of mainstream climate science while advocating for over-the-top technological fixes for the accumulation of atmospheric carbon (see Goodwin, "Volatile Spirits") and the work of free-market, physicist "merchants of doubt" (hired by the tobacco companies) to undermine the epidemiological studies establishing the risks of smoking are good examples (Oreskes and Conway, *Merchants of Doubt*).

Academic administrators are happy enough to encourage this sort of thing by promoting STEM education at the expense of ethics, history, and the arts, thereby cultivating the contempt and ignorance that encourage scientism. Still, it is hard to feel that this is an era where the cultural currency of science is being overestimated. Instead, at least in the United States, there is a new hammer in town. Now the presumption seems to be that the world would be a better place if only the marketer, the manager, or the businessman were in charge. This has all the risks of scientism in that it promotes narrowness of thought and fuels contempt for fields of inquiry that are important for sane and humane social and political development.

However, it is not clear that the businessman and the marketer must cultivate what ultimately made the scientist unfit for a life of enforced orthodoxy—intellectual integrity. If not, then perhaps we have entered the era of bullshit, when we embrace as our political model the mastery of self-deception, and we can all, finally, learn to love Big Brother.[1]

21
Controlling Thought through Tweets

Edwardo Pérez

How do you control someone else's thoughts? How do you get people to think what you want them to think and believe what you want them to believe—even if what you want them to think and believe is demonstrably false, defies logic, and is ultimately harmful to their individual psychology, natural instincts, and physical being?

And, how do you make someone think that everything you're wanting them to do is being done out of their own devotion to your cause? The genius of George Orwell's *1984* is that his answer wasn't simply brainwashing, nor was it some sort of fanciful science-fiction solution where people are mind-controlled by a mad scientist, programmed by evil computers, hypnotized by some being with psychic powers, or possessed by alien spirits. Orwell's solution was realistic, rooted in human history, and depicted with horrifying plausibility, rendering it not just possible but probable—perhaps this is why we still constantly refer to many aspects of our world as Orwellian.

Orwell's solution is also elegantly complex: guided by a political philosophy (Ingsoc), the Inner Party (symbolized by Big Brother) controls the Outer Party through a mixture of constructed language (Newspeak), cognitive dissonance (Doublethink), constant surveillance (telescreens), relentless enforcement (the Thought Police, the various Ministries), behavior modification (the Junior Anti-Sex League, Two Minutes Hate, Room 101), and revisionist history (the work of various Departments). The result is a society in which people believe what they know to be false and act in a manner that conforms to the Party's desires, not their own. Sounds a lot like what happens on social media, especially on Twitter.

Of all the social media platforms we have, Twitter is one of the most effective vehicles we can use for shaping the thoughts of users and followers—emojis have become Newspeak, hashtags have become Doublethink, and we're constantly tempted (if not ordered by the Twitter Thought Police) to follow, follow, follow.

As O'Brien tells Winston in *1984*, "Whatever the Party holds to be truth *is* truth. It is impossible to see reality except by looking through the eyes of the Party." Could we say that whatever our Twitter feed holds to be truth is truth? Is it impossible to see reality except through whatever hashtags are trending? Are our thoughts controlled by those we follow? Do we control the thoughts of those who follow us? Let's take a closer look at the relationship between Twitter and *1984* and let's begin with Speech Act Theory.

He Who Controls the Past Controls the Future

Speech Act Theory, outlined by J.L. Austin (1911–1960) and refined by John Searle, suggests that our communication doesn't just communicate, it performs. So, a speech act is defined as a *performative utterance* with three levels: the locution (what is said); the illocution (what is intended); and the perlocution (the effect of what is said). For example, consider the slogans of the Party: "War is Peace, Freedom is Slavery, Ignorance is Strength." As a locution, we can suggest that the literal meaning of each phrase is paradoxical. And, we can see how the intention (the illocution) is to produce an effect (a perlocution) of getting you to not just define peace as war (or freedom as slavery or ignorance as strength) but to feel as though these paradoxes are natural.

For the Party, war is natural, slavery is natural, ignorance is natural—because war is reality, slavery is the way things are, and ignorance is life in Oceania. An early scene between Syme and Winston illustrates this process.

Syme's job is to work on revising the Newspeak dictionary; he's working on the Eleventh Edition. As Syme tells Winston, the goal isn't to add words (as new editions of dictionaries often do), but to cut them. What's significant is that the process Syme describes resembles both the nature of Speech Act Theory and the nature of Twitter. Consider Syme's explanation: "Don't you see that the whole aim of Newspeak is to narrow the range of thought? In the end we shall make thoughtcrime literally impossible, because there will be no words in which to express it." Sounds like Twitter, doesn't it?

Although Twitter has expanded from one hundred and forty characters to two hundred and eighty characters, the range of thought possible on Twitter is limited. Even the use of links and jpegs function as a shorthand form of communication, focusing thought rather than expanding it. The advent of emojis replaces words with symbols (are we going back to hieroglyphics?) and Internet slang replaces words with abbreviations (like LOL and OMG), creating a whole new language (that arguably includes its own grammar, syntax, and protocol) that must be learned before being employed. Twitter functions like Newspeak by limiting the possibilities of thought to whatever fits in a tweet and by forcing users and followers to adapt to a new form of communication designed around symbols with fixed meanings. Everything is truncated, stripped of nuance and reduced to basic, fundamental reference.

For Speech Act Theory, if there are no words to express certain concepts, then locutions become limited, too. Logically, so do illocutions and perlocutions. The effect of all this diminishing of language produces a ripple effect throughout society. In *1984*, as Syme explains, this means the Party would eventually have to change their slogans. As he reasons:

> How could you have a slogan like 'Freedom is slavery' when the concept of freedom has been abolished? The whole climate of thought will be different. In fact there will be no thought, as we understand it now. Orthodoxy means not thinking—not needing to think. Orthodoxy is unconsciousness.

It's frightening to think that thinking will cease (or maybe, as some of our Twitter feeds show, it's already happened). In the framework of Speech Act Theory, if thinking is eliminated then perhaps so is locution and illocution—because what's said and what's intended is already determined. Only perlocution, the effect, would matter—or is that determined, too?

This is the orthodoxy Syme describes and what's important is that it recasts the very nature of a Speech Act. If the effect of language is all that matters—and language is reduced to a form where effects are predetermined to the point that thought is not necessary—then a Speech Act is no longer a Speech Act, it's a Speech Response. This is how the Two Minutes Hate works. Isn't this also how Twitter works? How many of us Tweet (or text) a single emoji or cyber-slang abbreviation in response to something? When tweets go viral, are we blindly following whatever hashtags are trending, retweeting popular tweets out of habit or because Twitter demands it? Do we think when we do this? Or is our response conditioned like the citizens in Oceania?

When we follow and retweet without thinking we don't act, we react, removing ourselves from any process of thought. If thought does remain, it's more declarative than deliberative as we parrot the positions of others. Tweeting becomes assertion, a way of claiming without demonstration or debate. Not only does thought no longer matter, neither does truth or fact. Tweeting makes it so. But if reality is created and thought is eliminated, what happens to meaning? Is meaning created or eliminated?

Happiness Is Better

The realm of the philosophy of language has seen several distinct theories of linguistic and non-linguistic meaning advanced in an effort to explain what is and isn't conveyed through communication. To keep things focused, let's look at two general theories of meaning: *semantic theory*, which tries to explain the meaning of specific utterances, and *foundational theory*, which tries to explain how languages (and the symbols used to create an utterance) derive their meaning.

Julia gives Winston a note which simply reads: "I love you." What does Julia's note mean? As a semantic theorist, we'd likely debate the possible meanings of the word "love" (because we'd assume the "I" refers to Julia and the "you" refers to Winston) and we'd take into account issues such as reference, relationship, and context—because assessing meaning isn't as simple or as clear as you might think (maybe that's why most of us simply assert it). We'd also realize that semantic meaning isn't universal when it comes to natural languages.

It's why things get lost in translation (or why emojis and cyberslang make no sense unless you're tuned in). No two languages contain the same set of words, so meaning is never fixed, it's always interpreted—and for a word like "love" (which borders on the ineffable) there are many possible meanings.

A quick search of "love" on dictonary.com and thesaurus.com yields twenty-one definitions and forty-seven main synonyms—there are also ninety-four adjectives, and another one-hundred and forty-eight additional synonyms (as well as fifteen antonyms) related to love. There's enough multiplicity of meaning that love is effectively rendered meaningless. Think about it, when Julia says "I love you," what does she really mean?

The best way to fix the meaning of a word like love is to do what Syme does with Newspeak: dictate only one possible definition and one possible opposite (love and unlove) and force everyone to learn it. Syme would probably define love as *adoration for Big Brother* and unlove as *unadoration for Big Brother* (or maybe as *adoration for someone other than Big Brother*, which would be strongly discouraged). Okay, but we still don't know what Julia's note means, at least not from a semantic perspective. Let's try *foundational theory*.

Staying focused on love, we'd want to understand the nature of the word and why Julia felt the need to use it—why not "I admire you" or "I fancy you"? We could delve into mental representation theories to examine Julia's mental state to understand her use of the word "love" and the meaning she intended. We could also investigate non-mentalist theories, which examine the use of expressions through causal origins and social norms, among other things. We could then ask: what caused the word love (and its way-too-many meanings) to be created in the first place?

We might be able to offer several answers to the mentalist question. Julia seemed nervous, anxious, rebellious, promiscuous, bold, risky, and insecure, to list a few possibilities. However, the non-mentalist question is difficult to address. How do we adequately explain the origin of any word, let alone a word such as "love"? And what are we explaining—the word or the concept? Etymologically, the word love can be traced to its Germanic and Latin roots. Conceptually, it's difficult to explain the idea of love and how this seemingly universal emotion came to be expressed in language. What we ultimately must admit is that words are arbitrary in their construction and conception because meaning is never fixed, it's always changing. We'd have to conclude—at least from a *foundational theory* standpoint—that the meaning of Julia's note is difficult to describe.

Returning to Twitter, if Julia had tweeted Winston it's doubtful the meaning of her note would be any clearer, especially if she'd framed it with a heart emoji. Which heart emoji could she have used? (💝, 💗 ,💟, 👫, 💜, 💘, 💙,☺) We'd ask the same set of questions from semantic and foundational theories of meaning and we'd be stuck trying to decipher her message. If we appealed back to Speech Act Theory, we'd be unable to figure out the intention and effect Julia was trying to achieve unless we first understood what she meant by "love" (is there really a difference in meaning between "I love you" and 😲?)

Even if we allow Julia to assert to Winston that she loves him, we can't say for certain what she means unless the meaning of the word "love" is fixed. And, if we judge the meaning based on Julia's actions and Winston's actions, we'd still be confused. Both Julia and Winston are in a rebellious mood, but Julia seems to be wanting physical love, while Winston desires an emotional bond. In other words, how Julia uses the word (as an invitation for sex) and how Winston reads it (as an affirmation of his defiance) are two different things. Winston wanted to viciously harm Julia before she passed him her note, which adds another layer of perplexity.

So, is meaning created or eliminated? Perhaps both are true if we consider that meaning is created and eliminated through assertion. To understand how this works, let's look at a concept called *mindcasting*, an idea conceived as a criticism of Twitter yet one that also seems to sum up the elaborate process used by the Party to control thought in *1984*—in a way that differs from concepts such as brainwashing, indoctrination, and conditioning, which use physically and psychologically harmful techniques.

Imagine a Boot Stamping on a Human Face Forever

New York University journalism professor Jay Rosen explains *mindcasting* as the sharing of substantial and significant thoughts, observations, and questions through tweets. If the

Party in *1984* had relied on Twitter instead of Telescreens to disseminate their messages, they would've simply tweeted *Freedom is Slavery* or *#Freedomisslavery*—and following the Party and Big Brother would've been mandatory (though it's doubtful they'd have more followers than Katy Perry or Taylor Swift).

What's paramount is that the Party isn't making an argument. They're just proclaiming *Freedom is Slavery* with enough rhetorical force that the assertion becomes truth. This is how *mindcasting* works. Its goal is to influence followers by broadcasting thoughts as facts, positions, or rhetorical questions and suggesting or implying that such claims (and inquiries) must be believed (or are believable at face value). Argument is absent, only assertion matters. This resembles Speech Act Theory, suggesting that what seems to matter most is the effect (the perlocution) of the tweet (the locution). This is how meaning is both created and eliminated. It's also how Julia's note worked.

While we concluded earlier that Julia asserting "I love you" to Winston doesn't answer the question of meaning, *mindcasting* doesn't seem concerned with semantic or foundational meaning. Rather, it's concerned with the meaning it creates or eliminates. The power of *mindcasting*, then, rests in its ability to claim truth and compel others to believe it. This is what Julia does to Winston. She effectively compels him to believe that she loves him. Consider how it happens: Julia, wearing a cast on her arm, falls down. Winston feels sorry for her and when she holds out her hand he helps her up. In this moment, Julia passes him a note. As Orwell narrates:

> Nevertheless it had been very difficult not to betray a momentary surprise, for in the two or three seconds while he was helping her up the girl had slipped something into his hand. There was no question that she had done it intentionally. It was something small and flat. As he passed through the lavatory door he transferred it to his pocket and felt it with the tips of his fingers. It was a scrap of paper folded into a square.

It takes Winston a while to read it and during his procrastination he considers the possibilities, thinking Julia is either working with the Thought Police or with the Brotherhood, believing that whatever was written on the note had political meaning and meant death. Even more telling is his reaction after reading it. Winston's stunned. Not only can he not work, he's consumed by the note to the point that his day becomes unbearable. He longs to be alone so he can think more clearly (especially about how to meet with Julia) and he begins to feel a deep desire to "stay alive."

In the end, the meaning of the note doesn't matter as much as its effect. Winston is a changed man and he conforms to every instruction Julia gives him so they can meet and eventually consummate their newfound relationship. Had Winston adhered to the Party, he would've simply put the note down the nearest memory hole and never given it a second thought and that's what's interesting about Winston's reaction. On one hand, he's overthinking the note to the point of become paranoid. On the other hand, he can't think clearly enough to discern a proper course of action. When he stops thinking and simply follows Julia, he becomes *mindcasted*. He believes she loves him and he then believes he loves her.

It's debatable whether they really love each other, but as far as *mindcasting* is concerned it doesn't matter. What matters is that Winston believes they love each other. Belief is perhaps the most important element when it comes to *mindcasting*, assertion, and the various theories we've discussed—because none of them would work without belief. Let's examine this though Winston's torturous encounter with O'Brien.

Orthodoxy Means Not Thinking

Winston does his best to resist O'Brien's horrific physical and psychological torture, heroically arguing with O'Brien often and getting tortured in return. Yet, O'Brien's observations on power are eventually proven true, at least for *1984*'s narrative (until you read the appendix, which suggests that the Party ultimately didn't succeed).

O'Brien eventually breaks Winston, causing Winston to betray Julia, not just because of his fear of rats, but because he finally chooses to accept the reality O'Brien constructs—not just accept it, but believe it. As O'Brien explains, "Power is in tearing human minds to pieces and putting them together again in new shapes of your own choosing." That's exactly what O'Brien does to Winston at the end of *1984*; he reshapes Winston's mind. He *mindcasts* him to the point that Winston actually believes he loves Big Brother.

First, O'Brien plants seeds of doubt in Winston, getting Winston to begin questioning what he knows and how he knows it. A great example of this is when O'Brien asks Winston to repeat the Party slogan regarding the past. Winston recites: "Who controls the past controls the future; who controls the present controls the past." Winston believes that the past (his knowledge of it) exists in written documents and in his memory. O'Brien counters by suggesting to Winston that since the Party controls all written documents and all memories, the Party (not the individual and not the books) controls the past.

Next, having convinced Winston that the Party controls memory, O'Brien proceeds to challenge Winston's belief that two plus two equals four. Winston fights this but after enduring enough pain, Winston eventually relents. But, O'Brien doesn't want Winston to just say two plus two equals five, he wants Winston to believe it, to actually see five fingers when O'Brien holds up four fingers—and, to be flexible enough to believe whatever O'Brien wants him to believe if the answer (on another day) is three instead of five. As O'Brien reasons: "Sometimes they are five. Sometimes they are three. Sometimes they are all of them at once."

O'Brien's point, as Winston later accepts, is that anything could be true so long as you believe it's true. This is how *mindcasting*, assertion, and Twitter work. We broadcast our likes, dislikes, beliefs, and thoughts on anything that captures our attention and everything that means something to us, planting our thoughts into other people's minds, hoping they'll believe not just what we believe, but what we want them to believe.

The Object of Power Is Power

So, what does all of this mean? For *1984*, O'Brien's torture, Julia's note, the Party's slogans and propaganda (along with the concepts of Newspeak and Doublethink) fundamentally change Winston, draining every last ounce of his identity and memory (and notions of rebellion) until he becomes a mindless follower of Big Brother.

Twitter might not be as horrific or as overtly dehumanizing (or is it?), but it's certainly efficient and effective. Given its nature, Twitter has the potential to be a more powerful tool for disseminating thoughts to a mass audience—and,

more importantly, for shaping the beliefs of a mass audience—
than any of the techniques used by O'Brien or the Party.
Twitter's current use in politics and news media illustrates
this all too well.

Certainly, the notion of intentionally *mindcasting* our
thoughts on Twitter presents an interesting commentary on
where our society is at, where it's been, and where it's headed.
Given the prevalence of so-called Twitter bots spreading disinformation and creating false realities throughout the world, as
University of Southern California researcher Emilio Ferrara
observes, Twitter seems to resemble the world of *1984* perhaps
more than we would like.

Ferrara finds that automated bots run nearly fifteen percent of all Twitter accounts. Studying the use of Twitter bots in
US, French, and German elections, Ferrara suggests that there
could be possible state and non-state actors utilizing bots for
political means and that such influence is just beginning. While
Ferrara suggests it's too early to combat Twitter bots directly
(because doing so might cause more damage), the mere contemplation of such a tactic suggests that our future wars may
not be fought with soldiers on battlefields, but rather with bots
in a virtual theater. Indeed, if we don't at least recognize the
danger Twitter (and social media) poses, we may all eventually
suffer Winston's fate.

To appropriate the Party's slogan: whoever controls Twitter
controls our thoughts, and whoever controls our thoughts controls our beliefs and our reality.

22
The Irrelevance of Truth

Jan Kyrre Berg Friis

We all lie! We lie because we believe we have *reasons* not to tell the truth, or are too embarrassed to be honest; for some it's a thrill to lie and get away with it. When we lie we know we're at odds with one of the most persuasive moral imperatives in our culture. Our trust is based on truth: the judicial system is too; in science and philosophy we pursue the true representation of the world; in religion it is what defines the essence of belief.

Nietzsche's insight on the matter is interesting. He says these "reasons" are due to our cause-creating drive: "we want to have a reason for feeling as we do"—it never suffices just feeling as we do—we only acknowledge this fact, and become conscious of it, when we have given it a motivation. And it is more—these "accompanying occurrences in consciousness", as he calls these ideas, are also brought up by memory. We have a "habituation to certain causal interpretation", which actually hampers and even prohibits any deeper understanding of this phenomena of *reason*. Sometimes we do not know why we lie, or that we lie, or tell the truth, or know what the truth is. Truth is only our own truths, nothing else.

It is necessary to understand more of the psychological basis of truth. Friedrich Nietzsche's view on truth and idols is inspiring. Nietzsche was throughout his relatively short life criticizing Western dogmatic thinking. His attacks were specifically directed towards dogma within "institutions of belief" like Christianity, Philosophy, and Science—all of these having various directions consisting of traditions subdivided into schools of thought with contradicting opinions on knowledge,

243

methodology, and God. But never mind these internal differences. All are at the bottom of it aiming at discovering the *truth* of the matter, of any matter. Nietzsche's own way of philosophizing was *Áskesis* and not the pursuit of truth. His Zarathustra sought personal transformation, his philosophy was as a meditative *praxis*—a process in which there is a gradual spiritual transformation of the philosopher. As the Japanese Zen master Dogen wrote in his *Shobogenzo*, "a Buddhist should neither argue superiority or inferiority of doctrines, but only be mindful of authenticity or inauthenticity of practice." Nietzsche, who was influenced by Theravada Buddhism and Arthur Schopenhauer's Buddhist leanings, rejected the truth-seeking paradigm. What is needed is instead a re-evaluation of all values:

> What then is truth? A mobile army of metaphors, metonyms, and anthropomorphisms—in short, a sum of human relations, which have been enhanced, transposed, and embellished poetically and rhetorically, and which after long use seem firm, canonical, and obligatory to a people: truths are illusions about which one has forgotten that is what they are; metaphors which are worn out and without sensuous power; coins which have lost their pictures and now matter only as metal, no longer as coins.
>
> We still do not know where the urge for truth comes from; for as yet we have heard only of the obligation imposed by society that it should exist: to be truthful means using the customary metaphors—in moral terms, the obligation to lie according to fixed convention, to lie herd-like in a style obligatory for all . . .
>
> Truth is in-between people; it is a *relation* that is played out between lovers and enemies, friends and colleagues. Truth is an event realized the moment we are talking and acting. That which was most real to us at some earlier time has during years of living, and of university, of professional training, lost its shine. Our *reasons* have taken on subtler shapes – we have taken refuge in idols—substituted that fragile lived illogical experience with theory, ideals, and beliefs, and our *will to truth* has become transformed, we have become pursuers of generalizations and abstractions.

Nietzsche rejected the claim that *truth is simple*. Truth is not simple, we try to define and apply it as if it is a straightforward matter of logic—as a validation of information sifted through rational discourse. Philosophers fail to agree on what truth is because of the complexities of the event that always will prompt us to redefine whatever is perceived to be contained in the event, and to which we would like to refer the value of truth. *All our efforts to simplify truth* must therefore be part of, to use Nietzsche's bold words, "a compound lie."

All this talk about the *nature* of truth is puzzling. As stated, truths are *relational*—in daily life a truth or its absence occurs in a communicative interaction between persons. Truths are embedded in speech-acts between persons. Truth is also something we consider when we think of ourselves; it is what I am telling myself that I am, *truth is in my belief*, and belief is conviction. Truth is what we make it out to be. Truth is within the context. Truth is a perspective.

We have to ask whether truth is just a figment of the human imagination and creativity: is it but a product of millennia of storytelling over the campfire? In that case, how much are we influenced and manipulated by the world around us—by people and the continuous Orwellian newsfeed of the internet and the news media? Are we able to dislodge from our socially and culturally determined likes and dislikes and still retain an authentic and spontaneous openness to the world and everything in it necessary for an authentic truth-relation to unfold?

Buddha said the world is an illusion, by that he meant the way we humans *perceive* and *conceptually distort* everything we sense and think. We don't *always* know when we're telling untruths. Besides having the best intentions or reasons to lie we are also telling untruths because our mind-bodies are biologically "pre-programmed" and culturally modified to *process* everything that is perceived and communicated. Information is lost in the processing. Also, the processing is tacit, it is silent, and unconscious. We have a personal history of social and cultural learning—we have been "formed", and we have acquired a "lifeworld"—a background of information for the thinking that determines everything perceived and said. The neurological "background" consists of all kinds of information, experiences, skills, and whatnot somehow stored in body and brain and from where the synapses of pre-conscious mind operate or fire up to fill in perceptual gaps and holes with meaning and context. The perceptual content—the content we are conscious of, is not always in accordance with that reality that is not us, not me, or you.

Knowing Ourselves

We have a conflicting self. We confuse the "self" with the identity of me. Nietzsche states, "We remain unknown to ourselves, we seekers after knowledge, even to ourselves: and with good reason. We have never sought after ourselves—so how should we one day find ourselves?"

Nietzsche continues in *Human, All Too Human*, "Direct self-observation is not nearly sufficient for us to know ourselves: we require history, for the past continues to flow within us in a hundred waves; we ourselves are, indeed, nothing but that which at every moment we experience of this continual flowing...." It is as the Zen masters teach: The Self is undetermined, which means not settled, indefinite. How can it be otherwise: we are, after all, ceaselessly in process!

Our social and cultural history, so important for the context of the truth-relation between persons, must be the one to blame for corrupting our minds. An essential episode in the cultural history of Western society happened when philosophy, science and Christianity absorbed the Cartesian notion of *ego cogito*, when we found that we have a consciously rational self, that we possess an *"I"* that is in control. It can be argued that we are *never* in control of the processes preceding consciousness, and that which is in consciousness cannot be controlled because it is the past.

Since the seventeenth century, truth has been bound up with truthfulness: what convinces us must *correspond* to our belief that it is true—in this context we are all like Hermann Hesse "confessors, obligated to truth and sincerity." Human interaction with the world is necessarily perceptual and communicative. Today science knows of 180 cognitive biases distorting perceptions, thought, and judgments—effectively blocking access to any "objective truth" and thus also makes us lie in absolute oblivion of whatever the truth is. What we encounter in our mind, what we *understand* is—as Nietzsche declared—only interpretations, mere models of the world—including the Self and its model, the "I."

Cognitive biases are like skills, they are tacit and present us with framings for every act of the "mind-body-being" we are. As hinted earlier, some biases are biological, others, like most skills —understood here as belonging to the domain of tacit knowledge, are social-cultural. Ironically, many "biases" have a function. For instance, information processing shortcuts connected with filling-in, which are conjoining the biological and cultural in almost perfect harmony, yet filling-ins are only capable of rendering probable outcomes, just enough to act upon, they are never truthful representations of the unfolding event. Again, this may indicate that mind's functions have little to do with representation at all. Whatever "representation" there is is of course a "distortion" and yet it is an *interpretation* we accept as "true" yet never will be able to reveal as "not entirely true."

Objective and Subjective

To forget (or rather to let ourselves get distracted from the fact) that each and every one of us, has a history that is very much present in its tacit potentiality as information source in our daily lives through our dreams and thoughts, is to *withdraw* from Being. A cultivation of reflectivity and logic is to embrace a thinking that has become *blind* to its preconscious ground of perpetual process. Martin Heidegger feared that the increasing dependency on technology and science would transform us as humans by the covering up of our personal background of lived experience.

To start with, emphasis is put on the objective world, making subjective experience into a problem of metaphysics and scientific methodology. Eventually we forget the importance of the background. The result is one-dimensional thinking oblivious to its basis, trained in calculative data-processing, finding technological technicalities the work of scientific reason and thus important. A thinking that is designing, building, calculating, systematizing, and computing has become, as John Caputo writes, a device to operate on a world of things already reified into a network of ends. What has been brought into scientific thinking is an understanding of a mind whose activity is directed towards the natural world understood as resource and human ingenuity as the mastery of it.

In Heidegger's view, it is the practical and solution oriented scientific and technological rationality that draws the curtain. What was worrying for Heidegger was the unbridled optimism among natural scientists, who believed that the natural sciences were the only way forward. For Heidegger, it was the objectifying, instrumental, and impersonal approach towards nature that constituted the threat to the future of humanity; as John Steffney writes, "traditional rationality (metaphysics) has been concerned with beings and not with the illumination process as such, with ontic matters at the expense of ontological ones." If this is correct, what happens to truth as truthfulness, to honesty, and sincerity? What is a rational world like?

Alternative Truth

George Orwell's view of a technological-totalitarian society bent on the manufacturing of alternative truth is described in the passages about the Ministry of Truth in his novel *1984*. The Ministry of Truth controls all news, entertainment, education, and the arts—all important areas concerning the formation of young minds. "War is Peace; Freedom is Slavery; Ignorance is Strength." Outrageous statements, yet we're not offended—not anymore. There are always a handful of regimes controlling their populations through terror, hate, and intolerance; there are democratically elected leaders of states lying in their teeth.

Getting attention and thereby the ear of people means you can influence big numbers of people to think in a certain way, that will support and strengthen the base and give credence to the purported "truth." Adam Gopnik in *The New Yorker*, has compared the alternative truther Donald Trump and his politics to Orwell's *1984*: "The blind, blatant disregard for truth is offered without even the sugar-façade of sweetness of temper or equableness or entertainment—offered not with a sheen of condescending consensus but in an ancient tone of rage, vanity, and vengeance. Trump is pure tagging authoritarian id." So Orwell got it right then, "that this kind of authoritarianism . . . rests on lies told so often, and so repeatedly, that fighting the lie becomes not simply more dangerous but more exhausting than repeating it. . . . It is, above all, a way of asserting power."

Trump and Nietzsche

Friedrich Nietzsche talks about truth as a *commitment to truthfulness*, to a "will to truth"—which is subordinated to the human *will to power*—which simply is the *will to life*—and this will to life is a power quite different from the Trumpian truthism scheme. It is after all humans who decide what is true or not true, the difference between Trump and Nietzsche is whether one is honest or not, truthful or not. People like Trump need to dominate and like to believe that they are in control; truth and lies become means to an end. Trumpists violate the trust people have to their fellow man being truthful and honest; okay, we can disagree what the truth may be, but the difference is not caused by an intentional lie, but by difference of perspective, personal knowledge, or background.

People are thus at all times living or coping with alternating realities each with their own inherent logic of truth. In this sense we can agree with Nietzsche when he stated that truth is an illusion that humanity has forgotten is an illusion. Truth "runs through practically every area of inquiry" and is now part and parcel of culture in general, according to Thomas Nagel, and because of this, we may add, we have the divide among scholars about its nature.

All this scholarly ambiguity makes us yawn and ask, is not everything relative anyway? Carlos Prado states that we cannot dismiss relativism altogether. It is after all difficult to prove that truth is a depiction of how things are, still more difficult is *what* is true, sentences or propositions? Nature or reality does not come neatly wrapped up in "convenient facts or state of affairs to which we can relate particular beliefs and sentences"—we don't even agree to what a "fact" relates to.

Torturers and Victims

In South Africa, it was the Truth and Reconciliation Commission which, according to Shiv Visvanathan, "raised some of the most profound philosophical questions of our time." The task of the commission was to retrieve the truth about the nature of violence that took place during the years of apartheid—"the relation between torturer and victim, the politics of memory, the question of forgiveness, and the reconstruction of justice . . . the aim was to salvage some truth and some justice." However, the attempts the Commission has made to bring tyrants and torturers to justice have in most countries failed.

Visvanathan is within the context of "truth and justice" also referring to the question of evidence and its relation to the observer. The scientific observer, observing from within a frame of scientific method and experimentation, is understood to have a privileged perspective to that which is about to be observed (let us not forget what already have been said about perception, bias, and background).

It is assumed that the split between the observer and that which is observed is important to the value-neutral outcome of the observation, it is therefore important to be "disembodied" and "methodologically distant," to use Visvanathan's words. The split between observers and observed is also strengthened by the use of technologies that enables the scientist to penetrate levels of matter unreachable by sense perceptions. That which is observed is not "nature" *per se* but a mediation, an image, a measure, a depiction of that which we want to investigate—and when the observer eventually is able to "read" (interpret) the mediation (after training and practice), the sheer quantity of information in the mediation is so huge that powerful computer technology is necessary in order to process it so that someone can make sense of it.

The split between the observer and the observed is twofold. What Shiv Visvanathan is directing our attention to is the new kind of observer introduced along with the work of the Truth Commissions, namely the witness as spectator. Here it is not objectified truth that is sought for. The witness is a spectator and sometimes even also a victim, as Visvanathan writes, the witness and victim not only sees but is acted upon, he is observer of but also a *site* for violence—crucial here is the state of the victim-observer's memory. We're all observers and victims; we observe but are also sites for truth ourselves, often the two don't correspond. Memory, operating at different times within the event that has unfolded, is adding nuances that are additions to the history. In this sense we're approaching a status of truth that is so personal and so immensely complex psychologically speaking that it is impossible to tell the outcome.

Truth and Post-Truth

Modern philosophical discussions, as already mentioned, reveal polar views on the question of truth. This has everything to do with truth being somehow a truth-to-nature relation or not since the first view concerns truth as accurate depiction of whatever is the case, whereas the other is for instance about truth as socially constructed. Following and tracing the arguments of Thomas Nagel, Richard Rorty, and Carlos Prado we end up with John Locke and Immanuel Kant as determining the modern problem of truth. According to Locke truth is agreement between concepts and the way we describe these concepts. We have placed our trust in a distinction about how we experience and represent realities and how these *represented* realities somehow also exist independently of the observer. Prado says this opens up a gap between "ideas and their objects that does not exist between words and ideas." How things are "in themselves" is something that Immanuel Kant introduces, which makes accessing the external reality as it is in-itself problematic, there is no truth, no reality that has not been sifted through the mind of the observer. Prado says Kant permanently changed the debate by turning our *understanding* of perception upside down—from having direct sense data of the world as it truly is to perception as a rather complicated interaction between perceiver and world. We are therefore not able to describe reality as it is in itself; we have instead a product of various processes of body, mind, and perception—knowledge or truth is thus a product of physical and neurophysiological as well as psychological and cognitive factors. What exactly is true is not so clear—that is, if truth is about reality and reality is a mind-independent bundle of matters of "fact." Humans shape everything that is *knowledge* about realities, or, if you prefer a more Wittgensteinian touch—it is not we who determine the language, it is the language that determines us. In the end, Thomas Nagel writes, "hiding at the bottom of everything" said or thought or acted on, is I, the thinking, perceiving individual. Prado continues: the problem of truth has morphed into the following questions: "Whose truth?" and "Which truth?" Or are there only interpretations, as Nietzsche claimed?

Many philosophers certainly don't agree with the modern conversion of truth: we are persons coping with weird circumstances in a "post-truth world" many of us not knowing what to believe, which means us coping with events in which facts does not influence us or other people—or normatively, should not influence us, since we know very well that it is personal belief spurred on by emotion that at least partially make people act. The use of truth, the manipulation of truth, is the use and manipulation of power. We humans have never really ever been very keen on facts anyway; as Elizabeth Kolbert writes "The vaunted human capacity for reason may have more to do with winning arguments than with thinking straight." It is not a total shocker anymore, is it? People are quite irrational—even when they think they behave rationally. What we define as reason is something that has evolved, Kolbert states, because we had to resolve frictions and problems caused by living in collaborative groups; reason is thus an adaptation to a social niche and its ways of interaction. There are, as we have seen, a few design flaws. We all condone information confirming our theories and reject information that contradicts them, a tendency known as "confirmation bias," which is a well-researched example that speaks against the belief that reason is designed to generate *reliable* judgments. We easily find faults about someone else's theories but not about our own position—because, as Kolbert claims, reason evolved to prevent us from getting screwed by other members of our group. Kolbert refer to cognitive researchers Hugo Mercier and Dan Sperber and their book *The Enigma of Reason*; here they shed light on the survival value of reason— which is *group control through work distribution*, about *winning arguments*. Reason is not so much about abstract speculation. For instance, hunting was a dangerous business and it was therefore necessary to have some kind of systematics as to whom did what each time—so that it was not the same person risking it all every time.

The "Post-Truth" findings of the cognitive scientists that Elizabeth Kolbert refers to, would be applauded by a thinker like Richard Rorty—"Post-Truth" relates to events in which objective facts does not have that impact on the public opinion instead the impact comes from the insurgence of sudden emotion but also the more long term personal beliefs that we already have established—yet here we have them confirmed by someone, perhaps someone important and powerful. This may very well be because "reason" is about sociability, as cognitive scientists Sloman and Fernbach argue in their book *The Knowledge illusion*. One of the great illusions is that we, *Homo sapiens*, believe we know more than we actually do. We stick to this belief because other people let us. This becomes very clear in view of the vast amount of technologies that surround us. Take any of them—look at it and try to describe its use, functionality and how it is put together. We realize we can't. We simply don't bother. Someone else has designed it so that I can use it easily, and my understanding of use, its perceived functionality and design melts together. Yet, there is something I clearly do not know. I do not master the engineering skills necessary to come up with all the parts needed and how they should be put together and "fueled" in order to work. So I don't know everything about the things I use.

What about politics? According to Kolbert, scientists Sloman and Fernbach insist that here we get into real trouble, they write that, as a rule, strong feelings about issues do not emerge from deep understanding. We depend on other minds that reinforce the problem. If your position is baseless and I rely on it, then my position is also baseless. However, that does not matter so much because the more people there is agreeing with us the smugger do we feel about our own position.

A third study by Jack and Sara Gorman—*Denying to the Grave*, points to the gap between what science tells us and what we tell ourselves. We resist vaccines that are made to save us from no other reason than our belief that they are dangerous. These are persistent beliefs we live by that may kill us—this is again confirmation bias. We really do not give a hoot about objective facts. So there is a split here, there are evolution generated traits pulling us toward the opinions of the crowd we identify with.

All we have is our personal history, the stories we have created for ourselves and others through life, but most importantly our imaginations. We could instead begin contemplating that there is no final authority for our beliefs and practices. Truth is prejudice. Rorty's solution, according to philosopher Eduardo Mendieta, is to give up all this truth talk and become mature and confront the contingency of our vocabularies—and we might add, confront what and why we think and act the way we do.

Hermann Hesse is definitely worth listening to when late in his long life, he wrote that "My story is not sweet and harmonious, like invented stories. It tastes of folly and bewilderment, of madness and dream, like the life of all people who no longer want to lie to themselves." And in *Demian* he concludes, "I have been and still am a seeker, but I have ceased to question stars and books; I have begun to listen to the teaching my blood whispers to me."

But that's probably not good enough if you're searching for the Truth.

23
oldthinkful duckspeak refs opposites rewrite fullwise upsub antefiling

KEITH BEGLEY

Nineteen Eighty-Four paints a picture of a terrifying dystopia. Perhaps the most disturbing thought that a philosophical reader encounters, beyond the brutalities and excesses of a totalitarian state, is the total subversion of the ideal of truth—the subversion of the notion that truth is something of intrinsic value, and that it is of value because it is an objective standard, and not merely a means to some end.

Indeed, this is a thought that George Orwell also found frightening, and one which motivated some elements of the dystopia depicted in *Nineteen Eighty-Four*. In his earlier essay, "Looking Back on the Spanish War" (1943), he put this in the following manner:

> Nazi theory indeed specifically denies that such a thing as "the truth" exists. There is, for instance, no such thing as "Science." There is only "German Science," "Jewish Science," etc. The implied objective of this line of thought is a nightmare world in which the Leader, or some ruling clique, controls not only the future but *the past*. If the Leader says of such and such an event, "It never happened"—well, it never happened. If he says that two and two are five—well, two and two are five. This prospect frightens me much more than bombs—and after our experiences of the last few years that is not a frivolous statement.

If truth were not an objective standard, most knowledge would be impossible, with perhaps the exception of an unconscious orthodoxy about what the Party demands. As such, philosophers and scientists would be out of a job or, worse, their jobs would be inconceivable. After all, there is no word for 'Philosophy' or 'Science' in Newspeak; there are merely blanket terms like 'oldthink' (logical and metaphysical concepts) and 'crimethink' (ethical and political concepts), the purpose of which is to destroy any notion of a systematic form of unorthodox thought.

Newspeak is central to the subversion of the ideal of truth. Its complete adoption allows for the possibility that we would be unable to say most of what we can say in Oldspeak. We would be unable even to think these things, in the sense of not being able to say them even silently to ourselves. This would also make it impossible for us to express certain truths and we would be unable to know them, even if we wanted to.

Despite the central place of Newspeak in the dystopia depicted in *Nineteen Eighty-Four,* the novel does not contain any actual Newspeak sentences. Instead, this is left largely to the reader's imagination with the help of a smattering of vocabulary and some examples of a hybrid language used for internal messages within the Ministry of Truth. In addition to these examples, we are provided with basic technical and theoretical descriptions of Newspeak. For me, what stands out in these passages and, indeed, throughout the novel, is the use of opposites and contradictions, and the way in which they contribute to Newspeak and underpin the central notion of doublethink.

A Word which Is Simply the Opposite of Some Other Word

In the canteen, Winston strikes up a conversation with Syme, who is a philologist of Newspeak, about his work on the Eleventh Edition of the *Newspeak Dictionary*. Syme reports that he is "on the adjectives," and then begins to expound enthusiastically about the destruction of words:

> It's a beautiful thing, the destruction of words. Of course the great wastage is in the verbs and adjectives, but there are hundreds of nouns that can be got rid of as well. It isn't only the synonyms; there are also the antonyms. After all, what justification is there for a word which is simply the opposite of some other word? A word contains its opposite in itself. Take "good", for instance. If you have a word like "good", what need is there for a word like "bad"? "Ungood" will do just as well—better, because it's an exact opposite, which the other is not. (p. 54)

Although using 'un-' to construct an opposite might be possible for some words it is not clear that it is possible or desirable for all. If you think that it's possible for something to be neither good nor bad, then you would take exception to someone saying that 'ungood' is a more than adequate replacement for 'bad'. This is because if someone were to say that something is 'ungood' or 'not good', then we would not necessarily have to interpret this to mean 'bad', because it could also mean 'neither good nor bad'.

The ethical nature of the example, at least as it appears to us in Oldspeak, somewhat muddies the waters here. A clearer example of this kind of relationship might be that between the words 'hot' and 'cold'; 'not hot' does not necessarily mean 'cold'. These kinds of opposites are called *gradable* because there is a gradation of meaning possible between them, which often matches up with a gradation or a spectrum in the world or in our experience. For example, the grades of temperature or how these temperatures feel to us, and the moral spectrum, which some people might have an intuition of, between good and bad.

Sentences that contain gradable opposites are often related to each other by what logicians call *contrariety*. For example, the sentence 'The water is hot' is *contrary* to the sentence 'The water is cold'. These sentences are said to be *contrary* to each other, rather than *contradictory*. Although 'The water is hot' implies 'The water is not cold', the reverse does not hold; the sentence 'The water is not cold' does not strictly imply 'The water is hot'. That is because the sentence 'The water is neither hot nor cold' might be true instead; the water could be neither hot nor cold.

In Newspeak, this kind of relationship cannot be constructed. The use of 'un-' to replace one side of an opposition degrades the relationship of opposition between those words and makes all of them of a similar kind logically. That is, all opposites become *ungradable* and sentences they are contained in, such as 'The water is cold' and 'The water is uncold' become logically *contradictory*.

In Newspeak, in contrast to Oldspeak, the sentence 'The water is uncold', *does* strictly imply that the water is hot or, perhaps, lacking coldness. That is because there is no gradation of meaning between 'uncold' and 'cold'. This is what Syme meant when he said that *exact opposites* are 'better' than others; they are better at restricting and destroying gradations of meaning.

Recognition of these logical relations is important to our understanding of what a speaker is saying. Indeed, some speakers seek to exploit unfamiliarity with these distinctions in order to cause us to think in an unnuanced manner, allowing them to convince us of their point of view by avoiding critical examination. For example, there are rhetorical strategies that employ the use of *false dichotomy* or *false dilemma*. These are to be found readily in political speech. Here are two famous examples from mainstream political leaders in the US and UK, which were slogans that were repeated often and in various forms:

> Either you're with us, or you're with the enemy; either you're with those who love freedom, or you're with those who hate innocent life. (George W. Bush, Fort Hood, Texas, January 3rd 2003)

This implies that someone can be either with or against and there are no neutral parties, and that either someone loves freedom or hates innocent life and there is no third position.

> It's a choice between strong and stable leadership under the Conservatives, or weak and unstable coalition of chaos led by Jeremy Corbyn. (Theresa May, at a campaign visit to Bolton, April 19th 2017)

This implies that only one of these two outcomes is possible and no others.

In light of these actual uses of opposites in Oldspeak, with-against, love-hate, stable-chaotic, it should be clear that Newspeak's use of 'un-' to degrade *gradable* opposites would create possible false dichotomies involving other *exact opposites* in the language. In fact, it would be even worse because it would be possible to express only the two sides of the dichotomy. A third or further option would not even be thinkable.

At least in Oldspeak we can communicate that there are more than two options. If this were not possible, we would not even be able to describe what a false dichotomy is, because in a certain sense there would not be any of them to describe. It is reasons such as these and others that would also prevent disciplines such as philosophy from getting started. There would be no possible critique to make of such sophistry, because the language required would not be available. Hence, oldthink and crimethink are entirely avoided in such cases.

The Spirit of Man

At first sight, it can seem like pairs of opposites are equal in their oppositeness, the only difference being which side of the opposition they name. However, opposites are often used in a way that is unequal in that one opposite can be used to refer to both sides of a distinction and, because of this fact, is used more often. This inequality of status between opposites is called *markedness*.

A simple example of markedness is the generic use of the word 'man' in Oldspeak to refer to all of humankind, for example, in the sentence 'The spirit of Man will defeat the Party'; that is, 'man' is *unmarked* because it can be used in this way while 'woman' is *marked* because it cannot. Markedness can also be found readily in questions; for example, we more often ask how tall (*unmarked*) someone is rather than how short (*marked*) they are, and we speak of 'height' as opposed to 'lowth' or '*shorth*'.

There are various complex reasons for these asymmetries, which we need not go into here, except to say that it is ubiquitous to language use in general. One reason for this is that it simplifies the vocabulary of a language to have fewer words denoting things that are relevantly similar to each other, and which can be distinguished by context. An *unmarked* word used generically can be thought of as the default position that could be modified as needed or distinguished further by the context in which it is used.

In Oldspeak, it is often the case that the marked side of an opposition is given a distinguishing mark on paper or in speech. For example, 'unhappy' is *marked*, while 'happy' is *unmarked*. The mark on paper in this case is the initial 'un-' of 'unhappy', which indicates that the word names an absence or negation of something, and that the word 'happy' is more primary or *unmarked*. So, in addition to 'un-' in Newspeak having the effect of degrading the normal relationships between opposites, it can also have a secondary effect of marking the *marked* side of an opposition. Orwell briefly mentions something akin to this in the appendix to the novel, entitled "The Principles of Newspeak":

> Given, for instance, the word *good*, there was no need for such a word as *bad*, since the required meaning was equally well—indeed, better—expressed by *ungood*. All that was necessary, in any case where two words formed a natural pair of opposites, was to decide which of them to suppress. *Dark*, for example, could be replaced by *unlight*, or *light* by *undark*, according to preference. (p. 315)

The choice of the *polarity* of the markedness, in each case the suppression of one opposite or the other of a pair, seems to be arbitrary. However, the Party may prefer to suppress one rather than the other for some reason. For example, if it wants to suppress or eliminate thought relating to badness, then it chooses the polarity that makes 'good' the *unmarked*, default, or root word.

It's unclear from the novel whether the Party reverses the polarity of the markedness whenever it wishes, along with, for example, whomever Oceania is at war with, or if it merely chooses one polarity and sticks with it. However, I think that most of the oppositions in Newspeak are always marked in the same way and do not change. The reason for this is that, as was mentioned earlier, one of the main characteristics of the development of Newspeak is the *destruction of words*. This undermines the possibility of reversing markedness, because there would be no other polarity to reverse to, since the use of 'un-' has completely replaced the required root word.

The political and societal function of markedness is not unique to Newspeak. Marked language can be used to oppress sections of a population, and this is often countered by a corresponding change in markedness. For example, some Feminists choose to alter the markedness between the words 'man' and 'woman' in Oldspeak by giving them alternative spellings and etymology. This has the effect of removing or altering their traditional markedness, which is seen as a consequence of, or even a contributory factor in, the oppression of women and other sections of society by *patriarchal* systems of power.

In the case of Newspeak, as we have seen, there is no possibility of using such a strategy to reverse markedness, at least in the case of opposites that are constructed upon a single root word using 'un-'. The goal of the Party and its systems of power, including its own apparent patriarch, Big Brother, is to oppress all humans, and to oppress humanity absolutely, or, as O'Brien puts it in more graphic terms: "If you want a picture of the future, imagine a boot stamping on a human face—forever" (p. 280).

Duckspeak

> It was not speech in the true sense: it was a noise uttered in unconsciousness, like the quacking of a duck.

Not only does Newspeak degrade the normal relations between opposites, or mark them differently, in some cases words can have two contradictory meanings. As Syme tells Winston, a little too plainly to be safe, this is the case with the word 'duckspeak', which means to speak like a quacking duck without any conscious thought, either in an orthodox or unorthodox manner:

> "There is a word in Newspeak," said Syme, "I don't know whether you know it: *duckspeak*, to quack like a duck. It is one of those interesting words that have two contradictory meanings. Applied to an opponent, it is abuse, applied to someone you agree with, it is praise." (p. 57)

This, of course, is not unique to Newspeak. Oldspeak also has what are called *auto-antonyms* or *Janus words* (after a two-faced Roman god). These are words that are either their own opposite or can be construed to have two opposed meanings in different contexts. A good example for comparison with 'duckspeak' is the Oldspeak verb 'sanction', which can mean either to approve or to disapprove of an action. Whole ambiguous sentences can be constructed using such words, and having a greater proportion of these words in a language would certainly lead to more ambiguous sentences. In the case of Newspeak, these would be sentences whose meaning could be easily reinterpreted in the context of other changes, such as changes to history and the doctrine of the Party.

Later in the novel, when Winston is reading Goldstein's book, another example of a Newspeak auto-antonym is discussed, 'blackwhite', which is especially interesting because its contradictory meanings are themselves about contradiction:

> Like so many Newspeak words, this word has two mutually contradic-
> tory meanings. Applied to an opponent, it means the habit of impu-
> dently claiming that black is white, in contradiction of the plain facts.
> Applied to a Party member, it means a loyal willingness to say that
> black is white when Party discipline demands this. But it means also the
> ability to *believe* that black is white, and more, to *know* that black is
> white, and to forget that one has ever believed the contrary. This
> demands a continuous alteration of the past, made possible by the sys-
> tem of thought which really embraces all the rest, and which is known
> in Newspeak as *doublethink.* (p. 221)

This part of Goldstein's book describes the mental training and
basic skills that the members of the Party must adopt as children. Blackwhite is the name for one of these basic skills. Black
and white are used as merely a simple instance of a pair of opposites; the same skill applies generally to any pair of opposites.

Philosophers undergo comparable training as children, or at
least training that corresponds to spotting and avoiding blackwhite. Blackwhite is essentially the habit of denying instances
of what philosophers call the *principle of non-contradiction.* If
there were to be a list of thought crimes in philosophy, then
denying or otherwise contravening this principle would be a
strong contender for thought crime number one. Assuming that
history is accurate, an early version of the principle was for-
mulated around two thousand four hundred years ago, by
Plato, and in terms of opposites:

> It is obvious that the same thing will not be willing to do or undergo
> opposites in the same part of itself, in relation to the same thing, at
> the same time. (*Republic* IV, 436c)

For example, something cannot be both black and white at the
same time and in the same way; although, something could be
black and white at the same time in different ways, like a
chessboard or an issue of *The Times,* or indeed at different
times, like hair turning from black to white.

As is the case with the word 'duckspeak', the only difference
between the two meanings of 'blackwhite' is the Party's attitude,
in this case, to black being white or not. 'Blackwhite' can mean
the ability to *suspend belief* in the principle of non-contradiction
and to believe or *'know'* that black is white if the Party demands

it. I put 'know' in scare quotes here to indicate the well-founded suspicion, held by many philosophers, that it is impossible ever to know a contradiction, even on pain of torture.

How Many?

I suppose there are four. I would see five if I could. I am trying to see five.

One reason that is given for why it's impossible to know a contradiction is that there could never be a contradictory state of the world to know. As Aristotle put it (*Metaphysics*, IV. 3), the principle of non-contradiction is a principle not just of our thought, or of logic, but also of the world itself; that is, it is a *metaphysical* principle that is true of all things. Although some modern philosophers unbellyfeel Aristotle on this point, we should for present purposes merely note this internal debate between oldthinkers and file it away for safekeeping using the nearest memory hole.

If someone attempted to deny the principle, then, roughly speaking, they would nonetheless need to make tacit use of the same principle; for what is denial without contradiction? The principle is not merely akin to a law of nature that we cannot break, like the laws that govern the climate or the force of gravity, it is a principle that is written into *what it is to be anything at all*. It's also the foundation of our ability to deny, or prove false, a statement that is made. If both a statement and its denial could be accepted without breaking the law, then there would be no real contest between them and no real reason to reject one of them.

A denial of the principle of non-contradiction would also entail that the world is radically indeterminate or that there isn't a certain way that it is. Although a radically indeterminate world is impossible to imagine, a useful substitute here is the description of the indeterminacy of Winston's experience under torture, when he is trying to see five fingers where he sees only four:

Behind his screwed-up eyelids a forest of fingers seemed to be moving in a sort of dance, weaving in and out, disappearing behind one another and reappearing again. He was trying to count them, he could not remember why. He knew only that it was impossible to count them, and that this was somehow due to the mysterious identity between five and four. The pain died down again. When he opened his eyes it was to find that he was still seeing the same thing. Innumerable fingers, like moving trees, were still streaming past in either direction, crossing and recrossing. He shut his eyes again.

"How many fingers am I holding up, Winston?"

"I don't know. I don't know. You will kill me if you do that again. Four, five, six—in all honesty I don't know."

"Better," said O'Brien. (p. 264)

Winston never sees five fingers and, indeed, how could he if he sees only four? In this situation, Winston's merely no longer being able to *know* was enough for O'Brien's approval. This is because doublethink, or 'reality-control' in Oldspeak, had started to affect Winston to the extent that his very experience of the world was becoming indeterminate, at least to some degree. It is a kind of "controlled insanity" that is imposed in order to accommodate the contradictions that he must accept. Goldstein explains the motivation for this in that, for the Party, "it is only by reconciling contradictions that power can be retained indefinitely" (p. 225).

There are, perhaps, philosophers who would be able to wriggle out of this and salvage some knowledge. Strictly speaking, there is no formal proof of the principle of non-contradiction that does not *beg the question* against the oldthinkers who unbellyfeel it, or the Party who deny it when they wish to—there's no proof that does not rely on or assume the principle to be proved. However, there are perhaps certain intuitive or performative elucidations. For example, a medieval Persian philosopher called Avicenna famously said that anyone who denies the law of non-contradiction should be tortured until they admit that there is a difference between being tortured and not being tortured:

Those who deny such things need punishment or perception, because—according to Avicenna *Metaphysics* I ch.9 (74vab)—those who deny a first principle need to be flogged or exposed to fire until they admit that to be burned and not to be burned, to be flogged and not to be flogged, are not the same thing. (John Duns Scotus, *Ordinatio*)

Similarly, Goldstein reports in his book that "Between life and death, and between physical pleasure and physical pain, there is still a distinction, but that is all" (p. 207). So, it seems that blackwhite, the denial of the principle of non-contradiction, and doublethink, which stems from this, may indeed have some limits involving basic human necessities, which cannot be avoided.

Here we can begin to see why the basic training of philosophers is so important, and why that of members of the Party is so important to the Party. Philosophers are engaged in investigation by means of reasoning and in search of knowledge, while the members of the Party are engaged in following the Ingsoc orthodoxy, even if that leads to a view of the world as indeterminate. Philosophers also combat illicit uses of *exact opposites*, suppression of one side of an opposition, ambiguity, duckspeak, blackwhite, doublethink, and other forms of fallacious or sophistic thinking.

In this way, philosophers are not unlike the Thought Police. We just won't kidnap you or try to persuade you by means of torture . . . that is, with perhaps the exception of Avicenna.

IV

Epilogue

24
Post-Factual Democracy

Vincent F. Hendricks and
Mads Vestergaard

> Before mass leaders seize the power to fit reality to their lies, their propaganda is marked by its extreme contempt for facts as such.
>
> —Hannah Arendt, *The Origins of Totalitarianism*

On the day of Donald Trump's inauguration, January 20th 2017, certain issues took center stage, caught the bulk of public attention and were subject of much heated debate about basic facts: Did the sun start to shine as the inaugural speech commenced? How big was the size of the crowd attending the inauguration? Was the attending crowd bigger or smaller than the one present at President Barack Obama's inauguration? Contrary to what is evident from the vast amount of footage from the inauguration ceremony—namely that the sun did not shine at any point during the speech—President Donald Trump claimed the opposite in his speech at the CIA headquarters:

> The rain should have scared them away. But God looked down and he said, "We're not going to let it rain on your speech." In fact, when I first started I said, "Oh no." First line, I got hit by a couple of drops. And I said, "Oh, this is, this is too bad, but we'll go right through it." But the truth is that it stopped immediately. It was amazing. And then it became really sunny, and then I walked off and it poured right after I left. (Jon Sharman)

Trump began his presidency with a false factual claim easily exposed: Examine the pictures and videos. The size of the crowd attending the inauguration was another issue of heated dispute. At the Salute to Our Armed Services Ball, the same day, Trump claimed:

> Even the media said the crowd was massive. That was all the way back down to the Washington Monument. (Jon Sharman)

Already during the speech, at the CIA headquarters, the crowd size had cropped up:

> We had a massive field of people. You saw that. Packed. I get up this morning. I turn on one of the networks and they show an empty field. I say, "Wait a minute. I made a speech. I looked out. The field was . . . It looked like a million, a million and a half people." Whatever it was, it was. But it went all the way back to the Washington Monument.

Photo materials from the inauguration unequivocally reveal that the crowd did not stretch that far and passenger data from the transportation authorities in Washington DC tell a different story too. All the same, at the first White House press briefing on January 21st, Press Secretary Sean Spicer doubled down. He attacked the media for "deliberately false reporting" on the size of the crowd and stated categorically "This was the largest audience ever to witness an inauguration, period, both in person and around the globe" (Matt Ford).

Later that day he was backed up by top Trump advisor Kellyanne Conway. On NBC's *Meet the Press*, confronted with the discrepancies between the publicly available evidence and Spicer's statement, she defended the statement as being not a lie or a falsehood, but a set of "alternative facts" provided by Spicer. When Spicer reappeared at a press Q&A on January 23rd, he made the statement that "Sometimes we can disagree with the facts" (David Smith).

Does it make sense at all to deny easily verifiable facts, appeal to "alternative facts" or "disagree with the facts"? Not from a logical and epistemological point of view. Logically, the concept of "alternative facts" is nonsense. As the NBC journalist Chuck Todd made clear to Conway, you can't give "alternative facts" without being wrong or lying. Facts are facts. Factual statements are either true or false. An alternative claim disputing a true statement is just a false claim. Epistemologically you just can't "disagree with the facts" without being wrong. You may surely disagree that they *are* in fact the facts. But to disagree *with* the facts is to disagree with reality. Whether you disagree or not, the sun is shining if and only if the sun is actually shining—like it or not. Now, as a *political strategy*, this dubious relation to the facts may actually make sense. It may indeed have become a winning strategy. Both the presidential election and the example just cited may be seen as symptoms of an emerging post-factual democracy.

Post-Factual Democracy and Post-Truth Politics

A democracy is in a post-factual state when opportune political narratives replace facts and evidence as the basis for political debate, opinion formation, and policymaking. In post-factual democracy, facts and evidence have lost their authority. When facts lose their authority, disregarding them or furnishing easily exposable lies may become a winning strategy.

According to Politifact, 70 percent of Donald Trump's statements made during the election campaign were false. For Hillary Clinton the proportion of factually false statements was 28 percent (Aaron Sharockman).

The British referendum on EU membership in 2016 is another example. The centerpiece of the victorious Leave campaign was the false and repeatedly debunked claim that the £350 million the UK dispatched to the EU every week, could and would be redirected to the National Health Service if Britain left the EU. UKIP leader Nigel Farage backed down on this promise the very night of the Leave victory calling it "a mistake" (Alan Travis).

It's nothing new that politicians cook up falsities, have lenient dealings with the truth, and sometimes lie. There was never a golden age of democracy in which politicians were honest and authentic. Politics has always been a somewhat dirty business with its fair share of deceit and masquerading. Yet, in the past, not being directly exposed was an essential part of the game. As Niccolò Machiavelli instructs: "if it be sometimes necessary to conceal facts with words, then it should be done in such manner that it shall not appear; or should it be observed, then a defense should be promptly ready."

What's new in post-factual democracy—and what makes it "post"—is that the political person doesn't even have to make an effort to hide lying or to excuse "disagreeing" with verifiable facts. Being caught lying is of little consequence if you can successfully blame the media exposing the lie for lying themselves and not being trustworthy. According to a recent survey, only a minority of the population in Germany or in the world now trust media institutions (Edelman).

If the media exposing the lies are successfully branded as partisan, as part of the opposition or a part of an illegitimate elite, or if the electorate doesn't even trust the fact checkers, then being caught lying carries no severe sanctions or blow to a person's political career or reputation. In post-factual democracy, to be in sync with the facts is of secondary importance. (According to a Rasmussen survey, just 29 percent of likely American voters trust fact checkers, and one-time White House chief strategist Stephen K. Bannon has stated: "The media here is the opposition party" (Michael M. Grynbaum).

The diagnosis of post-factuality points to the same phenomenon as the term "post-truth," as defined by Oxford Dictionaries: "Relating to or denoting circumstances in which objective facts are less influential in shaping public opinion than appeals to emotion and personal belief." The post-truth diagnosis has also been integrated in the World Economic Forum's Global Risk 2017. It lists post-truth politics as a challenge to democracy, global governance, and our ability to solve the pressing problems the world faces.

The preference here is to employ the term "post-factuality". It omits the controversial philosophical question of truth, which may also include questions of normative truth in the case of cognitivist meta-ethical positions. Post-factuality more narrowly denotes purely factual truth: A truth which may be decided upon via the traditional sources of sense experience, science, but also journalism, depending on the type of factual question at hand. Thus the thesis of post-factuality is less demanding than what is indicated by the term "post-truth."

The division of labor between political actors and the sources providing facts is nowadays challenged. Facts are not taken for granted or given, but have become a part of the political battlefield. Here everything is politicized. When solid verifiable facts are being politicized to suit the political logic of partisan opposition, there is no real fixed point for political debate. The facts, then, become something cherry-picked depending on whether they are in accordance with a political position or party affiliation. It is not only opinions that are chosen, but the facts too.

Selective cherry-picking of facts may be both a conscious tactical political maneuver and a consequence of the psychological phenomena of unconscious *confirmation* and *selection bias*. Psychological experiments have documented that people tend to allocate attention to, and believe in, the information already in sync with their political opinions (Manjoo, *True Enough*).

Even the question of whether the sun is shining is, in this extreme scenario, contingent on political opinion. If all is political, then everything is relative and factual reality has left the stage of politics. Enter post-factual democracy.

New Media and Fake News

Post-factuality is in no small part fueled by the media environment. A recent analysis from Buzzfeed of the current political debate on digital media in Germany shows a high level of online proliferation of false stories, fake news, and conspiracy theories. Negative stories about Chancellor Angela Merkel, her immigration policy, and its consequences, generated most Facebook engagement as to reactions, shares, and comments in the closing of 2016. Whether the stories actually reflect reality does not seem to matter much for their popularity and circulation. Rather the opposite. The top-scoring stories which created most engagement on Facebook in 2016 included unsubstantiated accusations of Merkel having mental problems or even being "insane," conspiratorial stories about Merkel controlling such mass media outlets as ZDF, and a fake news outlet producing a picture "showing" Merkel taking a selfie with the terrorist behind the Brussels attack.

The unscientific Buzzfeed analyses align with a scientific study from 2015 demonstrating that unsubstantiated conspiratorial claims reverberate, are circulated, and receive attention in time and volume on a par with verifiable factual information. When it comes to the potential for going viral, factuality is of secondary importance. In the new online media environment, it seems that rumors, false claims, and bogus stories live long and prosper. Sticking to the truth is not a necessary—let alone a suf- ficient—condition for stories and media content to be widely cir- culated receiving ample attention. Thumping online attention may have real impact on democratic debate, opinion formation and the political landscape, even if the content is debunked. Experiments show that correcting false information does not prevent it from having a measurable effect on participants' esti- mation of a political candidate (Emily Thorson).

The media landscape itself has changed dramatically with the Internet, digitalization, and social media. The traditional media institutions have lost their monopoly over disseminating information. Journalists and editors, the conventional gate- keepers of information and factual knowledge, have lost a lot of their power. This has been celebrated as the democratization of the media (Benkler, *The Wealth of Networks*). The new digital and networked media environment has made it possible, at lit- tle or no expense, to publish media content and information on online platforms, blog communities, and social media. Thus everyone is now a node in the networked public sphere and may voice their opinion. Contrary to the optimistic hope, empirical studies show that the allocation of attention is not more equally distributed between information sources, than it was when tra- ditional media had *de facto* monopoly of information distribu- tion. The allocation of attention still conforms with laws of scale (Webster, *The Marketplace of Attention*). When it comes to infor- mational impact on the Web, the winner takes it all—a few major news outlets and online platforms get the bulk of atten- tion and set the agenda. Yet this development has undermined the gatekeeping and informational filtering role of professional journalism. It comes at a price. The professional journalists and editors have guidelines for ethical conduct and virtues for good journalism. The Society of Professional Journalists in the USA considers the broad democratic purpose of journalism to be pub- lic enlightenment and enunciates a set of principles journalists should abide by, if they are to live up to that goal. To seek truth, and verify and report it accurately and fairly, is the very first principle. Journalists' gatekeeping function in the age of mass media included filtering out or exposing falsehoods, unsubstantiated rumors, and bogus stories as being exactly that. There has always been bad journalism, tabloidism and sensationalism, false claims, biases, and partisanship. Yet, media actors generally, to different degrees, were expected to subscribe—and were held professionally responsible—to values of truthfulness and (some measure of) objectivity and fairness. Now, political actors of all sorts, citizens and issue proponents, but also anonymous cynical actors with the sole purpose of making money, or concentrating power or status by attracting attention, do not have to go through the gate of the media institutions and the journalistic gatekeepers. The result: Fake News is beating verified news stories in social transmission.

The Market for Attention

Post-factuality emerges from a disproportionality between an overwhelming amount of available information and limited attention. In the information age, the amount of publicly available and easily accessible information is out of this world. Yet, if information is to matter, somebody needs to pay attention. Attention is the price paid for receiving information. The amount of attention is fixed and limited: Attention is a scarce resource (S.A. Herbert).

Individuals have a limited time each day and limited attention capacity. At the macro level, this is reflected in a limited amount of public attention each day. Even if the amount of available information is in overwhelming supply, the public *agenda* of a polity is limited. The aggregated attention of individual political, media or civil actors is curbed and the political system as such has limited informational carrying capabilities—an upper limit for the information attended to. This also goes for the major news media outlets with large audiences—they have a limited news agenda each day. Their carrying capabilities fix the limits for the information circulated and what receives broad public and political attention.

The scarcity of attention makes the *selection* of information decisive. Whether the individual actor is factually informed depends on how their limited attention is allocated. People allocating attention to unreliable information and epistemic unsound sources like conspiratorial, pseudo-scientific, political, or religious propaganda sites, will become less factually informed than people seeking factual information from more reliable sources. The same goes for individuals who disregard politically relevant information and consume entertainment media products instead. If the person's attention is spent on sports, then he is not reading a politically relevant or informative newspaper article in that period. Echo chamber and filter bubble effects and the potential resultant social fragmentation are also results of *information selection* and those phenomena may indeed be understood partly as issues of a suboptimal allocation of attention (Hendricks and Hansen, *Infostorms*).

The quality of information circulated is crucial for the factual quality of public deliberation. If politically irrelevant issues, junk evidence, and partisan contributions receive high levels of attention, then other relevant issues and sound information may not receive enough to actually inform democratic deliberation. In turn, the public agenda is dominated by narratives instead of facts, opinions instead of knowledge, stereotypes instead of representative instances, political bubbles instead of political substance. One outcome is post-factual democratic discourse, where facts and evidence are of secondary importance since they do not enjoy sufficient attention compared to unfounded narratives.

Attention is, besides being limited in supply, also in extremely high demand—attention is the most valuable asset online. The competition for attention is brutal. Media institutions and bloggers are competing for attention in terms of readers, listeners, viewers, and clicks. The currency of media institutions *is* attention. The huge amount of money companies spend on marketing and advertising is largely to gain consumers' attention. In this market of attention substantial money may be made by harvesting attention, by being an *attention merchant* (Wu, *The Attention Merchants*). The result is an economic incentive to get attention by all means necessary. The factual quality of the information does not matter from a monetary point of view. A click is a click and may be cashed into dollars or euros. In this environment the production of Fake News becomes a viable business strategy. When the public sphere is a market of attention, the viral narrative becomes the cash cow. Political populism and polarization may now be the winning political strategy.

Viral Narratives and the Rise of Populism

Political populism is characterized by employing narratives of exclusion and polarization. Populists' common claim is that they, and they alone, represent the true will of The People (Müller, *What Is Populism?*). Populism conceptually divides

1. the population into the real people and the "others", and

2. political actors into political representatives of the real people— the populists themselves—and "others," who are not representing the will of the people and thus according to the populists themselves lack democratic legitimacy.

This symbolic construction of The People, and the populists themselves as its only true representative, makes populism anti-pluralistic. In the framework of populism, political adversaries are not construed as representing legitimate challenging viewpoints and opinions—a basic condition for a pluralistic liberal democracy. Instead, they are branded as part of an elite betraying the people, neglecting their wishes, and not listening to their voices. If you are against the populist, you are against the people and thus lack democratic legitimacy, the meta-narrative goes.

Populist narratives of exclusion and polarization have a characteristic narrative structure of us-versus-them. This makes them very streamlined for attracting attention and setting the agenda in the current media environment. News stories feeding on anger (indignation) and fear have a high tendency to go viral and thus attract attention through social transmission (Berger, "What Makes Online Content Go Viral?" In his study, Berger uses the category "anger," but the news articles thus categorized feed specifically on indignation. Indignation is anger about a perceived injustice. This align with headlines such as: "What Red Ink? Wall Street Paid Hefty Bonuses" or "Loan Titans Paid McCain Adviser Nearly $2 Million."

Negative sentiments of anger and fear, together with positive feelings of awe and fascination, are referred to as activity mobilizing sentiments. They motivate agents to act—contrary to emotions of sadness or comfort, which are referred to as activity demobilizing. Acting also means sharing, retweeting, upvoting and other online acts fueling social transmission of media content. If you want your content to go viral, you make people angry or afraid. The narrative structure of us-versus-them with some "Other" as villain are effective in producing anger and fear. The "Other" in the populist narratives may refer to immigrants—who according to the populists are threatening national security, identity and values—or political elites in Brussels or Washington betraying the People by letting immigration happen and thereby selling out country and countrymen.

Populism may also target the elite of the mainstream media who are routinely blamed for hiding the truth with the intention of silencing the voice of the People. Different versions of this polarized narrative feed on indignation and fear and may thus mobilize people to act. In an online environment, this translates into high levels of social transmission, magnets of attention, and agenda setting effects. When it comes to the potential for virality, getting the facts right does not matter as much as getting the emotional effects of the narratives right. Whether or not they adequately represent the facts—and all of the available relevant facts—is of secondary importance for political impact.

The claim is not that populist narratives and communication do not relate to reality at all. Citizens supporting and voting for populists may of course be indignant and fearful for good reason with a solid foundation of (harsh) facts facing them. Rising inequality, social or cultural stigmatization or disintegration, the increasing divide between urban and rural areas, and so forth may all be very real reasons and motivations for indignant sentiments. A lot of facts and news stories may in isolation support the populist case. Yet, it is a trademark of populism to simplify complex programs, cherry-pick facts, and frame issues and information according to a stereotyped us-versus-them dichotomy.

In the Populist framework, stereotypes often replace facts. Culprits replace the complexity of the real world's causal relations. Political communication imbedding simplifications, stereotyping and symbolism is of course not reserved for political Populists. Because of the Populists' ideological anti-pluralism, they are much more free to employ clear-cut narratives structured on an exclusion of the stereotyped "Other" than political actors who are to some extent restricted by suvh basic values of liberal democracy as pluralism and individualism. With its selective use of facts, and its simplistic culprit framework well suited for boosting social transmission, Populism may just have become *the* winning political strategy in post-factual democracy. If that is the case, democracy may be facing a dire crisis.

Democratic Legitimacy

Whereas Populism and its claims of the democratic illegitimacy of opposing opinions and parties perform well in post-factual democracy, the legitimacy of post-factual democracy may itself be put into question. Depending on which model of democracy is subscribed to, the truthfulness of circulated information has different significance pertaining to the question of democratic legitimacy.

In deliberative models of democracy, legitimate democratic decisions ought to go through a process of rational deliberation in the public spheres of coffee shops, media outlets, and parliament. Citizens are supposed to form factually informed opinions on and rationally motivated attitudes to policy proposals (Habermas, "Political Communication in Media Society"). Factually informed deliberation is a necessary condition for democratic legitimacy. In post-factual democracy where facts are lost to partisan politics, to gain deliberative legitimacy through a demanding criterion of rational discourse is out of the question.

Even for less epistemically demanding theories of democracy, the lack of factuality undermines democratic legitimacy. Minimalistic democracy conceptions pay homage to the idea that the core of democracy is a procedure for the peaceful aggregation of individual interests. However, without any reference to facts or truth these nominal suggestions of democracy become at odds with what the procedure of voting is supposed to secure: Accountability in governance with checks-and-balances. According to minimalistic theories, democratic legitimacy consists in people's ability to elect their representatives in fair procedures of voting. The elections are mechanisms designed to hold the government and rulers accountable and replace them peacefully, if they are evaluated not to live up to their responsibility, their promises or in other ways perform badly according to the electorate. But void of a minimum of correct factual information and truth it is impossible to know or measure the government's performance. When the evaluation of *policies* becomes a matter of *politics,* what is lost is the factual basis from which to measure whether they work well or at all. A minimum of factuality is a necessary condition for democratic legitimacy.

Factual Democracy

Democracy has a minimum requirement of factuality. So does government. If policy-making is detached from reality, it becomes impossible to solve the real-world problems and global challenges facing us. To avoid a climate catastrophe, the first necessary condition is to acknowledge that man-made climate change in fact is real. It is necessary to grant authority to the facts. This means granting authority to institutions and agents that produce and procure factual knowledge by reliable methods: journalism and science. In the factual democracy, the epistemic authority of factual matters is delegated to the parties employing reliable methods for obtaining the factual knowledge in question.

That facts and experts have epistemic authority in factual democracy does not entail that experts are always right nor that what, at a given point in time, is considered facts does not change. Settling on the facts is in many cases a hard, complex and demanding ordeal. Science doesn't operate with absolute Cartesian certainty. It is also a historical, cultural, societal endeavor. Both science and journalism are fallible and both institutions sometimes produce false claims, incorrect theories, and junk evidence. But more and better science and journalism are able to correct those mistakes and falsehoods. The false claim that Iraq possessed WMDs before the invasion of the American-led coalition was, for example, heavily broadcast as a matter of fact by the major traditional mainstream media in the USA. But how can we correct such a claim if not with more and (much) better journalism, committed to uncover the facts and expose the truth?

There's a big difference between rejecting science and journalism as being untrustworthy branches of the elite and the internal critique of bad science or bad journalism coming from the parties themselves. Scientists do not always agree on the facts or on what the best methods for obtaining the facts are. On the backdrop of the recent financial crises, there is an emerging movement of students and scholars in economics— some even Nobel Laureates—who are critical of the current theoretical framework and methods in mainstream economics. The science of economics has, the claim goes, lost touch with the real world and does not take notice of, or measure, the relevant facts.

For instance George Akerlof and Robert Shiller wrote in 2009: "The public, the government, and most economists had been reassured by an economic theory that said we were safe. It was all OK. Nothing dangerous could happen. But that theory was deficient."

Also Paul Krugman: "As I see it, the economics profession went astray because economists, as a group, mistook beauty, clad in impressive-looking mathematics, for truth. . . . Unfortunately, this romanticized and sanitized vision of the economy led most economists to ignore all the things that can go wrong."

Sciences too, can lose the firm grip on reality. From *inside* the field itself there is thus a call for educational and theoretical reforms—and some even for a more radical paradigmatic shift. There's a world of difference between such scientifically based internal critique of a (neoclassical) paradigm and for example skepticism about man-made climate change. Climate skeptics have for the most part been unable to get through peer review and publish their "findings" in a scientific journal of the field.

Factual democracy is not a technocracy. Science is not epistemically infallible, and science does not provide normative guidelines for what *ought* to be done individually or collectively. In factual democracy, there is ideology, different visions for the good life and society, diversity among cultural traditions, moral viewpoints and religious doctrines. Forget about the ancient idea that modern-day Platonic philosopher-kings ought to rule because they know The Truth. Legitimate disagreement is a *sine qua non* for democracy. Factual democracy is pluralistic.

Yet, when *factual* questions arise in political debates, the facts to count are the ones produced by reliable and robust methods of inquiry. There should be a division of cognitive and deliberative labor, largely corresponding to the division between facts and values. Only by taking notice of the distinction between facts and values, and abiding by the division of labor, thus not politicizing facts obtained by solid state of the art inquiry methods, is it possible to engage in rational, enlightened and transparent dialogue. In a healthy democracy, such a dialog is the informational foundation for enlightened collective decisions and democratic checks and balances.

If the facts are politicized, we have post-factuality and potentially totalitarianism; if politics is reduced to factual questions and expert solutions, we end up with technocracy. Both extremes undermine democracy.

In Orwell's *1984* totalitarianism has won. Facts have lost all authority, and there is only one authority defining reality, truth and history. The Party:

> The Party told you to reject the evidence of your eyes and ears. It was their final, most essential command.

Such an order should never be obeyed—no matter who it comes from. Then we lose, then democracy is lost. Then reality is lost.[1]

---

[1] A revised German version of this chapter appeared in *Aus Politik und Zeitgeschichte* (October 2017).

Bibliography

The Collected Essays, Journalism, and Letters of George Orwell, edited by Sonia Orwell and Ian Angus (referred to here as CEJL) first appeared in 1968, and has been reprinted several times. It's a good four-volume selection of Orwell's important writings other than his nine book-length works. The Complete Works of George Orwell in twenty volumes, edited by Peter Davison (referred to here as CW) was published in London in 1986–1998. It includes everything by Orwell that could be found, including letters, diary entries, unpublished drafts, and jottings. The first nine volumes are Orwell's nine book-length works.

For the title of his last novel, Orwell preferred the spelling Nineteen Eighty-four (today Nineteen Eighty-Four would be more usual) but he reluctantly agreed to the use of 1984 for the American edition. In this volume, we have left the spelling as a free choice for each of the chapter authors.

Adorno, Theodor W. 1973 [1964]. The Jargon of Authenticity. Routledge.
———. 1973 [1966]. Negative Dialectics. Continuum.
———. 1998. Critical Models: Interventions and Catchwords. Columbia University Press.
———. 2006. Minima Moralia: Reflections on a Damaged Life. Verso.
Akerlof, G., and R. Shiller. 2009. Animal Spirits: How Human Psychology Drives the Economy and Why It Matters for Global Capitalism. Princeton University Press.
Alfano, M. 2013. Character as Moral Fiction. Cambridge University Press.

———. 2016. The Topology of Communities of Trust. *Russian Sociological Review* 15:4.

Arendt, Hannah. 1979 [1948]. *The Origins of Totalitarianism.* Harcourt.

———. 2006 [1961]. *Eichmann in Jerusalem: A Report on the Banality of Evil.* Penguin.

———. 2009. *Responsibility and Judgment.* Shocken.

Aristotle. 2014. *Nicomachean Ethics.* Hackett.

Asch, Solomon. 1951. Effects of Group Pressure on the Modification and Distortion of Judgments. In Harold Guetzkow, ed., *Groups, Leadership and Men.* Carnegie.

———. 1956. Studies of Independence and Conformity: A Minority of One Against a Unanimous Majority. *Psychological Monographs* 70.

Ascheim, Steven E. 2016. The (Ambiguous) Political Economy of Empathy. In Aleida Assmann and Ines Detmers, eds., *Empathy and Its Limits.* Palgrave Macmillan.

Austin, J.L. 1975. *How to Do Things with Words.* Oxford University Press.

Babiak, Paul, and Robert Hare. 2007. *Snakes in Suits: When Psychopaths Go to Work.* Harper Collins.

Baker, John. 1945. Science, Culture, and Freedom. In Hermon Ould, ed., *Freedom of Expression.* Hutchinson.

Barbera, Joseph. 2008. Sleep and Dreaming in Greek and Roman Philosophy. *Medicine* 9:8.

Bassetti, Claudio L. 2009. Sleepwalking (Sonambulism): Dissociation Between "Body Sleep" and "Mind Sleep." In Steven Laureys, Olivia Gosseries, and Giulio Tononi, eds., *The Neurology of Consciousness.* Elsevier.

Beck, Peter J. 2013. War Minus the Shooting: George Orwell on International Sport and the Olympics. *Sport in History* 33:1.

Bello, Walden. 2008. How to Manufacture a Global Food Crisis. *Development* 51:4.

Benkler, Y. 2006. *The Wealth of Networks: How Social Production Transforms Markets and Freedom.* Yale University Press.

Berger, J. 2012. What Makes Online Content Go Viral? *Journal of Marketing Research* 49:2.

Berlin, Isaiah. 2002 [1958]. Two Concepts of Liberty. In Isaiah Berlin, *Liberty.* Oxford University Press.

Bolton, W.F. 1984. *The Language of 1984: Orwell's English and Ours.* University of Tennessee Press.

Bowker, Gordon. 2003. *Inside George Orwell.* Palgrave Macmillan.

Brennan, Jason. 2016. *Against Democracy.* Princeton University Press.

Brown, Andrew. 2005. *J.D. Bernal: The Sage of Science.* Oxford University Press.

Brown, Wendy. 2006. American Nightmare: Neoliberalism, Neoconservatism, and De-Democratization. *Political Theory* 34:6.

Browning, Elizabeth Barrett. 2007. *Sonnets from the Portuguese: A Celebration of Love*. St. Martin's.

Burnham, James. 1941. *The Managerial Revolution: What Is Happening in the World*. Day.

Bush, George W. 2003. Remarks to the Troops at Fort Hood, Texas. January 3rd. Online at *The American Presidency Project* <www.presidency.ucsb.edu/ws/index.php?pid=261>.

Buss, Sarah, 2012. Autonomous Action: Self-Determination in the Passive Mode. *Ethics* 122:4.

Caputo, J.D. 1971. The Rose Is Without Why: The Later Heidegger. *Philosophy Today* 15:1 (Spring).

Carl, Noah. 2014. Verbal Intelligence Is Correlated with Socially and Economically Liberal Beliefs. *Intelligence* 44.

Cavell, Stanley. 1999. *The Claim of Reason: Wittgenstein, Skepticism, Morality, and Tragedy*. Oxford University Press.

Chakrabortty, A. 2016. I Hate Trump and Farage: But on Free Trade They Have a Point. *The Guardian* (October 19th).

Chapin, John, and Grace Coleman. 2009. Optimistic Bias: What You Think, What You Know, and Whom You Know. *North American Journal of Psychology* 11.

Clifton, Denise. 2017. Twitter Bots Distorted the 2016 Election— Including Many Likely from Russia. *Mother Jones* (October 12th).

Colls, Robert. 2013. *George Orwell: English Rebel*. Oxford University Press.

Conant, James. 2005. Rorty and Orwell on Truth. In Abbott Gleason, Jack Goldsmith, and Martha Nussbaum, eds., *On Nineteen Eighty-Four: Orwell and Our Future*. Princeton University Press. 2005.

Constante, Constantin. 2004. *Colindand prin Rusia Sovietica: Note i impresii de calatorie 1916–1918*. Curtea Veche.

Conway, Daniel. 2017. Banality, Again. In Richard J. Golsan and Sarah M. Misemer, eds., *The Trial That Never Ends: Arendt's "Eichman in Jerusalem" in Retrospect*. University of Toronto Press.

Corey, Gerald. 2016. *Theory and Practice of Counseling and Psychotherapy*. Tenth edition. Brooks Cole.

Craig, Jon. 2017. GE 2017: Corbyn Will Not Back Second EU Referendum After Confusion on Stance. *Sky News* (April 20th).

Crary, Jonathan. 2014. *24/7: Late Capitalism and the Ends of Sleep*. Verso.

Crick, Bernard. 1992 [1980]. *George Orwell: A Life*. Edinburgh University Press.

Dahlgren, P., and C. Alvares. 2016. Populism, Extremism, and Media: Mapping an Uncertain Terrain. *European Journal of Communication* 31:1.

Davison, Peter, ed. 1986–1998. *The Complete Works of George Orwell*. 20 volumes. Secker and Warburg.

————, ed. 2006. *The Lost Orwell: Being a Supplement to the Complete Works of George Orwell*. Timewell.

Desjardins, Jeff. 2017. Every Single Cognitive Bias in One Infographic. *Visual Capitalist* <www.visualcapitalist.com/every-single-cognitive-bias>.

Desmarais, Ralph. 2010. Science, Scientific Intellectuals, and British Culture in the Early Atomic Age: A Case Study of George Orwell, Jacob Bronowski, P.M.S. Blackett, and J.G. Crowther. PhD thesis, Imperial College London.

Dewey, John. 2004 [1916]. *Democracy and Education: An Introduction to the Philosophy of Education*. Dover.

Doris, J. (2015). *Talking to Ourselves*. Oxford University Press.

Dostoevsky, Fyodor. 1994. *Notes from Underground*. Vintage.

Edelman Trust Barometer. 2017. *Edelman Trust Barometer: Global Report*. <www.edelman.com/global-results>.

Elliott, K.C., 2017. *A Tapestry of Values: An Introduction to Values in Science*. Oxford University Press.

Fanon, Frantz. 2008. *Black Skin, White Masks*. Grove.

Federal Reserve. 2017. Changes in US Family Finances from 2013 to 2016: Evidence from the Survey of Consumer Finances. *Federal Reserve Bulletin* (September).

Ferrara, Emilio. 2016. How Twitter Bots Affected the US Presidential Campaign. *The Conversation* (November 8th).

Finlayson, L. 2014. Why I'm Not a Liberal. Unpublished seminar at Birkbeck, 1st July 2014.

Flusser, Vilém. 2000. *Towards a Philosophy of Photography*. Reaktion.

Ford, Matt. 2017. Trump's Press Secretary Falsely Claims: "Largest Audience Ever to Witness an Inauguration, Period." *The Atlantic* (January 21st).

Forrester, John. 1990. *The Seductions of Psychoanalysis: Freud, Lacan, and Derrida*. Cambridge University Press.

Foucault, Michel. 1978. *The History of Sexuality*. Pantheon.

————. 1988 *Politics, Philosophy, Culture*. Routledge.

Frankfurt, Harry G. 1988. *The Importance of What We Care About: Philosophical Essays*. Cambridge University Press.

————. 1998. *Necessity, Volition, and Love*. Cambridge University Press.

————. 2005. *On Bullshit*. Princeton University Press.

————. 2006. *Taking Ourselves Seriously and Getting It Right*. Stanford University Press.

Freud, Sigmund. 1989 [1900]. The Interpretation of Dreams. In Gay 1989.

Fromm, Erich. 1961. Afterword. In George Orwell, *1984*. Penguin

Gardiner, Stephen. 2011. *A Perfect Moral Storm*. Oxford University Press.

Gay, Peter, ed. 1989. *The Freud Reader*. Norton.

Gleason, Abbott, Jack Goldsmith, and Martha C. Nussbaum, eds. 2005. *On Nineteen Eighty-Four: Orwell and Our Future*. Princeton University Press.

Glover, Jonathan. 1984. *What Sort of People Should There Be?* Penguin.

Glover, Trudy. 1997. *Social Trust and Human Communities*. McGill-Queen's University Press.

Goldie, Peter. 2012. *The Mess Inside: Narrative, Emotion, and the Mind*. Oxford University Press.

Gopnik, Adam. 2017. Orwell's "1984" and Trump's America. *The New Yorker* (January 27th).

Greaney, Michael. 2015. "Observed, Measured, Contained": Contemporary Fiction and the Science of Sleep. *Contemporary Fiction* 56:1.

Greif, Mark. 2004. Against Exercise. *n + 1* (Fall).

———. 2016. Get Off the Treadmill: The Art of Living Well in an Age of Plenty. *The Guardian* (23rd September).

———. 2016. *Against Everything: Essays*. Pantheon.

Gross, Miriam, ed. 1971. *The World of George Orwell*. Weidenfeld and Nicolson.

Goodwin, William. 2017. Volatile Spirits: Scientists and Society in Gulliver's Third Voyage. In Janelle Pötzsch, ed., *Jonathan Swift and Philosophy*. Lexington.

Grynbaum, M. 2017. Trump Strategist Stephen Bannon Says Media Should "Keep Its Mouth Shut." *New York Times* (January 26th).

Guenther, Lisa. 2013. *Solitary Confinement: Social Death and Its Afterlives*. University of Minnesota Press.

Guerrero, Héctor Andrés Sánchez. 2016. *Feeling Together and Caring with One Another: A Contribution to the Debate on Collective Affective Intentionality*. Springer.

Haack, Susan. 2005. The Ideal of Intellectual Integrity in Life and Literature. *New Literary History* 36.

Habermas, Jürgen. 2006. Political Communication in Media Society: Does Democracy Still Enjoy an Epistemic Dimension? The Impact of Normative Theory on Empirical Research. *Communication Theory* 16.

Harman, Oren. 2004. *The Man Who Invented the Chromosome: A Life of Cyril Darlington*. Harvard University Press.

Harrington, Christine B., and Z. Umut Türem. 2006. Accounting for Accountability in Neoliberal Regulatory Regimes. In M.W. Dowdle, ed., *Public Accountability: Designs, Dilemmas, and Experiences*. Cambridge University Press.

Harvey, David. 2005. *A Brief History of Neoliberalism*. Oxford University Press.

Hegel, G.W.F. 1976. *Phenomenology of Spirit*. Oxford University Press.

Heidegger, Martin. 1966. *Discourse on Thinking*. Harper and Row.
————. 2008. *Being and Time*. Harper Collins.
Hendricks, V.F. 2016. In the Post-Factual Democracy Politicians Win by Getting the Feelings Right and the Facts Wrong. *Quartz* (July 5th).
Hendricks, V.F., and P.G. Hansen. 2016. *Infostorms: Why Do We "Like?" Explaining Individual Behavior on the Social Net*. Copernicus Books/Springer Nature.
Herbert, S.A. 1971. Designing Organizations for an Information-rich World. In Martin Greenberger, ed., *Computers, Communications, and the Public Interest*. Johns Hopkins University Press.
Hickel, J. 2017. *The Divide*. Penguin.
Hill, James. 2004. The Philosophy of Sleep: The Views of Descartes, Locke, and Leibniz. *The Richmond Journal of Philosophy* 6.
Hindman, M. 2008. *The Myth of Digital Democracy*. Princeton University Press.
Hitchens, Christopher. 2003. *Why Orwell Matters*. UK title: *Orwell's Victory*. Basic Books.
Honneth, Axel. 1996. *The Struggle for Recognition: The Moral Grammar of Social Conflicts*. MIT Press.
Horkheimer, Max, and Theodor W. Adorno. 2002. *Dialectic of Enlightenment: Philosophical Fragments*. Stanford University Press.
Huxley, Aldous. 2006 [1932]. *Brave New World*. Harper.
Insel, Thomas R., and Russell D. Fernald. 2004. How the Brain Processes Social Information: Searching for the Social Brain. *Annual Review of Neuroscience* 27.
Jasay, Anthony de. 2000. *Justice and Its Surroundings*. Liberty Fund.
Jones, Stanton L., and Richard E. Butman. 2011. *Modern Psychotherapies: A Comprehensive Christian Appraisal*. InterVarsity Press.
Kant, Immanuel. 2009. *Groundwork of the Metaphysics of Morals*. Harper.
————. 2016 [1784]. *Answering the Question: What Is Enlightenment?* <www.columbia.edu/acis/ets/CCREAD/etscc/kant.html>.
Kemmelmeier, Markus. 2008. Is There a Relationship between Political Orientation and Cognitive Ability? A Test of Three Hypotheses in Two Studies. *Personality and Individual Differences* 45:8.
Kligman, Gail. 1998. *The Politics of Duplicity: Controlling Reproduction in Ceausescu's Romania*. University of California Press.
Kolbert, E. 2017. Why Facts Don't Change Our Minds. *The New Yorker* (Book Issue, February 27th).
Korsgaard, Christine M. 2009. *Self-Constitution: Agency, Identity, and Integrity*. Oxford University Press.

Kring, Ann M., Sheri L. Johnson, Gerald C. Davison, John M. Neale. 2014. *Abnormal Psychology: DSM-5 Update*. Wiley.

Krugman, Paul. 2009. How Did Economists Get It So Wrong? *New York Times Magazine* (September 2nd).

Langton, Rae. 1993. Speech Acts and Unspeakable Acts. *Philosophy and Public Affairs*.

Levi, Primo. 1959. *If This Is a Man*. Orion.

Lewontin, Richard, and Richard Levins. 1976. The Problem of Lysenkoism. In Hilary Rose and Steven Rose, eds., *The Radicalization of Science*. Macmillan.

Lifton, Robert Jay. 2000. *The Nazi Doctors: Medical Killing and the Psychology of Genocide*. Basic Books.

Locke, John. 1979. *An Essay Concerning Human Understanding*. Oxford University Press.

———. 2000. *The Second Treatise of Government: An Essay Concerning the True Original Extent, and End of Civil Government*. In Locke, *Two Treatises of Government*. Cambridge University Press.

Lynn, Richard, and Tatu Vanhanen. 2012. National IQs: A Review of Their Educational, Cognitive, Economic, Political, Demographic, Sociological, Epidemiological, Geographic, and Climatic Correlates. *Intelligence* 40:2.

Machiavelli, Niccolò. 1882. *The Historical, Political, and Diplomatic Writings of Niccolò Machiavelli, tr. from the Italian, by Christian E. Detmold, Vol. 4*. <http://oll.libertyfund.org/titles/777>.

MacIntyre, Alasdair. 2007. *After Virtue: A Study in Moral Theory*. Third edition. University of Notre Dame Press.

MacKinnon, Catharine A. 1987. *Feminism Unmodified: Discourses on Life and Law*. Harvard University Press.

Manjoo, Farhad. 2008. *True Enough: Learning to Live in a Post-Fact Society*. Wiley.

Marchione, Tom. 2008. A Time to Rethink the Global Food Regime. *Anthropology News* 49:7.

Martin, Paul R. 2002. *Counting Sheep: The Science and Pleasures of Sleep and Dreams*. Dunne.

Mileck, J. 1978. *Hermann Hesse: Life and Art*. University of California Press.

Mill, John Stuart. 1978 [1859]. *On Liberty*. Hackett.

Mendieta, E. 2017. Rorty and Post-Truth. *Los Angeles Review of Books*.

Mocanua, D., L. Rossia, Q. Zhanga, M. Karsaib, and K. Quattrociocchi. 2015. Collective Attention in the Age of (Mis)Information. *Computers in Human Behavior* 51.

Moore, Jack. 2017. Dubai Jails Couple for Kissing in Service Station Restroom. *Newsweek* (May 17th).

Morocco World News. 2016. Moroccan Police Arrest Couple for Kissing in Public in Ramadan. *Morocco World News* (June 16th).

Muller, Herta. 1998. *Tod oder Knast oder Kinder*. Taz <www.taz.de/!565419>.

Müller, Jan-Werner. 2016. *What Is Populism?* University of Pennsylvania Press.

Nafisi, Azar. 2008. Reading *Lolita in Tehran*. Random House.

Nagel, Thomas. 1997. *The Last Word*. Oxford University Press.

———. 2002. *Concealment and Exposure*. Oxford University Press.

Nardelli, A., and C. Silverman. 2017. Hyperpartisan Sites and Facebook Pages Are Publishing False Stories and Conspiracy Theories about Angela Merkel. *Buzzfeed News* (January 14th) <www.buzzfeed.com/albertonardelli/hyperpartisan-sites-and-facebook-pages-are-publishing-false?utm_term=.wtaZgJ3Pr1#.kvN0RxoE36>.

Nietzsche, Friedrich. 1968. *The Will to Power*. Vintage.

———. 1968. *Twilight of the Idols / The Anti-Christ*. Penguin.

———. 1977. *The Viking Portable Nietzsche*. Penguin.

———. 1989. *On the Genealogy of Morals and Ecce Homo*. Vintage.

———. 1994. *Human, All Too Human*. Penguin.

———. 2001. *The Gay Science: With a Prelude in German Rhymes and an Appendix of Songs*. Cambridge University Press.

———. 2009. *On the Genealogy of Morals*. Oxford University Press.

Nussbaum, Martha. 1996. Compassion: The Basic Social Emotion. *Social Philosophy and Policy* 13:1.

Nyíri, J.C. 1996. Wittgenstein as a Philosopher of Secondary Orality. *Grazer Philosophische Studien* 52.

Oreskes, Naomi, and Erik Conway. 2010. *Merchants of Doubt*. Bloomsbury.

Orwell, George. 1940. Notes on the Way. CW, Volume XII; CEJL, Volume 2.

———. 1941. The Lion and the Unicorn. CW, Volume XII; CEJL, Volume 2.

———. 1943. Looking Back on the Spanish War. CW, Volume XIII; CEJL, Volume 2.

———. 1944. Arthur Koestler. CW, Volume XV; CEJL, Volume 3.

———. 1944 Letter to Noel (wrongly, "H.J.") Willmett (May 18th). CW, Volume XVI; CEJL, Volume 3.

———. 1945. Notes on Nationalism. CW, Volume XVII; CEJL, Volume 3.

———. 1945. The Sporting Spirit. CW, Volume XVII; CEJL, Volume 4.

———. 1945. What Is Science? CW, Volume XVII; CEJL, Volume 4 (brief excerpt).

———. 1946. Politics and the English Language. CW, Volume XVII; CEJL, Volume 4.

———. 1946. The Prevention of Literature. CW, Volume XVII; CEJL, Volume 4.

———. 1946 Editorial in *Polemic*, CW Volume XVIII, CEJL 4.

———. 1946. Second Thoughts on James Burnham (reprinted as the pamphlet *James Burnham and the Managerial Revolution*). CW, Volume XVIII; CEJL, Volume 4.

———. 1948. Letter to Roger Senhouse. CW, Volume XIX; CEJL 4.

———. 1948. Such, Such Were the Joys. CW, Volume XIX; CEJL, Volume 4.

———. 1948. Writers and Leviathan. CW, Volume XIX; CEJL, Volume 4.

———. 1949. Letter to Vernon Richards (22nd June). CW, Volume XX.

———. 1949. Reflections on Gandhi, CW, Volume XX; CEJL, Volume 4.

———. 1949. Letter to Francis A. Henson (Extract). CEJL, Volume 4.

———. 1949. Orwell's Statement on *Nineteen Eighty-Four*. CW, Volume XX.

———. 1961 [1949]. *1984*. Signet Classics.

———. 1962 [1940]. *Inside the Whale and Other Essays*. Penguin.

———. 1969 [1936]. *Keep the Aspidistra Flying*. Mariner.

———. 1972 [1933]. *Down and Out in Paris and London*. Mariner, 1972.

———. 1972 [1937]. *The Road to Wigan Pier*. Mariner.

———. 1974 [1934]. *Burmese Days*. Mariner.

———. 1981 [1949]. *1984*. New American Library/Penguin.

———. 1983 [1949]. *1984*. Plume.

———. 1983. *The Penguin Complete Novels of George Orwell*. Penguin.

———. 1986 [1933]. *Down and Out in Paris and London*. CW, Volume I.

———. 1986 [1934]. *Burmese Days*. CW, Volume II.

———. 1987 [1936]. *Keep the Aspidistra Flying*. CW, Volume IV.

———. 1987 [1937]. *The Road to Wigan Pier*. CW, Volume V.

———. 1987 [1938]. *Homage to Catalonia*. CW, Volume VI.

———. 1987 [1939]. *Coming Up for Air*. CW, Volume VII.

———. 1987 [1945]. *Animal Farm*. CW, Volume VIII.

———. 1987 [1949]. *Nineteen Eighty-Four*. CW, Volume IX.

———. 2004 [1949]. *Nineteen Eighty-Four*. Penguin Classics.

Orwell, Sonia, and Ian Angus, eds. 1968. *The Collected Essays, Journalism, and Letters of George Orwell*. Four volumes. Harcourt, Brace.

Oxford Dictionaries. 2017. Post Truth. Oxford University Press <https://en.oxforddictionaries.com/definition/post-truth>.

Park, Yeonmi, and Maryanne Vollers. 2015. *In Order to Live*. Penguin.

Parks, G., ed. 1991. *Nietzsche and Asian Thought*. University of Chicago Press.

Paul, R., and L. Elder. 2002. *Critical Thinking: Tools for Taking Charge of Your Professional and Personal Life*. Prentice Hall.

Persson, Ingmar, and Julian Savulescu. 2008. The Perils of Cognitive Enhancement and the Urgent Imperative to Enhance the Moral Character of Humanity. *Journal of Applied Philosophy* 25:3.

————. 2011. Unfit for the Future? Human Nature, Scientific Progress, and the Need for Moral Enhancement. In Julian Savulescu, Ruud ter Meulen, and Guy Kahane, eds., *Enhancing Human Capacities*. Wiley-Blackwell.

————. 2012. *Unfit for the Future: The Need for Moral Enhancement*. Oxford University Press.

Pinker, Steven, 2011. *The Better Angels of Our Nature: Why Violence Has Declined*. Viking.

Plato. 1997. *Complete Works*. Hackett.

————. 2004. *Republic*. Hackett.

Popper, Karl R. 2002 [1944]. *The Poverty of Historicism*. Routledge.

————. 2013 [1945]. *The Open Society and Its Enemies*. Princeton University Press.

Prado, C.G. 2006. *Searle and Foucault on Truth*. Cambridge University Press.

Prescott, Orville. 1949. Books of the Times. *New York Times* (June 13th).

Rachels, James. 1975. Why Privacy Is Important. *Philosophy and Public Affairs* 4.

Rand, Ayn. 1964. The Ethics of Emergencies. In Rand, *The Virtue of Selfishness*. Signet.

Rasmussen Reports. 2016. Voters Don't Trust Media Fact-Checking. September 30th. <www.rasmussenreports.com/public_content/politics/general_politics/september_2016/voters_don_t_trust_media_fact_checking>.

Rawls, John, 1971. *A Theory of Justice*. Harvard University Press.

Reso, Paulina. 2010. Man Gets 90 Lashes, 4 Years in Prison—for Kissing Woman in Mall. *New York Daily News* (June 10th).

Ricoeur, Paul. 1990. *Time and Narrative*. University of Chicago Press.

Roberts, David D. 2006. *The Totalitarian Experiment in Twentieth-Century Europe: Understanding the Poverty of Great Politics*. Routledge.

Robinson, Paul. 2002. *Opera, Sex, and Other Vital Matters*. University of Chicago Press.

Rodden, John. 2003. *Scenes from an Afterlife: The Legacy of George Orwell*. ISI.

————, ed. 2007. *The Cambridge Companion to George Orwell*. Cambridge University Press.

————. 2011. *The Unexamined Orwell*. University of Texas Press.

Rorty, Richard. 1989. *Contingency, Irony, and Solidarity*. Cambridge University Press.

Rosen, Jay. 2009. Mindcasting: Defining the Form, Spreading the Meme. <http://jayrosen.tumblr.com/post/110043432/mindcasting-defining-the-form-spreading-the-meme>.

Russell, Bertrand. 1905. On Denoting. *Mind* 14:56.

Sartre, Jean-Paul. 1992 [1943]. *Being and Nothingness: A Phenomenological Essay on Ontology*. Washington Square Press.

Scarry, Elaine. 1985. *The Body in Pain: The Making and Unmaking of the World*. Oxford University Press.

Schechtman, Marya. 1996. *The Constitution of Selves*. Cornell University Press.

Schmid, Hans Bernhard. 2014. The Feeling of Being a Group: Corporate Emotions and Collective Consciousness. In Christian von Scheve and Mikko Salmela, eds., *Collective Emotions: Perspectives from Psychology, Philosophy, and Sociology*. Oxford University Press.

Schneier, Bruce. 2015. *Data and Goliath: The Hidden Battles to Collect Your Data and Control Your World*. Norton.

Scotus, John Duns. 2013. *Ordinatio* I <www.aristotelophile.com/current.htm>.

Searle, John R. 1969. *Speech Acts: An Essay in the Philosophy of Language*. Cambridge University Press.

Sharman, Jon. 2017. Donald Trump: All the False Claims 45th President Has Made Since His Inauguration. *Independent* (January 23rd).

Sharockman, Aaron. 2016. The Truth about the 2016 Presidential Campaign. *Politifact* (September 26th).

Sigman, Marian, and Shannon E. Whaley. 1998. The Role of Nutrition in the Development of Intelligence. In Ulric Neisser, ed., *The Rising Curve: Long-Term Gains in IQ and Related Measures*. American Psychological Association.

Smith, David. 2017. Sean Spicer Defends Inauguration Claim: "Sometimes We Can Disagree with Facts." *The Guardian* (January 23rd) <www.theguardian.com/us-news/2017/jan/23/sean-spicer-white-house-press-briefing-inauguration-alternative-facts>.

Society of Professional Journalists. 2014. Code of Ethics. Eugene S. Pulliam National Journalism Center <www.spj.org/ethicscode.asp>.

Stangroom, Jeremy. 2017. *Philosophical Health Check*. Philosophy Experiments <http://www.philosophyexperiments.com/health>.

Steffney, J. 1977. Transmetaphysical Thinking in Heidegger and Zen Buddhism. *Philosophy of East and West* 27:3 (July).

Steele, David Ramsay. 2017. *Orwell Your Orwell: A Worldview on the Slab*. St. Augustine's Press.

Stokes, Patrick. 2015. *The Naked Self: Kierkegaard and Personal Identity*. Oxford University Press.

Sunstein, Cass R. 2005. Sexual Freedom and Political Freedom, In Gleason, Goldsmith, and Nussbaum 2005.

Szanto, Thomas. 2014. How to Share a Mind: Reconsidering the Group Mind Thesis. *Phenomenology and the Cognitive Sciences* 13:1.

Taylor, Charles. 1992. *Sources of the Self: The Making of the Modern Identity*. Harvard University Press.

Taylor, D.J. 2003 [2002]. *Orwell: The Life*. Holt.

Thomson, Judith Jarvis. 1975. The Right to Privacy. *Philosophy and Public Affairs* 4.

Thorson, Emily. 2013. Belief Echoes: The Persistent Effects of Corrected Misinformation. Publicly Accessible Penn Dissertations 810. University of Pennsylvania. <http://repository.upenn.edu/edissertations/810>.

Travis Alan. 2016. The Leave Campaign Made Three Key Promises: Are They Keeping Them? *The Guardian* (June 27th).

Van der Braak, A. 2011. *Nietzsche and Zen: Self-Overcoming Without a Self*. Lexington.

Visvanathan, S. 2003. Progress and Violence. In A. Lightman, D. Sarewitz, and C. Desser, eds., *Living with the Genie: Essays on Technology and the Quest for Human Mastery*. Island Press.

Walpole, Horace. 1769. *Letter to Sir Horace Mann*. <https://en.wikiquote.org/wiki/Horace_Walpole>.

Webster, J.G. 2014. *The Marketplace of Attention. How Audiences Take Shape in a Digital Age*. MIT Press.

Werskey, Gary. 1978. *The Visible College*. Holt.

Whitman, James Q. 2004. The Two Western Cultures of Privacy: Dignity versus Liberty. *Yale Law Journal* 113.

Wittgenstein, Ludwig. 2010. *Philosophical Investigations*. Wiley.

Wolin, S. 2010. *Democracy Incorporated: Managed Democracy and the Spectre of Inverted Totalitarianism*. Princeton University Press.

Wong, D. 2006. *Natural Moralities*. Oxford University Press.

World Economic Forum. 2017. *The Global Risks Report 2017*. <http://www3.weforum.org/docs/GRR17_Report_web.pdf>.

Wu, Tim. 2016. *The Attention Merchants: The Epic Scramble to Get Inside Our Heads*. Knopf.

Zimbardo, Philip G. 2005. Mind Control in Orwell's *Nineteen Eighty-Four*: Fictional Concepts Become Operational Realities in Jim Jones's Jungle Experiment. In Gleason, Goldsmith, and Nussbaum 2005.

Unpersons

MARK ALFANO is Associate Professor of Philosophy at Delft University of Technology and Professor of Philosophy at Australian Catholic University. His first book, *Character as Moral Fiction*, was published in 2013, and his second book, *Moral Psychology: An Introduction*, in 2015. He's now working on a project to extract patterns of virtues and values from the text of obituaries, as well as a project to combat fake news. Feel free to try to seduce him, but maybe don't do it the way it was done to Winston Smith.

KEITH BEGLEY is an Adjunct Assistant Professor in Philosophy at Trinity College Dublin, Oceania. His current research interests include an unorthodox obsession with opposites, and using computers to disprove some trivial duckspeak about hidden patterns in the old-think of Heraclitus. He's a suspected thought criminal. He was born in 1984, and so, for most of his life, he's been preparing to write his chapter by working as an unpaid undercover operative in the dystopia known as modern Ireland. There, two political forces are locked into a permanent civil war. They are not divided by any genuine ideological difference. Their aim is no longer to achieve a decisive victory over one another, rather, it is to maintain their power entirely for its own sake. This is not a joke; please send help!

DARREN BOTELLO-SAMSON is an associate professor of political science at Pittsburg State University (Kansas, Oceania) where he teaches administrative law, constitutional law, and political philosophy. He dreams of being a bartender in a dystopian watering hole, where he will develop the Orwelltini: 2 oz. Victory Gin, 1 oz. juice boiled cabbage, 1 saccharine tablet (Inner Party members may have this drink shaken with ice).

JASON MATTHEW BUCHANAN lives in the city of New York, Oceania, with his family and two dogs. When not worrying about the possibility of Orwell's world coming true, he's trying to fit a good night's sleep between being a partner, parent, and professor of English at The City University of New York. He has also written about the role philosophy plays in the anti-Orwellian show *Futurama*. He knows that the worst thing in the world isn't rats, but won't let anyone know what it is.

JOSIP ĆIRIĆ is assistant professor at Zadar University, Eurasia. He's a person with a disability, ham-radio enthusiast, sci-fi fanatic and non-monotic logic lunatic. He has studied philosophy, sociology, psychology and a bit of psychotherapy, but he's feeling better now. He teaches philosophy of information, information ethics, science fiction and philosophy and, yes, logic. In his spare time he leads RPG sessions, and on special occasions types logic proofs using telegraphy. Informed by his dentist that he has a cavity, he feels a strange urge to cry out "Do it to Julia!"

BRUNO ĆURKO is assistant professor at the University of Split and President of the Association "Petit Philosophy." He writes articles about philosophy with children, philosophy of education, and critical thinking. He travels around dealing with EU projects, symposiums, and conferences. He attends hard rock and heavy metal concerts and festivals. You can regularly find him at Metal Days (Tolmin). He likes philosophizing, heavy metal, and the Mediterranean. After drinking a bottle of slivovitz, he can't tell whether someone is holding up four fingers or five.

DANIEL CONWAY directs the Brotherhood from an undisclosed Wal-Mart in Texas. He also plays lead guitar for an indie-techno-thanatonic garage band known as The Singing Proles.

JAMES CROSSLEY is Professor of Bible, Society, and Politics at St Mary's University London.

EZIO DI NUCCI is Associate Professor of Medical Ethics at the University of Copenhagen. He was not born in 1984 nor did he grow up behind the iron curtain. He left Italy ages ago because of Berlusconi and never returned because of, well, it's Italy ain't it? This book was Stefan's idea—and that's praise rather than blame. After watching reality TV, Ezio has concluded that if there's hope, it doesn't lie in the proles.

ISKRA FILEVA is an assistant professor of philosophy at the University of Colorado in Boulder. She specializes in ethics, moral psychology, and issues at the intersection of philosophy and psychiatry.

JAN KYRRE BERG FRIIS is a philosopher—or so he believes, some-times awake, sometimes asleep but never in oblivion because he is always in the process of becoming—or so he believes. His most vivid fantasies include people and places, conversations and books, or a piece of music by Handel or Pergolesi, of eternal summers and the coolness of the afternoon breeze. He walks, he eats, he senses, and he *knows* he will die, yet he ponders from whence this certainty comes.

WILLIAM GOODWIN is Associate Professor of Philosophy at the University of South Florida. He is a philosopher of science who focuses on applied and constructive sciences such as chemistry and climatology. Much of his work considers how standard philosophical topics such as the nature of explanation, mechanisms, and modeling present differ-ently in these philosophically under-investigated fields. Additionally, he has on ongoing project investigating the interactions of science and society through literature, of which this Orwell chapter is part.

VINCENT F. HENDRICKS is Professor of Formal Philosophy at the University of Copenhagen. He is Director of the Center for Information and Bubble Studies (CIBS) has been awarded the Elite Research Prize by the Danish Ministry of Science, the Roskilde Festival Elite Research Prize and the Rosenkjær Prize. He is the author of numerous books and articles on bubble studies, attention economics, fake news, logic and epistemology. His favorite quote is from *The Deer Hunter*: "This is this, this ain't something else, this is this," although in post-factual times, even this tautology may be called into doubt.

JARNO HIETALAHTI was born in 1984, and he is now fully committed to serve the machine at the University of Jyväskylä, Eurasia. Well, at least the Kone (in English "machine") Foundation funds his post-doctoral research on humor and utopian thinking. Finally, he has realized the beauty of Doublethink, and follows its ideals in his life. Hietalahti is a devoted vegetarian who eats meat on a weekly basis. He is very strict never to drink coffee but enjoys at least a couple of cappuccinos every day. For him, controversies are something to be embraced. They provide food for thought, be those thoughts silly and nonsensical. Sometimes paradoxes make great sense, and that's what Hietalahti follows day after day. Nights, obviously, are a com-pletely different matter.

POLARIS KOI is a doctoral candidate in Philosophy at the University of Turku, Eurasia. He's interested in human abilities. Like Winston, he likes to think his resistance isn't futile.

GREG LITTMANN bio doubleplus ungood. DELETE: "Greg Littmann is an associate professor at SIUE. He has published on metaphysics, epistemology, and the philosophy of logic, and has written numerous chapters for books for the general public, including volumes on Dracula, *Dune, Frankenstein, Game of Thrones*, Stephen King, and Jonathan Swift." REPLACE WITH: "Greg Littmann was an associate professor at SIUE. He published denunciations of metaphysics, epistemology, and the philosophy of logic, and wrote numerous chapters for books for Party members, including volumes denouncing freedom, democracy, Stephen King, and Jonathan Swift. Just before his sudden and unexpected death while assisting the Ministry of Love with enquiries, he expressed the hope that he would be remembered for his dictum, "Never leave your echo-chamber or question your reality-bubble. Your Party can never be wrong."

LAVINIA MARIN is one of those researchers who thinks that, just by saying the truth publicly, philosophers can enforce the public sphere. She also realizes that, without an educated public, any kind of truth utterance will not matter. In her home country, Romania, people are screaming untruths on all TV channels, in news bulletins and talk shows, day and night, and the viewers are starting to believe all this. A lie repeated a thousand times becomes the truth. The art of lying via the telescreen has been brought to perfection in the land of Romania, once freed from the threat of totalitarianism in 1989, now closer than ever to a future that looks like 1984.

CHRISTOPHER MARKOU is a PhD Student at the Faculty of Law of the University of Cambridge.

DIANA ADELA MARTIN is an assistant lecturer at Dublin Institute of Technology, researching engineering ethics and philosophy of technology. She is also cofounder of the educational NGO Link Education and Practice focused on improving youth employability. She was born in 1985 in Bucharest, Romania, and lived in *1984* until 1989. Whenever her partner starts reading aloud from *The Society of the Spectacle*, she suddenly feels very sleepy.

KAYCE MOBLEY is an assistant professor of political science at Pittsburg State University (Kansas, Oceania). After studying politics and Latin at the University of the South in Sewanee, Tennessee, she completed her PhD at the University of Georgia in 2015. Her research broadly concerns ethical issues in conflict, and her latest publication is in the *Journal of Military Ethics*. She's confident that her history of Internet searches related to international relations

landed her on a government watch-list well before she even regis-
tered for a driver's license.

ERIN J. NASH is an advanced doctoral candidate at the Centre for
Humanities Engaging Science and Society/Department of Philosophy
at Durham University, Airstrip One. Erin also holds an undergradu-
ate degree in Science (with Honours) and a master's in Philosophy
and Public Policy. Her research interests lie at the interface of the philosophy of science, epistemology, and political/social/moral philosophy.
In her doctoral thesis, Erin examines the social and political implications of misleading speech about scientific issues, and the responsibilities different actors have when communicating scientific
information. Before returning to academia she had a career as a policy analyst and adviser. She unfortunately injured her arm while
operating the machine that wrote her chapter for this volume.

EDWARDO PÉREZ is an Associate Professor of English at Tarrant County
College in Hurst, Texas, where he specializes in controlling the thoughts
of students through torturous readings, horrific group assignments, and
mind-altering exams. A secret member of the Thought Police, Edwardo
specializes in Doublethink and Newspeak (what Prolos might call
rhetorical theory), looking for thoughtcrimes in every paper he grades.

ELIZABETH RARD is currently working on her PhD in Philosophy at
UC Davis, and is a Philosophy Instructor at Reedley College. In addition, she works part-time for the Ministry of Truth, producing training documents and correcting historical records. As a small child
Elizabeth would amuse herself by redacting objectionable material at
the local public library. She was directly responsible for the official re-
education of no fewer than three of her school instructors. In her
spare time, she practices holding inconsistent thoughts in her head
and dusts her rather large collection of rubber stamps, which say
things like "CLASSIFIED" and "DELETED."

ALBA MONTES SÁNCHEZ is currently an independent scholar, until
recently employed as a postdoctoral researcher at the Center for
Subjectivity Research (University of Copenhagen, Eurasia). She specializes in the philosophy of emotion and has written various academic articles on shame, and more recently also pride and envy. If you
found her on Airstrip One, she would certainly be doing her best to get
some good contraband coffee.

TIMOTHY SANDEFUR is a lawyer at the Goldwater Institute in
Phoenix, Arizona, where he holds the Duncan Chair in Constitutional

Government. He is the author of several books, including *Frederick Douglass: Self-Made Man* (2018), *Cornerstone of Liberty: Property Rights in 21st Century America* (co-authored with Christina Sandefur, 2016), *The Permission Society* (2016), and *The Conscience of The Constitution* (2014), as well as dozens of articles on subjects ranging from Indian law to antitrust, slavery, and the Civil War, and political issues in Shakespeare, ancient Greek drama, and *Star Trek*.

OSHRAT C. SILBERBUSCH holds a PhD in Philosophy from Tel Aviv University, Eurasia. Her book *Thinking as Resistance: Theodor W. Adorno's Philosophy of the Nonidentical* comes out in 2018 (she's hoping it will make people think and resist). She has published papers on Theodor W. Adorno, Jean Améry, and post-Shoah philosophy, and likes to philosophize about the candles in the dark: the people who do good when everything is bad. She read *1984* first in 1984, when she was in second grade, and has never fully recovered from that premature introduction to the perverse potential of the human mind.

STEFAN STORRIE has written the *Routledge Guidebook to Berkeley's Three Dialogues* (2018) and is the editor of *Berkeley's Three Dialogues: New Essays* (2018). He is Big Brother to four long-suffering siblings. They have learned to love him.

TORBJÖRN TÄNNSJÖ is Professor of Practical Philosophy at Stockholm University, Eurasia. He has published extensively in moral philosophy, political philosophy, and bioethics. Some of his most recent books are *Understanding Ethics* (third edition, 2013), which is a simple introduction to normative ethics, *Taking Life: Three Theories on the Ethics of Killing* (2015), and *Setting Health Care Priorities: What Ethical Theories Tell Us* (forthcoming). His views have sometimes been considered controversial such as when *Vox* refused to publish a solicited piece because it was feared that it would offend some of their readers. He is consequently a member of the editorial board of the recently founded *Journal of Controversial Ideas*. Torbjörn is a very moderate social democratic reformist, but only above the waist.

MADS VESTERGAARD is a PhD Fellow at Center for Information and Bubble Studies (CIBS), University of Copenhagen, Eurasia. He has an MA in philosophy. He debates and communicates philosophy and social science through the press, radio, and television. He has also applied philosophy in untraditional contexts. As founder and former leader of the Danish satirical project Nihilistisk Folkeparti (The Nihilist Democratic Party), Mads made the absurdity of post-factual politics into the election slogan: *Let's look at the hard facts: Reality is pure spin!*

Destroy These Words